Pictures and Texts
Henry James, A.L. Coburn, and
New Ways of Seeing in Literary Culture

Studies in Photography, No. 2

Diane M. Kirkpatrick, Series Editor

Associate Professor, History of Art
The University of Michigan

Other Titles in This Series

Pictures and Texts
Henry James, A.L. Coburn, and
New Ways of Seeing in Literary Culture

by
Ralph F. Bogardus
Associate Professor of American Studies
University of Alabama
University, Alabama

UMI RESEARCH PRESS
Ann Arbor, Michigan

Produced and distributed by
UMI Research Press
an imprint of
University Microfilms International
A Xerox Information Resources Company
Ann Arbor, Michigan 48106

Library of Congress Cataloging in Publication Data

Bogardus, Ralph F., 1938-
  Pictures and texts.

    (Studies in photography ; no. 2)
    Revision of thesis–University of Mexico, 1974.
    Bibliography: p.
    Includes index.
    1. James, Henry, 1843-1916–Aesthetics. 2. James,
Henry, 1843-1916–Illustrations. 3. Coburn, Alvin
Langdon, 1882-1966. 4. Illustration of books–United
States–History. 5. Photography–United States–History.
6. Frontispiece. 7. Literature and photography–United
States. I. Title. II. Series.
PS2127.A35B63 1984   813'.4   84-8844
ISBN 0-8357-1471-3 (alk. paper)

To the Memory of my Father, Ralph W. Bogardus
and
to Professor George W. Arms

Contents

List of Illustrations

Acknowledgments

Mark Twain once said, "Soap and education are not as sudden as massacre, but are more deadly in the long run." In a manner of speaking, Twain was correct, for it is often the Aunt Pollys of the world who do the scrubbing and educating. I have been fortunate, however, to work with people who—unlike Aunt Polly—have not urged upon me either soap or education in the sense that Twain meant. These people, in large and small small ways, have generously offered help, suggestions, criticisms, and pointed out directions without circumscribing or getting in the way of my own ideas.

This work began over ten years ago, but has subsequently undergone a great deal of rethinking, revision, and expansion. The subject grew out of my work in a seminar on Howells and James, taught by George W. Arms. Professor Arms gently but critically helped nurture the idea, and it grew and developed into a book-length work. Over the years, he has read new materials that have found their way into the book, and he has made countless suggestions and criticisms. His guidance and his example as a scholar have provided me with a most instructive model of what intelligent and interesting scholarship should be. Others, too, helped in various, important ways, reading and criticizing my work and providing me with the encouragement, materials, and skills necessary for me to complete the task: Joel M. Jones, Ferenc M. Szasz, Beaumont Newhall, and Ann Noggle, all of The University of New Mexico. Van Deren Coke (San Francisco Museum of Modern Art), Richard Rudisill (Museum of New Mexico, Santa Fe), Alan Trachtenberg, (Yale University), and Peter C. Bunnell (Princeton University) graciously provided me with sources, ideas, and directions. Alan Trachtenberg, especially, gave me encouragement regarding the value of the subject at a time when I was not certain about its potential.

I have also been generously aided by a number of individuals over the past few years. Leon Edel (New York University, and the University of Hawaii) permitted me to use the mostly unpublished James-Coburn correspondence, located at the University of Virginia; Louis Budd (Duke University) thoughtfully provided me with some useful sources; William Taylor (SUNY at Stony Brook) and Bill Stott (University of Texas, Austin) both astutely criticised the contents of a paper that eventually found its way into this study; and Hugh Kenner (Johns Hopkins) helped me clarify in my own mind some important ideas that bear on this book. Sara deSaussure Davis, Fred Hobson, and Elliott Gorn (all of the University of Alabama) read portions of the manuscript and offered many shrewd and useful criticisms. Fred and Elliott, along with colleague Rose Gladney, also provided me with close friendship and intellectual solace over the past few years at Alabama. One other person in particular deserves special mention. Margaret Vines not only shared many of the burdens of the program while I was buried deeply in my world of words, but generously gave me indispensable help in the typing and compiling of the manuscript and made it possible for me to complete this project by the last deadline; her calm and good humor also helped keep me relatively sane throughout.

All of the above-named persons have my deepest gratitude and thanks.

Much of the research for this book was conducted at The General Library, Special Collections, University of New Mexico, Albuquerque; the Amelia Gayle Gorgas Library, the University of Alabama, Tuscaloosa; and the Houghton Library, Harvard University. Thanks go to the staffs of these institutions and particularly to the following: Barron K. Oder, Special Collections Department, New Mexico; and William Bond, Librarian (retired), Rodney G. Dennis, Curator of Manuscripts, and F. Thomas Noonan, Curator of the Reading Room, all of the Houghton. Additional research was conducted through the mails, and a number of libraries and archives as well as individuals provided much needed aid. Thanks go to the following for their indispensible help in making available unpublished letters and manuscripts, copies of important illustrations and photographs, and scarce periodicals and books: the staff of the Clifton Waller Barrett Library, University of Virginia; Richard M. Ludwig, Assistant University Librarian for Rare Books and Special Collections, and Jean F. Preston, Curator of Manuscripts, The Library, Princeton University; Thomas F. Barrow, Professor of Art, and Neil Morganstern, Assistant to the Curator of Collections, University Art Museum, University of New Mexico; Rachel Stuhlman, Head Librarian, and Barbara Puorro Galasso, Print Service, the International Museum of Photography at George Eastman House; David Schoonover and Mary Maturo, both of the Beinecke Rare Book and Manuscript Library, Yale University; Kay Jones, Interlibrary Loan Librarian, Amelia Gayle Gorgas Library, University of Alabama; and Sir Brian Botsford, Lamb House, Rye.

I have received generous support for research expenses and time, for gathering materials, and for completing the manuscript from the University of Alabama: the Presidential Venture Fund made it possible for me to visit important research archives and to secure copies of essential materials from their collections; the University Research Grants Committee, the University of Alabama, awarded me two summer research grants, making it possible for me to complete the initial research on, and writing of, sections of the manuscript; and most importantly, Dean Douglas E. Jones and his staff, of the College of Arts and Sciences, aided my effort in both large and small ways, helping to underwrite the cost of illustrations and the manuscript, providing that modern scholar's *deus ex machina*—the dedicated word processor—for my use, and giving encouragement all along the way.

The following have generously permitted me to use published and unpublished sources, and I gratefully acknowledge their kindness: Alexander R. James, currently head of the James family, for permission to quote from unpublished letters by Henry James to Alvin Langdon Coburn, in the James Collection, Clifton Waller Barrett Library, University of Virginia; Charles Scribner, Jr., and Princeton University Library, for permission to quote from unpublished letters in the Charles Scribner's Sons Archive, Princeton University; the International Museum of Photography, at George Eastman House, Rochester, New York, for permission to use an unpublished photograph, "Dumping Ground, Boston," by Alvin Langdon Coburn; Houghton Library, Harvard University, for permission to use two photographs of Henry James, both in the James Family Collection, Henry James, Jr., Papers; and the editors of *Centennial Review*, and *History of Photography*, for permission to use materials that were previously published in those journals.

The other illustrations appear here through the courtesy of the Special Collections Department, General Library, and the University Art Museum, both of the University of New Mexico; and the Amelia Gayle Gorgas Library, University of Alabama. Special thanks goes to Hank Herrera, who made most of the excellent copy prints.

I wish to end by thanking those closest to me—my family. My children saw less of their father than they ordinarily do and projects for them did not get built, yet they did not complain more than usual. My wife, Ann, helped by proofreading the manuscript and correcting my verbal infelicities (in English) and my misplacement of diacritical marks (in French); but she helped most by just being with me. They all have my love and respect.

Our fine arts were developed, their types and uses were established, in times very different from the present, by men whose power of action upon things was insignificant in comparison with ours. But the amazing growth of our techniques, the adaptability and precision they have attained, the ideas and habits they are creating, make it a certainty that profound changes are impending in the ancient craft of the Beautiful. In all the arts there is a physical component which can no longer be considered or treated as it used to be, which cannot remain unaffected by our modern knowledge and power. For the last twenty years neither matter nor space nor time has been what it was from time immemorial. We must expect great innovations to transform the entire technique of the arts, thereby affecting artistic invention itself and perhaps even bringing about an amazing change in our very notion of art.

— Paul Valéry, *Aesthetics*

Prologue

"There are readers," began the anonymous reviewer in an early 1908 issue of *Literary Digest*, "who have come too late upon the scene to have been able to gather one by one . . . the novels of Henry James. The search for some of the earlier volumes, now become rare, may have been to some a fascinating pursuit, but one to be rewarded only after patient and persistent endeavor. . . . To all such then," the reviewer announced, "the new subscription edition embracing the output of Mr. James's various publishers is a real boon. Nothing could be more satisfactory to the lover of a great writer's work than the fine, ample, and dignified volumes that make up this edition."[1] Another reviewer, Edward E. Hale, Jr., agreed, noting in the pages of *Dial* his "pleasure in viewing, in thinking of, the stately volumes [of Henry James's newly re-issued works], even aside from the pleasure of reading such good print on such good paper."[2] At last, the first six volumes of James's carefully wrought New York Edition had emerged. By the following year, the remaining books in the edition would be published, and James's monument would finally be complete.

Two years earlier, in 1906, James had begun work on the New York Edition. At this time in his career, according to biographer Leon Edel, James was very concerned about "his own literary reputation," so he sought "to shore up, against the ravages of posterity, a great part of his oeuvre — in the New York Edition, the 'definitive edition' he had planned for years."[3] The edition itself was not meant to be merely a collection of complete works, however. As James projected it, his "'handsome' collective (and *se*lective) Edition Définitive of writings" was to be a carefully edited one, designed to include special prefaces written for the occasion and unique frontispieces ornamenting each volume.[4] James embarked on the creation of his "definitive edition" because he wished to exercise full control over the publication of his collected works. He simply could not leave his literary fate to others — as had, for example, Balzac. For the most part, James succeeded in realizing his plans, and his effort must seem to us both inspired and sensible as well as rewarding. To begin with, his decision provided him an opportunity to refine many of his individual tales and novels. Also, it led to the creation of, and plea for, intelligent criticism found in the prefaces.[5] Yet, there was another, less heralded consequence, too: the appearance of photogravure frontispieces in each volume. These frontispieces were made from photographs taken by a young American pictorial photographer, Alvin Langdon Coburn, in collaboration with Henry James.[6]

Though by no means unprecedented, the illustration of fiction with photographic frontispieces was still a risky endeavor. Whether James fully appreciated this or not is unclear, for no such awareness was divulged in the preface to *The Golden Bowl*, where Coburn's contribution was praised.[7] Manifested instead was an explanation of the consciously conceived purpose that underlay the act — a critical statement by James that formulated a new aesthetic for uniting pictures and texts into a single work of art. James's aesthetic innovation, implicit both in the use of single photographs to illustrate individual works of fiction and in the symbolic manner of this use, was somewhat at odds with his age's conventions regarding illustration. Nonetheless, when James's thinking is examined carefully, it becomes evident that the problem of how to use illustrations had concerned — one might better say, plagued — him for a long time, and his chosen means of illustration — photography — turned out to be a logical, masterful solution to the problem as he had long conceived it. The medium was utterly compatible with James's extraordinarily visual sensibility as well as his method of gathering materials for his art; and the images Coburn and he produced perfectly complemented James's late manner prose style.

The climate of attitudes regarding the proper practice of illustration and the status of photography provide the context which makes James's use of photographic illustration somewhat radical and, on its face, enigmatic. During James's lifetime, illustration was widely used in book, newspaper, and magazine publication, and it was immensely popular.[8] Photography, too, was ubiquitous and quite popular. Yet, it was not the popularity of either of these that made James's act bold. Its audaciousness instead arose from the fact that James's use of photographic illustration was both an affirmation and a disavowal. By the time the collaboration itself took place during 1906-07, photography had long been the center of a vigorous controversy over whether the medium was an art; and the final judgment regarding its status was not yet in.[9] Hence James's risk in using it as the pictorial medium to illustrate his "definitive edition." If photography was ultimately judged not an art by the critical powers that be, then the artistic quality of the entire New York Edition would be forever compromised. Since Henry James was a writer who considered himself a supremely conscious artist, his inclusion of photographic frontispieces put him implicitly on the side of those who believed photography capable of being an art.

Unlike photography, illustration was considered one of the fine arts (albeit a modest one), so there was no danger that its use would be regarded as inappropriate by James's contemporaries.[10] Still, certain conventions were common in the proper practice of illustrating good literature. Victorian fiction was usually illustrated with pictures made by the hand of an artist, and the images sketched were designed to work as visual representations of specific scenes, characters, or actions found in the texts. Certainly, these were expected to be charming decorations too; but pictures accompanied texts in order to clarify or amplify the writers' verbal pictures—just in case the words themselves failed. James, however, believed that if written language alone could not convey the mental picture it was meant to, then it was not successful as literature.[11] So instead of admitting the conventional, hand-drawn "explanatory pictures"[12] into the pages of his "definitive edition," James reinvented another approach. He actively collaborated with Coburn on the creation of frontispieces that would serve as symbols of the texts they were designed to accompany. James was the director in this collaboration, Coburn the cameraman; and together the two artists made twenty-four images designed to function not only as complementary, noninterfering, and generalizing illustrations of the texts but also stand alone as beautiful pictures.

By the time of the New York Edition collaboration, James was aware of the uses to which both illustration and photography had been put. His work had often been illustrated, and he himself had been photographed many times. He had made references to photography and photographing in his various writings, and he had authored a book of essays on illustrators and illustration. It is clear that, though James liked the work of certain illustrators, he disliked having his own work illustrated; and it is equally clear that before the collaboration he did not regard photography an art of any particular merit or consequence. Why, then, did Henry James choose to illustrate his "definitive edition" with photographic frontispieces? And did the frontispieces work in the manner he had planned, contributing beautiful new symbols to each work they related to without interfering with the prose? Although at first these sorts of questions—even the question of the collaboration itself—may seem too restricted, they lead us into the complex, ambiguous territory of James's own nineteenth-century background. This, in turn, demands a consideration of broader matters that reflect on the age's evolving modernist forces, clarify the author's developing consciousness within his milieu, and illuminate the quality of his achievement.

Part One: The Collaboration

*These photographs are taken by Mr. Alvin Langdon Coburn
. . . and Mr. James thinks these so highly successful that he is
anxious that Mr. Coburn should do as much more of the
work as is possible. There is, for instance, in Paris an old
house which Mr. James suggests would make an appropriate
frontispiece for "The American," and this Mr. Coburn could
photograph under Mr. James' direction.*

—James B. Pinker to Charles Scribner's Sons,
13 July 1906

I greatly rejoice in . . . everything you've done. . . .

—Henry James to Alvin Langdon Coburn,
27 December 1906

1

Henry James Directs Some Films

On 26 April 1905, a meeting took place in New York City between two gifted artists—Henry James and Alvin Langdon Coburn. James had just turned sixty-two-years-old and was considered by many to be the "Master" of contemporary English prose literature, while Coburn, almost twenty-three, was only beginning to be recognized both in England and America as a leading artist-photographer. The two met because Coburn had been commissioned by Richard Watson Gilder, the prominent New York editor, to make photographic portraits of famous writers for publication in *Century*. Using a letter of introduction from Gilder, Coburn made an appointment with James and photographed him.[1] With this meeting, Coburn later reminisced, "it all began."[2] Of course, what Coburn was referring to here was the collaboration between the two artists to create the photogravure frontispieces for James's New York Edition.

Leon Edel writes that James took it for granted that his definitive Edition would be illustrated with frontispieces, "telling Scribners that he would appreciate 'a single good plate, in each volume.' To make certain there would be no mistake about it he [James] added, 'only one, but of thoroughly fine quality.' "[3] In the correspondence surrounding the Edition, Scribner's editor W. C. Brownell urged James to use hand drawn pictures, once even suggesting that Albert Sterner be retained for this purpose. Though undecided about the question of illustration, James nonetheless knew what he did not want. "I like Albert Sterner," he wrote Scribners, "but are twenty Albert Sterners desirable or even thinkable—???" Moreover, James explained bluntly, he was opposed to the inclusion of ordinary magazine type illustration in the Edition, preferring in its place "some scene, object or locality, and associated with some one or other of the tales in the volume, both consummately photographed and consummately reproduced."[4] Unfortunately, James feared, taking on such a project would require more effort and time than he felt could be spared. Yet, despite his dread, he embarked on a collaboration with Coburn, and Scribners honored his decision and paid for the picture-making.[5]

The exact reasons for James's rejection of hand rendered illustration and choice of the photographer Coburn are ambiguous. So too is the precise time when James decided to collaborate with Coburn on the entire project. Unquestionably, Henry James and Alvin Langdon Coburn liked each other from the beginning. "There are some people you cannot help liking the moment you see them," Coburn later said, "and Henry James was, for me, such a person. I met and photographed him and even at this first meeting we seemed to become friends."[6] Still, more than friendly feeling was necessary in order for James to retain Coburn as a collaborator.[7] Edel asserts that because James found Coburn "sympathetic" during their first meeting, the author conceived "the idea of trying him out" on the project.[8] Coburn himself seems to affirm this, later recalling that James suggested to him during this occasion that he visit Rye when they both returned to England.[9] Yet, despite the success of their initial meeting in New York, James was only entertaining the possibility of a collaboration with Coburn. As Edel correctly implies, James did not decide to engage the photographer before seeing more of his work — "not only his portraits but his pictures of London, his landscapes, photographs of docks at Liverpool and arches in Rome."[10] From Edel's description, it is evident that James attended Coburn's first one-person show that opened in London at the Royal Photographic Society in February 1906.[11] Even then, however, James's decision to use Coburn was not finally settled but instead continued to emerge slowly, tentatively, and somewhat sporadically during the subsequent six months of 1906.[12]

A letter from James to Coburn indicates that the two artists probably met next in London at the Reform Club in early May 1906.[13] The reasons for that meeting are not fully clear. Doubtless James wished to probe the possibility of collaboration more deeply. It is likely, too, that this was the occasion of the first — and, as it turned out, unsuccessful — sitting for a portrait that could be used as the *Roderick Hudson* frontispiece.[14] Then, on 8 June 1906, James telegraphed Coburn and invited him to Rye for another round of photographing.[15] Coburn made the trip on 12 June and made more pictures of James.[16] Shortly after this second sitting, James saw the outcome and was pleased. "We seem to have produced between us," James wrote, "some very queer results, but the three profiles are interesting and the smallest (which is quite beautiful, I think) is the best for my purpose and will do very well indeed."[17] The sitting *was* successful, and the profile James referred to now decorates the pages of *Roderick Hudson* (figure 1). Obviously, a collaboration of sorts had begun. Still, the question of whether or not Coburn should do the entire set of illustrations remained unsettled in

James's mind, for he continued to try out the young photographer on other scenes and even discussed with Scribner's the possibility of using a hand drawn illustration for another volume.[18]

Despite James's hesitation, the collaboration was gradually becoming a fact; and true to James's working style, it was coming into being only after careful testing and reflection on the author's part. Though the collaboration was from the beginning a two-sided endeavor with both artists contributing to it in distinctive ways, it is clear that James was the director, scenarist, and editor of these films — as both Coburn and Scribner's would understand completely. In the same letter where he praised Coburn's portraits (26 June 1906), James revealed his role, making several suggestions that set the tenor and practice of the collaboration. There, James urged that the *Roderick Hudson* portrait be cropped at the middle of the torso — and so it appears in the New York Edition. James also wrote down the instructions for the next image Coburn was to make: "It is now important that you should do my (this) little house (for the same use) — and could you come down for the purpose someday early next week?"[19] Following his director's instructions, the gifted cameraman travelled to Rye on 3 July 1906 and made photographs of James's house, one of which became "Mr. Longdon's," the frontispiece to *The Awkward Age* (figure 9).

Though James was clearly the director in this venture, it is equally clear that Coburn's role was indispensible to its success. As the literary agent, James B. Pinker, wrote to Scribner's regarding the photographs already taken by Coburn, "Mr. James thinks these so highly successful that he is anxious that Mr. Coburn should do as much more of the work as is possible. There is . . . in Paris," Pinker continued, "an old house which Mr. James suggests would make an appropriate frontispiece for 'The American,' and this Mr. Coburn could photograph under Mr. James' direction."[20] Obviously, Coburn was the creative photographer who knew exactly how to achieve the artistic results that James envisioned. But it must also be understood that Coburn was not merely an unthinking assistant who simply replicated James's orders on film. Coburn made important aesthetic decisions during the collaboration, deciding how best to photograph and print each desired scene. On occasion, Coburn did even more. It was he, for example, who suggested that a St. Paul's scene might do for the first volume of *The Princess Casamassima* (figure 5). James agreed, and it became the one image that Coburn made without the instigation or presence of the Master.[21]

The collaboration lay dormant for the remainder of the Summer of 1906, while Coburn vacationed. It picked up again in September. On 3 September, James wrote Coburn another letter, emphasizing how anxious he was for

Coburn to go to Paris for more frontispieces.[22] Subsequently, Coburn left for Paris on 2 October 1906, taking along a detailed shooting script for the Paris picture-making.[23] To reassure an apparently nervous young artist, James posted an additional letter that would await Coburn in Paris. "But I really think it exaggerates difficulties to assume at all that you won't be able to worry through by yourself, after the various talks we have had, the indications I have given and the natural facility and feasibility of the place," James wrote. "I have no doubt whatever that I shall find enough right things in the number you do."[24] James was correct in his confidence in, and reassurance of, Coburn; but he was also shrewd enough to insure good results by sending thorough instructions. As Coburn later put it, "I went there . . . armed with a detailed document from James explaining exactly what he wanted me to photograph."[25]

In their completeness, the instructions typified the character of the collaborative relationship—of the director and his photographer. James knew in his mind's eye the Paris he wanted for his Edition. It was the one he so vividly recalled from his many times spent there as a resident and visitor. It was also the one he had filtered through his imagination to provide a backdrop for so many of his novels and tales. Indeed, in these instructions there is clear evidence of James's extraordinary sense of visual memory. For just one frontispiece—that of the *porte-cochère* which symbolizes the barrier between Madame de Cintré and Christopher Newmann in *The American*—James had his secretary type one-and-one-half pages of notes that were designed to help Coburn capture the sense of what James visualized as the right image. There, James specified numerous Paris streets where he believed Coburn might find examples of the type of thing he wanted. James instructed Coburn to drive through these streets in order to begin to get an idea of the type. Then, James told Coburn to walk and slowly look in order to obtain a fuller and more precise view. James even suggested and partly described an explicit example—the British Embassy in the *Rue de Faubourg Saint Honoré*—which, though too big and modern, he thought would help Coburn get the picture exactly.[26]

Coburn followed James's instructions well, and James chose the image entitled "Faubourg St. Germain" for *The American* (figure 2). It was precisely the *porte-cochère* James had envisioned. But again note that once Coburn had found the right type, the photographer's own talent and artistry took up where his director's left off. At this point, it was Coburn who selected the point of view, lighting, and framing that would transform the object into a beautiful image. That James himself was aware of, and accepted fully, Coburn's role in the creative effort is clear, for the Paris instructions explicitly urged the photographer to exercise his own judgment.

Sending Coburn to the Place de la Concorde, James advised, "Look out *there* for some combination of objects that won't be hackneyed and commonplace and panoramic; some fountain or statue or balustrade or vista or suggestion . . . that will serve in connection with *The Ambassadors*, perhaps; just as some view, rightly arrived at, of Notre-Dame would also serve — if sufficiently bedimmed and refined and glorified."[27] With regard to *The Tragic Muse*, James again gave evidence of his trust in Coburn's creative responsibility. He suggested a photograph of the facade of the Thèâtre-Français, transformed through "some ingeniously-hit-upon angle of presentment of its rather majestic big square mass and classic colonnade."[28] Finally, James stressed, "do bring me something right, in short, from the Luxembourg."[29] Again the photographer followed closely his director's shooting script, upholding his end of the collaboration by bringing back "something right," an "ingeniously-hit-upon angle of presentment," another "view, rightly arrived at," as well as a "generalizing" glimpse of the Arc de Triomphe (the frontispiece appearing in volume two of *The Princess Casamassima*).[30] Yet, exercising greater creative license than perhaps expected by James, Coburn also returned with a view not "of Notre-Dame" (as James had directed), but with an image "By Notre Dame" — the photograph of a bridge, leading from Notre Dame to the Left Bank, which was picked by James for volume one of *The Ambassadors*. Obviously, James recognized when his cameraman had found a better image than he himself had suggested, and he accepted it gladly.

Not only does the creative relationship become illuminated through the Paris instructions, but we are also given insight into James's early-formed aesthetic for conjoining the frontispieces and texts in the New York Edition. He would later articulate this aesthetic more systematically in his Preface to *The Golden Bowl*. In the Paris instructions, James directed Coburn to go to the Luxembourg Gardens and look for a scene that corresponded to a passage from *The Ambassadors* — the one where the hero is "sitting *there* against the pedestal of some pleasant old garden-statue, to read over certain letters with which the story is concerned. Go into the sad Luxembourg Gardens . . . to look for my right garden-statue (composing with other interesting objects) — against which my chair was tilted back."[31] At the outset, as James subsequently wrote, the frontispieces were conceived as "optical symbols or echoes," "small pictures of our 'set' stage with the actors left out" whose purpose was to convey "the ideal . . . of an aspect of things or the combination of objects that might, by a latent virtue in it, speak for its connexion with something in the book, and yet at the same time speak enough for its odd or interesting self."[32] In the literary sense, then, the frontispieces were visual equivalents of things or places that were linked in the texts to important turning points in major characters' lives. In using illustration in this manner, James was experimenting with a fresh approach—something which he neither quite seemed to realize nor note, even in *The Golden Bowl* preface.

Meanwhile, on 9 October 1906, James again wrote to Coburn in Paris. He indicated that he was anxious to see the results of Coburn's work but reassured the photographer, "I have no doubt of my being able to make my pick, for each required plate."[33] After Coburn returned to England and printed the Paris photographs, James saw the results on 2 November 1906 and was satisfied.[34] In all, six images were selected: "Faubourg St. Germain" for *The American*; "Splendid Paris, Charming Paris" (the "generalizing" image of the Arc de Triomphe that James had wanted) for *The Princess Casamassima*; "The Comédie Français" for *The Tragic Muse*; "The Court of the Hotel" for *The Reverberator*; and finally for *The Ambassadors*, two images—"By Notre Dame" for volume one and "The Luxembourg Gardens" for volume two (figures 2, 6, 7, 13, 21, and 22).

The next trip Coburn needed to take was to Italy to secure images in Venice and Rome. While preparations were being made for that sojourn in early December 1906, Henry James sought permission for Coburn to photograph a room of the "Wallace Collection" at Hertford House. He desired an image of a group of objects in this prominent collection as the frontispiece to *The Spoils of Poynton*.[35] During this time, Coburn and James also planned the photographing of some of the other English scenes deemed necessary for the Edition. But at this moment in the collaboration, it is evident that James was still not certain what all of the subjects for the frontispieces were to be—partly because the textual selection for, and organization of, the Edition had not been completed.

James dictated and sent Coburn the instructions for the Italian journey on 6 December 1906, however another letter sent the next day indicates that James was still unclear regarding whether there were to be twenty-three or twenty-four volumes in all.[36] There James explained that he had looked carefully at the list of images needed, but it was still not quite right. Despite the fact that most of the frontispiece plates had been decided on, James said he had completely forgotten about the one for *The Awkward Age* (in fact, he had not, since Coburn had already made "Mr. Longdon's" the previous July); besides that image, something was needed—James was not quite sure what—for "In the Cage." He wanted the thing settled, but it had to be satisfactory, and this meant further discussion with Coburn. Though James hoped that all the images except perhaps the American scenes could be decided on before Coburn left for Italy, nothing was to be left to chance.[37]

James's efforts to complete the Edition's order continued. On 9

December 1906, he was still juggling the tales around, and this meant he was also rethinking and refining the shooting script. In a letter of that date, James informed Coburn that permission to photograph the "Wallace Collection" had been given and so he should go there immediately. True to his practice, James instructed Coburn to shoot the objects at an oblique angle and to get a lot of the damask wallpaper as background. He also stressed that Coburn should go to Italy as soon as possible after making this picture and reiterated his wish to have a photograph of the Palazzo Capello in Venice for "The Aspern papers." James explained that his desire for this particular image necessitated a change in the order of the tales, for if this particular frontispiece was to be used, "The Aspern Papers" had to be placed in a different volume than was originally planned.[38] Surfacing for the first time in the collaboration was James's conscious recognition that the frontispieces were beginning to help determine the order in which certain of the shorter works were to appear in the Edition. Clearly, as Edel observes, the Edition was becoming "a living organism possessing an identity all its own."[39] The frontispieces were a force affecting its growth and shape.

While James was busy refining the Edition's organization, Coburn had been busy photographing English scenes, some of which might serve as an aid to James's planning. He photographed and printed some Sheffield views to show James so the author could work out his ideas better,[40] though it is not clear what help these were or what texts they were connected with. "Some of the Spoils" was also photographed, and James was elated when he saw the results (figure 10).[41]

Finally, in mid-December 1906, Coburn left for Italy. This trip, as the photographer later put it, "yielded four subjects, two in Rome and two in Venice. The Roman pictures were: 'The Roman Bridge' for the second volume of *The Portrait of a Lady* and 'By St. Peter's' for *Daisy Miller*. The Venetian pair were 'Juliana's Court' for . . . *The Aspern Papers*, and the 'Venetian Palace' for the second volume of *Wings of the Dove*" (figures 4, 18, 12, and 20).[42] Regarding the Venice shooting, Coburn recalled that he carried with him "most careful instructions as to my pictures . . . exactly where I was to find it [the Palazzo Barbaro, for *Wings*], and how to approach it."[43] The instructions were just as precise regarding the scene for "The Aspern Papers" frontispiece. Once again, Coburn's director knew in his mind exactly what he wanted—and where the subjects could be found.

One of James's friends, Constance Fletcher, was to be Coburn's guide in Venice. James had written her, giving her instructions regarding her mission. Coburn's Italian shooting script—like that of Paris—reveals once more the directoral control which James had exercised in order to get the desired results. It also reveals a quality in James which has been discussed by Edel and others — that James was a keen observer, a walker in cities, a kind of Baudelairean *flâneur*.[44] As James wrote Coburn, an "extremely tortuous and complicated walk — taking Piazza San Marco as a starting point — will show you so much, so many bits and odds and ends, such a revel of Venetian picturesqueness, that I advise your doing it on foot as much a possible."[45] Clearly, James himself had walked this and other cities mar times, though his expressed observations were not always like Baudelaire' Often it was the picturesqueness that he most noticed and later wanted f his Italian frontispieces. Yet, they were not to be too picturesque. "It is tl old faded pink-faced, battered-looking and quite homely and plain (a things go in Venice) old Palazzino on the right of the small Canal," James instructed Coburn. "It has a garden behind it, and I think, though I am not sure, some bit of a garden wall beside it; it doesn't moreover bathe its steps, if I remember right, directly in the Canal, but has the small paved Riva or footway in front of it, and *then* water-steps down from this little quay."[46] James, the *flâneur* and keen observer, displayed here — as he had in the Paris instructions — that his working methods and perceptual approach were like a photographer's. For photography is a selective art, and the street is one of the richest places for finding raw materials for photographs. Of course, the photographer's mind and eye must be alert enough to catch the moments or things worth recording. James, like some of the ablest photographers of his and later times, walked and searched for images and ideas that might some time serve as sources for his art. Like photography, James's art — as he practiced it — was selective.

Upon careful examination of the Italian instructions, we might again ask whether Coburn was allowed much creative room in the collaboration. But comparing them with the Paris and English directions, it is clear that there was. Apparently, James provided Coburn with written instructions only for the Venice photographs, since no written instructions exist pertaining to the Rome images. Very likely the latter were only discussed orally with Coburn, and so we shall never know how thorough they were — although we may guess as to that, given the other examples. Still, the written instructions for the Venice photographs gave Coburn creative room. Coburn had to translate James's "mental films" into photographic images on real film.[47] And James understood where the director's art ended and the cameraman's began: "You must judge for yourself, face to face with the object," James wrote regarding the Venetian garden wall ("Juliana's Court"), "how much, on the spot, it lends itself to a picture. I think it *must*, more or less, or sufficiently; with or without such adjuncts of the rest of the scene (from the bank opposite, from the bank near, or from wherever you can damnably manage it) as may seem to contribute or complete — to be needed in short, for the interesting effect."[48] Next, explaining what he wanted for *The Wings*, James wrote that he "had vaguely in mind the Palazzo Barbaro . . . the very old Gothic one . . . [with] water steps beside it . . . a little gallery running beside a small stretch of side-canal . . . [and] a beautiful range of old *upper* Gothic windows," and suggested that Coburn photograph an outside view. Still, James acknowledged,

> you must judge best if you can take the object most effectively from the bridge itself, from the little campo in front of the Academy, from some other like spot. . . . If none of these positions yield you something you may feel to be effective, try some other palace. . . . And do any other odd and interesting bit you can, that may serve for a sort of symbolized and generalized Venice in case everything else fails; preferring the noble and fine aspect, however, to the merely shabby and familiar . . . yet especially *not* choosing the pompous and obvious things that one everywhere sees photos of."[49]

All went well in Venice and Rome, and James looked forward to seeing the results.[50] He was able to see them by the beginning of the new year, and on 2 January 1907, he wrote Coburn that the photographs "had huge success with my highly tasteful friends last p.m. — and they will go, a full set at market price (for I shall insist on paying the whole figures for each mother's son — or rather grandson — of them) of all our pictures without exception. I want the complete array."[51] Obviously, James was satisfied with the way the collaboration was working out. Otherwise he would not have displayed the results to his "highly tasteful friends." Moreover, his desire for a full set of the prints, at market price, indicates his pleasure. And finally, James referred to them as "our pictures." He was confident that each artist shared in their making, and he was proud to take partial credit for a first-rate effort. He never responded that way to the work of any of the other artists who illustrated his work.[52]

Only a few photographs remained to be taken — some English scenes and the images in America. The English photographs were the most memorable ones for James and Coburn, because both participated directly in the search for the right scenes.[53] This time, the director and his cameraman walked the streets together, seeking out possible places where the right images might be found. Here, perhaps more than at any other moment in the collaboration, the appropriateness of photography as an inclusive art — as well as a selective one — becomes fully evident. A sketcher would have had the option of searching for the right illustrative scene or simply inventing one. In any case, he would likely have created alone. He would have imposed his own subjective interpretation on the scene, his hand and imagination being the creative mechanisms that would allow him to alter as radically as he wished the contents and form of the world in front of his eyes. But because of the nature of photography, Coburn did not have the sketcher's option. He was much less likely to interpose his own interpretation on the scene in a way that would interfere with the author's directions. The camera, after all, is relatively more objective than the sketching hand. Its image-making capacity is more delimited by the actual contents of the world before the lens. The image's content and form are selected and framed by the eyes from that world; and the picture-making mechanism, the viewfinder, can be shared — as a sketcher's hand cannot be — with another's eyes.

James seems to have understood these things explicitly, for he commented on them at some length in his preface to *The Golden Bowl*. There he asserted bluntly that he had initially "looked much askance at the proposal . . . to graft or 'grow,' at whatever point, a picture by another hand of my own picture — this being always, to my sense, a lawless incident." Though he often found illustrations charming, he nonetheless resented what he termed the " 'picture-book' quality" of "contemporary English and American prose." As James argued, an author's "own garden . . . remains one thing, and the garden he has prompted the cultivation of at other hands becomes quite another." Ordinarily, illustration was a "garden" cultivated by the "hands" of another, and it threatened one's own garden. It competed by offering readers another's "frame" for seeing the story. And whatever relieved "responsible prose of the duty of being . . . good enough, interesting enough . . . pictorial enough . . . *in itself*, does it the worst of services." So, James concluded, he sought "a contribution in as different a 'medium' as possible," illustrations that would not keep "dramatic step with their suggestive matter." This set of images was to work as "optical symbols or echoes . . . of the type or idea of this or that thing . . . small pictures of our 'set' stage with the actors left out."[54] What becomes clear from a careful reading of James's discourse on illustration is that he recognized that he could eliminate the "other hands" by entering into a collaboration with a photographer to produce the frontispieces for the New York Edition. "Hands" were not central to making photographs. Eyes were, and James's visual sense and memory were extraordinary. His gift made him perfectly suited for the photographic enterprise and enabled him to participate on an equal basis in the cultivation of the garden of illustrations for his definitive edition. Whatever place James envisioned as being an appropriate "set stage" for the novel or tale to be illustrated could be found in the world. If James already had an object or scene in mind, he could direct his cameraman to it and suggest the qualities required in the image. Coburn would know how to record it. If James was not sure where or what the right scene might be, he could either describe the right type and send Coburn to find it or, in the case of the England images, accompany Coburn in the search. Indeed, James exclaimed in his preface, "Nothing in fact could more have amused the author than the opportunity of a hunt for a series of reproducible subjects."[55] For the first time, James had found a visual medium that he could participate in and master, thereby exercising creative control over the making of the illustrations that were to accompany his prose.

The London pictures were made both before and after the Italian images — in mid-fall 1906, and early January 1907. Coburn alone had photographed "The Dome of St. Pauls' " and "some of the spoils," but as he later recalled, "the others we found or 'discovered' together." Coburn described the enterprise best:

> The afternoon that we went to St. John's Wood to photograph the little gateway and house which was to serve as the illustration for the second volume of *The Tragic Muse* was an unforgetable experience. It was a lovely afternoon, I remember, and H. J. was in his most festive mood, and I was carefree because I did not this time have to hunt for the subject, for I had the most perfect and dependable guide, the creator and author himself.
>
> I had not even read *The Tragic Muse*, but I shared his enthusiasm when, after considerable searching, we came upon exactly the right subject for his purpose.
>
> Where the house is located I do not now recall, it may in fact no longer exist, for so much of London has passed away into the domain of forgotten things, but in the photograph it is preserved, crystallized as a memento of what Henry James had meant it to be.[56]

They were looking, in James's words, for an "aspect of things or the combination of objects that might, by a latent virtue in it, speak for its connection with something in the book, and yet at the same time speak enough for its odd or interesting self."[57] Like each of the other frontispieces, "St. John's Wood" was precisely the "aspect of things" that James had envisioned (figure 8).

Sometimes, as in the case of "St. John's Wood," James knew exactly where and how to look. This was true of the making of "Portland Place," frontispiece to the second volume of *The Golden Bowl*. James realized, as he put it, that "nothing would so nobly serve as some generalized vision of Portland Place. Both our limit and the very extent of our occasion, however, lay in the fact that, unlike wanton designers, we had, not to 'create' but simply to recognize — recognize, that is, with the last fineness. The thing was to induce the vision of Portland Place *to* generalize itself." James understood "that at a given moment the great featureless Philistine vista would itself perform a miracle, would become interesting, for a splendid atmospheric hour, as only London knows how; and that our business would be then to understand."[58] So James and Coburn went to Portland Place and waited. The right moment occurred when a black coach suddenly appeared, heading into the receding hazy vista. Coburn then caught this perfect moment and created one of the most strikingly beautiful as well as symbolically appropriate images to appear in the whole of the Edition (figure 24).

Other times, however, the physical location of the needed scene had to be discovered. "Saltram's Seat," frontispiece to "The Coxon Fund," was fictionally placed at Wimbledon; but unfortunately, as Coburn explained it, "there was not such a group of trees as his [James's] imagination had visualized," so they had to search until they finally found such a scene at Hampstead Heath (figure 15).[59] "The Curiosity Shop" (made for volume one of *The Golden Bowl*) was, in James's words, completely "a shop of the mind, of the author's projected world in which objects are not primarily related to each other and therefore not 'taken from' " anywhere in particular.[60] So a real shop had to be found and photographed, one that corresponded to the author's imagined world (figure 23). The frontispiece for "In the Cage," titled simply "The Cage" (figure 11), was also "a shop of the mind," and Coburn remembered, it too "required patience and perseverance before it was discovered."[61] Nonetheless, in every instance the right objects and scenes were found; and when they were, all James had to do was direct his cameraman to capture them on film. As Coburn later said, "it was the thing itself which was important rather than the actual location."[62] And without question, only a photographer could have depicted the "thing itself" in a manner that accorded with James's own vision.

In February 1907 Coburn travelled to America to photograph the American scenes for the Edition. Little is said regarding these photographs, either by James or Coburn. At first, James thought that only two images would be needed — one for "Europe" and another for "Lady Barbarina." And though he evidently did not dictate any detailed instructions regarding them, Coburn recalled that the "illustrations were made according to H. J.'s suggestions."[63] From among the American shots Coburn took, James selected two for the Edition: " 'On Sundays, now, you might be at Home?' " for "Lady Barbarina," and "The New England Street," for "Europe" (figures 14 and 16). After this, the two artists then believed, only two English scenes remained to be made before the series would finally be complete.[64] These images — "The English House" (frontispiece to volume one of *The Portrait of a Lady*) and "The Doctor's Door" (frontispiece to volume one of *The Wings of the Dove*) (figures 3 and 19) — were evidently made shortly after Coburn returned from America.

The Edition, however, did not end with the twenty-three volumes James had so carefully planned. It grew to twenty-four. On 17 August 1908, James wrote his old friend W. D. Howells and lamented, "there may have to be a couple of supplementary volumes"; he then indicated that Scribner's was the party who had originally prescribed the plan for twenty-three.[65] In spite of this attribution of blame, we know it was James who had settled on this number. The twenty-fourth came about, according to Edel, because James "had not counted his wordage carefully; his volumes of tales proved too long. They spilled over into a 24th volume."[66] When his publisher gave him this news, sometime in 1908, James was upset.[67] Nonetheless, he wrote Coburn near the end of 1908, asking the photographer—who happened to be in America—to contact Scribner's about an additional frontispiece.[68]

True to form, James once again entered into the old spirit of the collaboration, making suggestions about the scene. "Fortunately," James wrote, "a New York subject is required and you by good luck are there. The story in question is 'Julia Bride.' [69] James then suggested that Coburn read the story and proceeded to list possible scenes for Coburn to consider. The fact that this frontispiece connects with the last story in the volume seems odd, but as James remarked, "This extra volume is unexpected and . . . the picture is rather a makeshift at the best."[70] The photograph ("The Halls of Julia") was then made and in James's hands by 22 January 1909, and James responded with grateful but disappointed enthusiasm: "This morsel of the Museum will quite serve our turn—it had all your technical merit, and it's not your fault if the subject, quite prescribed and imposed by our fatal conditions, isn't more entrancing" (figure 17).[71]

Only once more did the possibility of the need for another image arise. In 1913, some speculation regarding an additional volume occurred. Hearing of this, Coburn wrote to James from Paris, offering to do the frontispiece. James responded with a letter considering the offer and reflecting on the possibilities surrounding it.[72] James mentioned two scenes that might do—one, a Paris image that he believed technically impossible and the other, a New York skyscraper.[73] Coburn evidently responded with yet another suggestion as to scene, because James quickly wrote Coburn again: "Yes, my dear Alvin, I think the view from Monmartre, at as great a height as possible, would do as well as anything else I am able to suggest."[74]

Nothing came of this, however, for reasons that remain unexplained. It may have been partly due to James's age and increasingly poor health. But very probably it was because James was tired of the Edition and disappointed with its poor reception.[75] His monument, he subsequently wrote Edmund Gosse near the end of his life, not only failed to bring any profit to him but worse it "has never had the least intelligent critical attention at all paid it—and the artistic problem involved in my scheme was a deep and exquisite one, and moreover was, as I held, very effectively solved."[76] And regarding the Prefaces and revisions, James continued, "it took such time—*and* such taste—in other words such aesthetic light. No more commercially thankless job of the literary order was (Prefaces and all—*they* of a thank-lessness!) accordingly ever achieved."[77]

After James's death the two additional volumes that make up the Edition were brought out. *The Ivory Tower* and *A Sense of the Past* were unfinished novels, and they were published with short prefaces by Percy Lubbock and included Henry James's extensive notes regarding each novel. They also were accompanied by frontispieces—but not Coburn's. It is uncertain who made these photographs, which may be just as well. As images of artistic quality, they would probably have disappointed James, for they are not quite so beautifully realized as Coburn's work in the other volumes.

Given Henry James's bitter disappointment at the Edition's final reception, it is also just as well that he knew nothing of the final two volumes. The twenty-four that he so passionately and intelligently nurtured into existence were, in spite of his later feelings, a major achievement. James, it is clear, was utterly satisfied with Coburn's contribution. In a letter to Coburn, James promised that he would not attempt to urge Scribner's merely to note their authorship. On the contrary, he asserted, "I shall commemorate it myself, charmingly and appreciatively, in the last Preface of the lot; that of *The Golden Bowl*."[78] And so he did, considering the frontispieces "a contribution of value" to the Edition.[79] Though James felt that some of the reproductions of "Coburn's beautiful photographs" suffered through reduction in size, "those that have suffered least, the beauty, to my sense, remains great."[80]

In spite of the fact that the structure of James's monument was altered—"disturbed" was his word[81]—the monument is still quite sturdy and imposing. The Prefaces, the revised texts, and, finally, the beautiful frontispieces merge to achieve a well conceived whole. "The architectural form of the monument was preserved," Edel correctly urges, for "it constitutes in the totality of Henry James's writings, a work of art in itself."[82]

2

So Salient a Feature: A Portfolio of the Frontispieces

At the end of his 1908 review of the first few volumes of the New York Edition, Edward E. Hale, Jr., noted:

> It was a very happy idea to illustrate each volume with "portraits of some scene, situation, etc., representative of the locality of the text," and the execution has admirably carried out the plan: the pictures are an immense addition to the novels. Such as are accustomed to impressions of the spirit of place will look long and with intense pleasure at the picture of the Faubourg Saint Germains [*sic*] in "The American," — it almost takes the place of the novel. People who feel that they have lost something in the modernistic text may feel that they have gained something here, and so almost with some of the others. The spirit of place, — how much it may be in a novel!![1]

Henry James was not alone in recognizing the beauty and power of Coburn's photographic images, though the author must surely have been disquieted at Hale's suggestion that the frontispiece to *The American* "almost takes the place of the novel."

Since James's public acknowledgment of the frontispieces did not appear until the following year (in the preface to *The Golden Bowl*), his views regarding their creation and purpose were not available to Hale at the time the *Dial* review was written. Yet, James's conscious approach to illustration as well as the aesthetic quality of Coburn's images were made manifestly clear in the earliest volumes published. In *The Golden Bowl* preface, James wrote appreciatively but candidly of Coburn's contribution: "I have so thoroughly 'gone into' things, in an expository way, on the ground covered by this collection of my writings, that I should still judge it superficial to have spoken no word for so salient a feature of our Edition as the couple of dozen decorative 'illustrations.' "[2]

Indeed, they were truly a "salient" feature that was much appreciated. But James made it clear exactly what role the illustrations were to serve. In his preface, he wrote that he welcomed "illustration . . . with pride and joy; but also with the emphatic view that, might one's 'literary jealousy' be duly deferred to, it would quite stand off and on its own feet and thus, as a separate and independent subject of publication, carrying its text in its spirit, just as that text correspondingly carries the plastic possibility, become a still more glorious tribute."[3] If, despite his "literary jealousy," James "could still make a place for the idea of a contribution of value by Mr. A. L. Coburn to each of these volumes—and a contribution in as different a 'medium' as possible—this was just because the proposed photographic studies were to seek the way, which they have happily found, I think, not to keep, or to pretend to keep, anything like dramatic step with their suggestive matter."[4] The images were not to be "competitive" with the literary texts. Recall that they were to be "optical symbols or echoes, expressions of no particular thing in the text, but only of the type or idea of this or that thing. They were to remain at the most small pictures of our 'set' stage with the actors left out."[5] The frontispieces were to embody the "idea . . . of an aspect of things or the combination of objects that might, by a latent virtue in it, speak for its connexion with something in the books, and yet at the same time speak enough for its odd or interesting self."[6] And, James noted, when the photographic "quest was rewarded, it was, I make bold to say, rewarded in perfection."[7]

Without question, James intended that the frontispieces should work as complements to their respective texts. But he also intended that each image should be able to "speak enough for its odd or interesting self," and "stand off and on its own two feet." The frontispieces do work successfully as symbols; yet, as James also wished, they work equally well as images viewed separately from their texts. They are formally striking and communicate their content forcefully but discretely. To date, no portfolio of Coburn's entire set of twenty-four photographic frontispieces has been published. Their only publication has been in James's Edition itself.[8]

Though the pictures' connections with their respective texts must eventually be discussed, it is entirely appropriate that the pictures be exhibited separately in portfolio form. What follows is a facsimile reproduction of Coburn's twenty-four photogravures in the order that they originally appeared in the New York Edition.

Figure 1. A. L. Coburn, *Henry James*
[Facsimile Signature] Frontispiece to *Roderick Hudson*,
The Novels and Tales of Henry James, I.
(Courtesy of Special Collections Department, General
Library, University of New Mexico.)

Figure 2. A. L. Coburn, *Faubourg St. Germain*
Frontispiece to *The American, The Novels and Tales of Henry James*, II.
(Courtesy of Special Collections Department, General Library, University of New Mexico.)

Figure 3. A. L. Coburn, *The English Home*
Frontispiece to *The Portrait of a Lady*, *The Novels and
Tales of Henry James*, III.
(Courtesy of Special Collections Department, General
Library, University of New Mexico.)

Figure 4. A. L. Coburn, *The Roman Bridge*
Frontispiece to *The Portrait of a Lady*, *The Novels and Tales of Henry James*, IV.
(Courtesy of Special Collections Department, General Library, University of New Mexico.)

Figure 5.   A. L. Coburn, *The Dome of St. Paul's*
Frontispiece to *The Princess Casamassima, The Novels
and Tales of Henry James*, V.
(Courtesy of Special Collections Department, General
Library, University of New Mexico.)

Figure 6.   A. L. Coburn, *"Splendid Paris, Charming Paris"*
Frontispiece to *The Princess Casamassima, The Novels
and Tales of Henry James*, VI.
(Courtesy of Special Collections Department, General
Library, University of New Mexico.)

Figure 7.   A. L. Coburn, *The Comédie Français*
Frontispiece to *The Tragic Muse*, *The Novels and Tales
of Henry James*, VII.
(Courtesy of Special Collections Department, General
Library, University of New Mexico.)

Figure 8. A. L. Coburn, *St. John's Wood*
Frontispiece to *The Tragic Muse*, *The Novels and Tales of Henry James*, IX.
(Courtesy of Special Collections Department, General Library, University of New Mexico.)

Figure 9.   A. L. Coburn, *Mr. Longdon's*
Frontispiece to *The Awkward Age*, *The Novels and
Tales of Henry James*, IX.
(Courtesy of Special Collections Department, General
Library, University of New Mexico.)

Figure 10. A. L. Coburn, *Some of the Spoils*
Frontispiece to *The Spoils of Poynton, The Novels and Tales of Henry James*, X.
(Courtesy of Special Collections Department, General Library, University of New Mexico.)

Figure 11. A. L. Coburn, *The Cage*
Frontispiece to *In the Cage, The Novels and
Tales of Henry James*, XI.
(Courtesy of Special Collections Department,
General Library, University of New Mexico.)

Figure 12.　A. L. Coburn, *Juliana's Court*
Frontispiece to *The Aspern Papers*, *The Novels and Tales of Henry James*, XII.
(Courtesy of Special Collections Department, General Library, University of New Mexico.)

Figure 13.   A. L. Coburn, *The Court of the Hotel*
Frontispiece to *The Reverberator*, *The Novels and
Tales of Henry James*, XIII.
(Courtesy of Special Collections Department, General
Library, University of New Mexico.)

Figure 14. A. L. Coburn, *"On Sundays, now, you might be at Home?"*
Frontispiece to "Lady Barbarina," *The Novels and Tales of Henry James*, XIV.
(Courtesy of Special Collections Department, General Library, University of New Mexico.)

Figure 15. A. L. Coburn, *Saltram's Seat*
Frontispiece to "The Coxon Fund," *The Novels and
Tales of Henry James*, XV.
(Courtesy of Special Collections Department,
General Library, University of New Mexico.)

Figure 16.   A. L. Coburn, *The New England Street*
Frontispiece to "Europe," *The Novels and Tales of
Henry James*, XVI.
(Courtesy of Special Collections Department, General
Library, University of New Mexico.)

Figure 17   A. L. Coburn, *The Halls of Julia*
Frontispiece to "Julia Bride," *The Novels and Tales of
Henry James*, XVII.
(Courtesy of Special Collections Department, General
Library, University of New Mexico.)

Figure 18.   A. L. Coburn, *By St. Peter's*
Frontispiece to "Daisy Miller," *The Novels and Tales
of Henry James*, XVIII.
(Courtesy of Special Collections Department, General
Library, University of New Mexico.)

Figure 19.   A. L. Coburn, *The Doctor's Door*
             Frontispiece to *The Wings of the Dove*, *The Novels
             and Tales of Henry James*, XIX.
             (Courtesy of Special Collections Department, General
             Library, University of New Mexico.)

Figure 20. A. L. Coburn, *The Venetian Palace*
Frontispiece to *The Wings of the Dove*,
The Novels and Tales of Henry James, XX.
(Courtesy of Special Collections
Department, General Library, University
of New Mexico.)

Figure 21. A. L. Coburn, *By Notre Dame*
Frontispiece to *The Ambassadors, The Novels and
Tales of Henry James*, XXI.
(Courtesy of Special Collections Department,
General Library, University of New Mexico.)

Figure 22.   A. L. Coburn, *The Luxembourg Gardens*
Frontispiece to *The Ambassadors*, *The Novels and
Tales of Henry James*, XXII.
(Courtesy of Special Collections Department, General
Library, University of New Mexico.)

Figure 23. A. L. Coburn, *The Curiosity Shop*
Frontispiece to *The Golden Bowl*, *The Novels and
Tales of Henry James*, XXIII.
(Courtesy of Special Collections Department, General
Library, University of New Mexico.)

Figure 24.　A. L. Coburn, *Portland Place*
　　　　　Frontispiece to *The Golden Bowl, The Novels and*
　　　　　Tales of Henry James, XXIV.
　　　　　(Courtesy of Special Collections Department, General
　　　　　Library, University of New Mexico.)

Part Two: The Picture-Book Age

"I guess we can make it work in America — with illustrations."
"Going to have illustrations?"
*"My dear boy! What are you giving me? Do I look like the
sort of lunatic who would start a thing in the twilight of the
nineteenth century* without *illustrations? Come off!"*
— W. D. Howells, *A Hazard of New Fortunes*

*I have always hated the magazine form, magazine conditions and manners,
and much of the magazine company. I hate the hurried little subordinate
part that one plays in the catchpenny picture-book — and the negation of all
literature that the insolence of the picture-book imposes.*
— Henry James to W. D. Howells,
22 January 1894

3

James and the Art of Illustration

In his letters, published writings, and ultimately, in his use of photographic frontispieces for the New York Edition, Henry James exhibited what might appear on the surface to be a curious ambivalence toward the art of illustration. He delighted in his early and continuing love for the satirical illustrations of "Phiz" (H. K. Browne), George Cruikshank, Gavarni, Daumier, and George DuMaurier. He publicly professed an admiration for "realistic" illustrators such as Edwin Abbey, Charles S. Reinhart, and Alfred Parsons. Yet, he openly expressed dislike at having his own work illustrated, and though his serialized work was often accompanied by pictures, the art of "black and white" was kept out of nearly all his fiction when it appeared in book form. In 1893 James published *Picture and Text*, a collection of previously published essays honoring several artists and illustrators; but couched amidst his plaudits were many criticisms of illustration. About this same time, moreover, he wrote a masterful story, "The Real Thing," in which he unfolded a subtle discourse on literary realism and launched a critique of both illustration and photography—developing these through the consciousness of an artist-hero who illustrates for a living but believes his work to be mere "pot-boiling."

Most important, though, Henry James turned down the proposal to use hand drawn illustration in the New York Edition, deciding instead to use photographic frontispieces by Alvin Langdon Coburn and becoming consciously involved in the collaboration in a manner that insured the desired results. From this experience emerged a cogent picture-text aesthetic. "I should in fact be tempted here," James wrote in his preface to *The Golden Bowl*, "but for lack of space, by the very question itself at large—that question of the general acceptability of illustration coming up sooner or later, in these days, for the author of any text putting forward illustrative claims (that is producing an effect of illustration) by its own intrinsic virtue and so finding itself elbowed, on that ground, by another and a competitive process." James continued:

The essence of any representational work is of course to bristle with immediate images; and I, for one, should have looked much askance at the proposal, on the part of my associates in the whole business, to graft or "grow," at whatever point, a picture by another hand on my own picture—this being always to my sense, a lawless incident. Which remark reflects heavily, of course, on the "picture-book" quality that contemporary English and American prose appears more and more destined, by the conditions of publication, to consent, however grudgingly, to see imputed to it. But a moment's thought points the moral of the danger.

Anything that relieves responsible prose of the duty of being, while placed before us, good enough, interesting enough and, if the question be of picture, pictorial enough, above all *in itself*, does it the worst of services, and may well inspire in the lover of literature certain lively questions as to the future of that institution. That one should, as an author, reduce one's reader, "artistically" inclined, to such a state of hallucination by the images one has evoked as doesn't permit him to rest till he has noted or recorded them, set up some semblance of them in his own other medium, by his own other art— nothing could better consort than *that*, I naturally allow, with the desire or pretention to cast a literary spell. Charming, that is, for the projector and creator of figures and scenes that are as nought from the moment they fail to become more or less visible appearances, charming for this manipulator of aspects to see such power as he may possess approved and registered by the springing of such from his seed. His own garden, however, remains one thing, and the garden he has prompted the cultivation of at other hands becomes quite another, which means that the frame of one's own work no more provides place for such a plot than we expect flesh and fish to be served on the same platter. One welcomes illustration, in other words, with pride and joy; but also with the emphatic view that, might one's "literary jealousy" be duly deferred to, it would quite stand off and on its own two feet and thus, as a separate and independent subject of publication, carrying its text in its spirit, just as that text correspondingly carries the plastic possibility, become a still more glorious tribute.[1]

Clearly by 1906, when work on the Edition began, James possessed a cogent sense regarding how illustration should and should not be used. And a close study of his evolving attitudes toward illustration and its uses suggests that James's thought regarding the "picture-book" art was never confused nor subject to radical shifts. His viewpoint was consistent throughout his artistic maturity and was the product of a clearcut, sophisticated understanding of the differences between written and visual language. This enabled James to decide when and how pictures ought to be used with *his* texts.

By the time James's fiction was first illustrated (in the initial serialization of *Washington Square* in 1880), the art of "black and white" as a decorative and informational mode was a well established practice; and its ubiquitousness and controversial status among writers had long been the case, as is evidenced by Wordsworth's 1846 sonnet, "Illustrated Books and Newspapers":

> Discourse was deemed Man's noblest attribute,
> And written words the glory of his hand;

Then followed Printing with enlarged command
For thought—dominion vast and absolute
For spreading truth, and making love expand.
Now prose and verse sunk into disrepute
Must lacquey a dumb Art that best can suit
The taste of this once-intellectual Land.
A backward movement surely have we here,
From manhood,—back to childhood; for the age—
Back towards caverned Life's first rude career.
Avaunt this vile abuse of pictured page!
Must eyes be all-in-all, the tongue and ear
Nothing? Heaven keep us from a lower stage![2]

Of course, the convention of illustrating texts had existed for centuries, and it is clear from the history of illustration that the use of pictures with texts was as varied in manner, function, and extent as in the style of the pictures accompanying the words. So far as we know, the first illustrated book is an Egyptian papyrus roll dating from roughly 1980 B.C.—though the *Book of the Dead* (ca. 1300 B.C.) may be the best known ancient example.[3] More recently, however, illustration was an integral part of fifteenth-century illuminated manuscripts and "block books."[4] Subsequently, during the sixteenth and seventeenth centuries, books such as the Bible, travel literature, romances, and poems were commonly illustrated. The practice continued throughout the eighteenth century, reaching its zenith in the works of William Blake.[5]

The illustration of novels was not extensive prior to 1830, when the practice burst upon the scene along with the monthly part-novel.[6] John R. Harvey, in *Victorian Novelists and Their Illustrators*, attributes its inception to the publication of Charles Dickens's *Pickwick*, beginning in early 1836, which utilized caricatures by Seymour and "Phiz."[7] However, Harvey is not strictly correct. In the eighteenth century, the caricaturist Thomas Rowlandson made illustrations for Henry Fielding's *Tom Jones* and *Joseph Andrews*; later, during the 1830s and 1840s, a group of illustrators called "*les vignettistes*" worked in France, illustrating novels by LeSage and Cervantes.[8] So it is probably more accurate to say, as Percy Muir puts it, that "wildfire success in this medium began with Dickens," and *Pickwick* was the first.[9]

Before the 1830s, the most common use of graphic art, in relation to the novel, was probably as a reference—though a quite direct reference as in the example of the use of William Hogarth's art. Since Hogarth's engravings were so widely distributed and popular during the eighteenth century, writers such as Fielding and Smollett often verbally alluded to his work instead of describing a particular character's appearance. Moreover, as Harvey puts it, "Hogarth was still used as a short cut in the 19th century, especially if the scene to be described was chaotic."[10] Writers knew that graphic art, in general—as well as Hogarth's, in particular—was immensely popular and taken quite seriously; and so the custom of referring to well known pictures in the midst of narratives may have helped perpetuate a visually oriented audience that balked at reading words alone.[11]

Whatever the case, illustration became extraordinarily popular when it was introduced directly into literature through the rise of the monthly part-novel in the 1830s and the birth of the illustrated weekly newspaper in the 1840s. During the 1840s and 1850s, the illustrated press blossomed. The first illustrated *Punch* appeared in 1841. Next came the *Illustrated London News* (1842), *L'Illustration* (1843), and *Illustrierte Zeitung* (1843). In America, *Frank Leslie's Illustrated Newspaper* began in 1855 and *Harper's Weekly* in 1857. Back in England, *Once a Week* and *Cornhill Magazine* were born in 1859 and 1860, respectively. "Others," Muir notes, "followed thick and fast: *Good Words* (1860), *London Society* (1862), *The Sunday Magazine* (1865), *Argosy* (1866), *The Quiver* (1867)."[12] By the 1850s, illustrated literature was in such demand that the process became more mechanized. Firms such as Dalziels Brothers, in England, were established for the sole purpose of producing illustrations for literary publications. In mass production fashion, they created illustrations for publication under their name and even kept stocks of pictures that could be used over and over again. "By the 1880s," Betsy Jablow asserts, "illustrated books were in such demand that publishers often took charge of the illustration process and produced books in which the text served primarily to explain or illustrate the pictures."[13] It has been estimated that between 1870 and 1900 the space allocated to illustration in magazines such as *Harper's Monthly*, *Century*, and *Scribner's* increased over 50 percent.[14] By 1900, Edward Bok's *Ladies' Home Journal* was publishing monthly halftone "picture-stories" in which words were almost nonexistent.[15]

The extraordinary growth and popularity of illustrated literature occurred for various and complex reasons, the bases of which were the scientific, industrial, and political revolutions of the eighteenth and nineteenth centuries. These revolutions gave rise to phenomenal psychological, social, and political changes. The birth of new urban, democratic, mass culture certainly contributed to the shift in, and growth of, the audience of the writer. Whereas in the eighteenth century this audience was limited, after the French Revolution it broadened greatly to include not only the newly empowered middle class but also the working class.[16] And it may be, as Harvey argues, that the "author and artist worked for a public which did

not easily imagine what it read, and so found illustrations a valuable aid" —
that a mass audience suddenly existed "which was accustomed to 'read' its
pictures."[17]

Though illustration did not consistently attract nineteenth-century artists of
truly major importance, the best illustrators were nonetheless very gifted.[18]
The most talented were the caricaturists who worked mainly between the
1830s and the 1860s. Among the greatest of them were Cruikshank, Seymour, and "Phiz" (in England) and Daumier and Gavarni (in France). These
artists were brilliant social satirists, whose deftly drawn pictures suggest a
penetrating comprehension of human nature and the human condition.
Their work was published widely — some of it, almost weekly — during their
productive lives.[19]

  Cruikshank, Seymour, and "Phiz" are probably best remembered for
their illustration of Charles Dickens's works, and it was through the fiction
of Dickens that a youthful Henry James first encountered them. The importance of Dickens — and, by implication, his illustrators — to an "early consciousness" was recalled by James in *A Small Boy and Others*, where he
recorded that Dickens had a "presence and a power. . . . He did too much
for us surely ever to leave us free."[20] James made it clear in his memoirs that
he loved to look at illustrations throughout his childhood. As he put it, "my
bent for gaping at illustrations and exhibitions, was absorbing and genuine
. . . the picture, the representative design, directly and strongly appealed to
me, and was to appeal all my days, and I was only slow to recognize the
kind, in this order that appealed most."[21] Of course, he had plenty of
opportunity to look at illustrated literature, for it was readily available in
his home. In *Notes of a Son and Brother*, James noted that his father took
Cornhill's, *Once a Week*, and *Punch*; and in his essay, "London," he
recalled the "old volumes of the 'Illustrated London News' turned over in
childhood."[22] As a small boy, James even wrote a little drama, and as the
adult James related it, "When the drama itself had covered three pages, the
last one, over which I most laboured, served for the illustration of what I
had verbally presented. Every scene had thus its explanatory picture."[23]
Unfortunately, James continued, despite the fact that the little boy "was
capable of learning, though with inordinate slowness, to express ideas in
scenes," he "was not capable, with whatever patience, of making proper
pictures; yet I aspired to this form of design to the prejudice of any other,
and long after those primitive hours was still wasting time in attempts at it. I
cared so much for nothing else, and that vaguely redressed, as to a point,
my general failure of acuteness."[24]

  For a young Henry James, illustration was a delightful and perpetual adventure, and in his half-conscious mind it took on an aspect of almost lifelike proportions. Again and again in *A Small Boy and Others*, James revealed his childhood practice of perceiving his experience of reality through the filter of illustrations. As a child in New York City, James remembered, he passed the hours at home partly "by a study of a great store, as it seemed to me, of steel plated volumes devoted mainly to the heroines of Romance, with one in particular, presenting those of Shakespeare, in which the plates were so artfully coloured and varnished, and complexion and dress thereby so endeared to memory, that it was long afterwards a shock to me at the theater not to see just those bright images, with their peculiar toggeries come on."[25] And reminiscing about a childhood visit to a Dickens adaptation, James recalled that he had to make the characters in the theater poster "conform to the illustrations of Phiz."[26]

The omnipresence of illustrations not only affected a youthful James's theater going but also pervaded his everyday life. A New York schoolmaster to the young boy "was not at all funny . . . but he was to remain with me a picture of somebody in Dickens, one of the Phiz if not the Cruikshank pictures."[27] A once-visited dentist, to James's "mind's eye," resembled "certain figures in Phiz's illustrations to Dickens."[28] Indeed, Londoners seen during an 1850s trip to England, reminded young James,

of Cruikshank's Artful Dodger and his Bill Sikes and his Nancy, only with the bigger brutality of life, which pressed upon the cab, the early-Victorian fourwheeler, as we jogged over the Bridge, and cropped up in more and more gas-lit patches for all our course, culminating, somewhere far to the west, in the vivid picture, framed by the cab-window, of a woman reeling backward as a man felled her to the ground with a blow in the face. The London view at large had in fact more than a Cruikshank, there still survived in it quite a Hogarth, side — which I had of course then no name for, but which I was so sharply to recognise on coming back years later that it fixed for me the veracity of the great pictorial chronicler.[29]

The numerous allusions made in James's memoirs to illustrators and illustration indicate just how important the art was to the sensibility developing in James during his formative years; and it becomes clear that seeing was a central experience in the formulation of the artist's consciousness. So, it is important to note also that James's childhood included the experience of looking at painting. As a youth, James saw firsthand the work of many important painters when he visited some of the major museums in Paris and London. Moreover, when the James family moved to Newport, Rhode Island, in 1859, young Henry studied art in the studio of the American artist William Morris Hunt.[30] The work of many painters attracted the eyes of a very visually minded child and, in the process, reinforced and further developed his interest in, and proclivity towards, an intensely visual approach to the world. Of course, it would be a mistake to argue that as a small boy James was fully conscious of the implications of his broad visual experience. Not until he became a young writer did he begin to reflect critically on his visual background and its importance to his evolving mind. As a professional author, he wrote many essays on painting in which he proved himself to be a perceptive and articulate critic of the visual arts.[31] More important, though, the author's assimilation of his visual experience consciously surfaced in his own art. This experience made it possible for him to forge an extraordinarily pictorial prose style. It also contributed to his definite attitudes towards illustration and its use in his own work.

The satirical mode of illustration, so prevalent during James's childhood in the 1840s and 1850s, was quite different from the style that came to be practiced during his adulthood. In the 1860s, J. R. Harvey notes, caricature's exaggerated manner fell from fashion, and the formerly "delicate communication of relationships" — found, for example, in "Phiz's" work in Dickens's *Dombey and Son* (figure 25) — were no longer predominant. As the style shifted from caricature to realistic representation (figure 26), vital, expressive qualities were lost.[32] Yet, illustration became even more widely used than before and reached its peak in popularity during the 1890s.[33] Accompanying the stylistic change was the victory of the Victorian high art concern for book decoration, and credit for this triumph is given by Holbrook Jackson to the influence of William Morris's "Arts and Crafts" movement and to the work of pre-Raphaelite painters such as Rossetti, Millais, and Hunt. Jackson explicitly dates the inception of the new style with the publication of the famous Moxon edition of Tennyson's *Poems* (1857), while Harvey credits Millais with the introduction of the new mode in 1855.[34] Whatever the exact date, the work of "Phiz," Cruikshank, and other such artists was suddenly deemed inferior art by the new illustrators, editors, and publishers. Joseph Pennell, one of the leading illustrators in the new manner, summed up their attitude when he wrote in 1895, "I suppose that among artists and people of any artistic appreciation, it is generally admitted by this time that the greatest bulk of the work of "Phiz," Cruikshank, Doyle, and even many of Leech's designs are simply rubbish." Critic Gleeson White agreed, explaining that those artists' illustrations lacked "academic accomplishment," "literal imitation of nature," and "beauty of truth."[35]

As the new artistic style took hold and as James himself matured as a writer and critic, his youthful enthusiasm was replaced by a strong skepticism regarding the illustration of literature. Leon Edel tells us that, insofar

Figure 25. "Phiz," Illustration in *Dombey and Son* by Charles Dickens (1846–48). (Courtesy of Special Collections Department, General Library, University of New Mexico.)

"YOU MAKE MY REPARATION—MY EXPIATION—DIFFICULT!"—[SEE PAGE 349.]

Figure 26.   C.S. Reinhart, Illustration in "Louisa Pallant,"
by Henry James, *Harper's Monthly* (January 1888).
(Courtesy of Special Collections Department, General
Library, University of New Mexico.)

as his own writing for magazine serialization was concerned, James "did not like the illustrated ones, because he considered illustration an affront to the written word. Therefore *Scribner's*, which later became *Century*, continued to receive what he regarded as his poorer efforts. His best was still reserved for the *Atlantic Monthly*."[36] Elsewhere, Edel elaborates on this, noting that though James seemed to like the work of some illustrators, he disliked having his own words illustrated because the publication of his stories was held up "in order to give the artists time to do their work."[37]

Evidence found in James's letters and essays indicates that Edel is correct; James indeed had an aversion toward having his seriously intended prose illustrated, even though he did admire certain illustrators who were active during his adult lifetime. This seemingly ambivalent viewpoint might best be summed up by James himself in a letter to a *Century* editor: "Ah, your illustrations — your illustrations; how as a writer one hates 'em; and how their being as good as they are makes one hate 'em more! What one writes suffers essentially, as literature, from going with them, and the two things ought to stand alone."[38] In a letter to his friend, Howells, James was much harsher: "I have always hated the magazine form, magazine conditions and manners, and much of the magazine company. I hate the hurried little subordinate part that one plays in the catch-penny picture-book — and the negation of all literature that the insolence of the picture-book imposes."[39] On another occasion, James wrote a more good natured attack on the medium in a letter to Clement Shorter, the editor of the *Illustrated London News*: "I confess I am afraid your artist — although I regard my story as essentially and absolutely dramatic — won't find in my situations a great deal of suggestion for variegated or panoramic pictures. But I *like* so little to be illustrated (I resent it so, amiably speaking, on behalf of good prose and *real* writing) that I won't hypocritically pretend to pity him too much."[40] But subsequently to Howells, James again denounced illustrations as "loud simplifications and *grossissements*, the big building . . . the 'mounted' play, the prose that is careful to be in the tone of, and with the distinction of a newspaper or bill-poster advertisement."[41]

If James's attitudes toward illustration had never been expressed outside the privacy of letters, we might conclude that though he hated to be illustrated, he sat back and quietly suffered it, bending his will to popular pressures. But he did not do that. He wrote and published essays about illustration, and several of these were collected in a small edition called *Picture and Text* (1893). Most of these essays are appreciations of individual illustrators and their illustrations. Among the artists discussed are Edwin A. Abbey, Charles S. Reinhart, Alfred Parsons, George DuMaurier, John Singer Sargent, and Honoré Daumier — of whom all but one were friends of

James.[42] Much of *Picture and Text* contains James's pictorial analyses of the work of these — and other — artists, analyses in which James's critical approaches are unusually clear, penetrating, and shrewd if often impressionistic. Imbedded in his criticisms are also cultural observations that are intelligently related to his analyses. But more to the point of this inquiry are his comments — often negative — on the art of illustration.

Edel calls *Picture and Text* a "subtle and delicate" book.[43] Yet, it is also a reticent and ambiguous one when considered within the entire context of James's attitudes about illustration. James began the book with an obliquely laudatory statement tinged with irony:

> If there be nothing new under the sun there are some things a good deal less old than others. The illustration of books, and even more of magazines, may be said to have been born in our time, so far as variety and abundance are the signs of it; or born, at any rate, the comprehensive, ingenious, sympathetic spirit in which we conceive and practice it.
>
> If the centuries are ever arraigned at some bar of justice to answer in regard to what they have given, of good or of bad, to humanity, our interesting age (which certainly is not open to the charge of having stood with its hands in its pockets) might perhaps do worse than put forth the plea of having contributed a fresh interest in "black and white." The claim may now be made with more confidence from the very evident circumstance that this interest is far from exhausted. These pages are an excellent place for such an assumption. In *Harper* they have again and again, as it were, illustrated the illustration, and they constitute for the artist a series of invitations, provocations and opportunities. They may be referred to without arrogance in support of the contention that limits of this large movement, with all its new and rare refinement, are not yet in sight.[44]

Throughout much of the book, James proceeded to interweave his sometimes curious compliments of illustration with his appreciations of the individual artists.

Illustration, James wrote, has conferred "great distinction on our magazines."[45] And though a few pages later he admitted that the medium was limited because of its lack "of color," James suggested that such a flaw was minute compared to its real value. The illustrator

> purchases a freedom which enables him to attack ever so many ideas. It is by variety and numerosity that he commends himself to his age, and it is for these qualities that his age commends him to the text. The twentieth century, the latter half of it, will, no doubt, have its troubles, but will have a compensatory luxury, that of seeing the life of a hundred years before much more vividly than we — even happy we — see the life of a hundred years ago. But for this our illustrators must do their best, appreciate the endless capacity of their own form. It is to the big picture what the short story is to the novel.[46]

Not only was illustration oddly praised with overtones of tongue in cheek, but it was accorded a kind of duty toward the future that implied that its real value lay in its factuality instead of its artfulness. Illustration could convey information vividly, suggesting that its function was reportorial—a charge often made against photography.

On many occasions, James did bestow compliments on the illustrators. Beginning in his introductory essay, "Black and White," James treated illustration through the examples of several of the illustrators. He spoke of Frederick Barnard's work as having "so remarkable a sense of English types and attitudes," of Alfred Parsons as being an artist who reproduced "with remarkable discrimination and truth,"[47] and of Charles S. Reinhart as being "the observer of the immediate, as Mr. Abbey is that of the considerably removed."[48] Also, Frank Millet's illustrations were credited with having variety and being "artistically interesting."[49] Immediately following his general introductory essay, James went on to discuss separately and with greater fullness the work of Abbey, Reinhart, and Parsons as well as the historically more important Daumier and Sargent. James continued to analyze the work of the now lesser known illustrators in language that praised—but praised in rather modest, narrow terms. Abbey, for instance, "enlarged the idea of illustration" as his variety of efforts indicated.[50] Parsons was "a masterly contributor" to *Harper's*.[51] And of Reinhart's work, James thought "no work of art is absolutely little."[52]

Only when James encountered the more outstanding art of Daumier, Sargent, and (perhaps) DuMaurier, did his prose expand and clarify, utilizing more precise, superlative language and less qualified phrasing. DuMaurier, James wrote, "has a brilliant history, but it must be candidly recognized that it is written or drawn mainly in an English periodical."[53] In that periodical, *Punch*, James saw "for so many years" DuMaurier's "interpretation" of "the social life of England that he interpretation has become the text itself."[54] DuMaurier made vivid the stupidities, the falseness, and the shallowness of so many people. It was DuMaurier, we recall, who first illustrated James's fiction.[55] Along with Gavarni, "Phiz," and Cruikshank, DuMaurier was very special to Henry James.

Daumier, too, was treated in a large manner in *Picture and Text*. Where Parsons was guardedly described as communicating "to us something of the thrill of the whole," when representing nature,[56] Daumier was discussed in grander, more certain terms: "There is an admirable page—it brings the idea down to 1851—in which a sordid but astute peasant, twirling his thumbs on his stomach and looking askance, allows his political adviser to urge upon him in a whisper that there is not a minute to lose—to lose for action, of course—if he wishes to keep his wife, his house, his field, his heifer and his calf. The canny skepticism in the ugly, half averted face of the typical rustic who considerably suspects his councellor is indicated by a few masterly strokes."[57] It was in Daumier's "masterly" drawn types that James sensed "universality."[58]

Sargent was highly praised also—but neither as an illustrator nor as a painter whose work exhibited a literary tendency. Indeed, it is unclear just why he was discussed in a book on illustration. Perhaps James needed another essay to fill the book, and since James respected and liked Sargent as a painter and a friend, it may have seemed appropriate to include the piece. Whatever the reasons, the Sargent essay was included and James's high opinion of the portraitist's work made for an interesting contrast to his views of the work of the illustrators. To James, Sargent was a painter of complex sophistication, whose visual expressions would not ever likely appeal to a broad public.[59]

In James's opinion, Sargent was a gifted painter, and Daumier and DuMaurier were illustrators of a very special kind—caricaturists and satirists. They all were able to penetrate and convey truths about social life and human nature. That James should honor these three men is not surprising, for he greatly esteemed painting and believed caricature to be an unique, distinctive form of illustration—probably the highest achievement possible in it.[60] Rarely did James's discussions of these artists contain the kind of indirect criticism that he leveled at illustrators such as Abbey, Parsons, or Reinhart.

Elsewhere in *Picture and Text*, the criticism of the minor artist-illustrators—and of illustration—came closer to the attitudes that James revealed in his letters. About one of the illustrators, James wrote, "The superficial view is, after all, the natural one for the picture-maker."[61] And of another, James said, he probably does not regard "himself, in the first place as an illustrator, in the sense to which the term is usually restricted."[62] Finally, a clue to James's real reservations about illustration emerged: "A charming story-teller indeed he would be who should write as Mr. Abbey draws. . . . It is true that what the verbal artist would like to do would be to find out the secret of the pictorial, to drink at the same fountain."[63] Taken together, James's views make it clear so far that the did not particularly object to the work of illustrators per se but instead, in Viola Hopkins Winner's words, was concerned with "the fact that illustrations invaded the writers domain."[64]

It is this attitude that emerged in complete, though again indirect, form in the last essay in *Picture and Text*, "After the Play." Concealed in that imaginary dialogue over the issue of the proper use of stage decoration in the theater is the real issue that concerned James—the appropriate use of illustration alongside good literature. At the beginning of the dialogue, a small party of people has just left an afternoon performance of a play. They are having a conversation about it, and following a discussion on the relation of fiction to life, they begin talking about stage decoration. One of the characters (clearly speaking for James) is Dorriforth who says,

> There is evidently a corrosive principle in the large command of machinery and decorations—a germ of perversion and corruption. It gets the upper hand—it becomes the master. It is so much less easy to get good actors than good scenery and to represent a situation by the delicacy of personal art than by "building it in" and having everything real. . . . [The actor] hasn't a decent respect for his art unless he be ready to render his part as if the whole illusion depended on that alone and the accessories didn't exist. The acting is everything or it's nothing. It ceases to be everything as soon as something else becomes very important.[65]

A moment later Dorriforth adds, "Good scenery and poor acting are better than poor scenery with the same sauce. Only it becomes then another matter: We are no longer talking about the drama."[66] Substitute "writing" for "acting," and it follows that, "We are no longer talking about" *literature.* Obviously, James was suggesting that good illustration was easier to find than good literature. And though there often was "good scenery" accompanying the writing of his day, it did not convert the poor writing into literature; even worse, it often corrupted the good literature that did appear by getting "the upper hand." To James, writing was "everything or it's nothing."

James, through Dorriforth, reemphasized his point again and again.[67] Yet, ultimately, he did qualify himself—making it clear that he was concerned only with "the abuse of scenery. I never said anything so idiotic as that the effect isn't helped by an appeal to the eye and an adumbration of the whereabouts."[68] When the question of how to determine this arose, James had Dorriforth answer in words that foreshadowed the aesthetic principle underlying his own use of illustration in the New York Edition: It must simply give "the essence of the matter," leaving "the embroidery to the actors."[69]

In just one piece of fiction did James touch upon the question of illustration, and that is in his short tale, "The Real Thing" (1892).[70] Though this story deals mainly with the questions regarding art, life, and literary realism, illustration is commented upon, and James's attitudes on the art of "black and white" again emerge. The story's center of consciousness is an unnamed artist who aspires to be a serious portrait painter. Meanwhile, however, he makes his living as an illustrator.

"The Real Thing" concerns this artist's reflections upon an experience he has had with an impoverished genteel couple, Major and Mrs. Monarch. The Monarchs ask the artist for work as models. Since they are the real thing, they assume themselves to be supremely suited as models for the illustrations of ladies and gentlemen that the artist needs to sketch for a "projected *édition de luxe*." Feeling sorry for them, the artist takes them on, but they do not prove to be nearly as satisfactory as two others — Miss Churm, a Cockney, and Oronte, an Italian immigrant. So, ironically, the servant class pair become models for the illustrations of the refined characters while the genteel, refined Monarchs become temporary, real life servants of the artist and his models.

It is at the beginning of the story that the artist reveals his — and James's — attitude toward illustration and its importance in the hierarchy of art forms:

> I worked in black and white, for magazines, for storybooks, for sketches of contemporary life, and consequently had frequent employment for models. These things were true, but it was not less true (I may confess it now — whether because the aspiration was to lead to everything or to nothing I leave the reader to guess), that I couldn't get the honors, to say nothing of the emoluments of a great painter of portraits out of my head. My "illustrations" were my potboilers; I looked to a different branch of art (far and away the most interesting it had always seemed to me), to perpetuate my fame.[71]

To this artist — and to James — illustrations were "potboilers" and painting was "far and away the most interesting" branch of art. Obviously implied here is the notion that there is a hierarchy among art forms, with painting at the top and illustration at, or near, the bottom. This implication sums up succinctly the general nineteenth-century attitude: painting was accorded a very high — often the highest — status among all the arts, visual and literary. Apparently, this was even James's view for a time. As Leon Edel makes clear, James grew up believing in such a hierarchy in the palace of art, and at one time in his life, when he was studying in William Morris Hunt's studio (1859-60), it was difficult for James to come to the realization that he himself had no talent as a sketcher and painter. Subsequently, of course, he set out to become a novelist bent on making his writing an art that would equal any painting.[72]

As an artform, then, illustration could not be taken too seriously. Yet James did not leave it there. In "The Real Thing," his artist — though engaged in illustrating — is an aspiring painter who believes himself capable of seeing the truth about the Monarchs: "I had immediately *seen* them. I had seized their type — I had already settled what I would do with it. Something that wouldn't absolutely have please them, I afterwards reflected."[73] The artist goes on to tell the reader that the Monarchs failed to serve as good models for his illustrations because they were stiff and had no variety. Indeed, Mrs. Monarch "was singularly like a bad illustration."[74] The couple possessed insufficient imagination to guide the artist's eye and hand and thus help him create the illustrations that the texts demanded. Here James asserted that the artist, as a painter, would have had no trouble painting them truthfully, for he had "*seen* them." And as a painter, he would have been free to interpret what he saw through his own critical eye and imagination. But no such freedom existed for the illustrator, who had to bind his own imagination with the cord of the text. Thus limited, the illustrator needed the help of good models possessing enough variety to act the parts written for them in the text. Obviously, James was pointing out that in any picture-text combination either the sketcher's or the writer's picture will inherently dominate, and as far as James was concerned, the proper practice of illustration called for the picture to be subordinate to the word. Otherwise it would interfere. James's artist understood that he was not free to develop his talents and reputation so long as he engaged in his "potboiling" art. And his frustrated ambition provided James with a brilliant vehicle for putting illustration in its place within the hierarchy in the palace of art.

It must now be evident that Henry James was quite clear in his views regarding the illustration of literature. To admire the work of certain illustrators—indeed, to be friends with several of them—and still believe that illustration was a threat to good literature must have been somewhat uncomfortable for James. Nonetheless, he maintained this stance over the years, because he believed deeply in the uncompromised value of good literature. As will be seen, he managed to keep illustration out of most of his books, in spite of the pressures exerted by his editors and the general climate in the publishing industry. And when he finally decided how he wished to illustrate his definitive Edition, he knew exactly what he wanted from illustration and set about to make sure that his ideas were carried out to perfection.

4

The Illustrated James

To Henry James, the illustration of someone else's literature was one thing. To have one's own work illustrated, however, was quite another. Like that of so many other authors, James's writing did not escape being accompanied by illustrations; but an analysis of the extent to which his texts were illustrated as well as the manner in which pictures were linked with his words indicates that James's views on illustration were derived in great part from his own experience.

James's fiction was first illustrated in 1880, beginning with the serialization of *Washington Square*. George DuMaurier, James's good friend, provided the drawings, and this joint picture-text effort initially appeared in *Cornhill Magazine* from June through November 1880. Immediately following this, on 1 December 1880, the first book edition of *Washington Square* was published by Harper and Brothers in America. This edition, it is interesting to note, also contained DuMaurier's illustrations, making it one of just three of James's book editions of fiction to be illustrated besides that of the New York Edition (1907–09).[1] These facts suggest one of the important points that must be stressed regarding the illustration of James's writings. Until the New York Edition, James's fiction was — with the exceptions cited — illustrated only in its premier magazine serialization, and even then it was not always accompanied by illustration.[2] When it was, however, the results must have helped form, and further confirm, both James's doubts and aesthetic views about illustration, contributing to his attempt to create an exceptional approach to illustration in the New York Edition.

Though few of James's books of fiction were illustrated, many of his nonfiction books and essays were. Yet, even here the pattern of not including illustration in books is often evident. James's early essay on George DuMaurier, appearing in the May 1883 issue of *Century*, contains examples of DuMaurier's *Punch* caricatures. But in the subsequent reprinting of this essay, in *Partial Portraits* (1888), the illustrations are absent.[3] On the other hand, *Picture and Text* (1893) contains many of the same illustrations that appeared in the original magazine edition of each essay contained in it. These illustrations include portraits of the illustrators discussed and examples of their work. What is especially interesting about this latter edition is the fact that several of the portraits of the artists are retouched photographic reproductions, images in which the shirts, coats, and ties have obviously been drawn in by hand.[4]

As was common, James's travel literature was often illustrated. But again, it was just as often not. *Transatlantic Sketches*, James's first collection of travel essays, was not illustrated either in its first English edition (1875) or in its Tauchnitz revised edition (1883).[5] *Portraits of Places* (1883), another collection of travel sketches, was likewise unillustrated.[6] And *A Little Tour of France* (1884), originally planned as an illustrated work with drawings by Joseph Pennell, was first published without them. Not until the 1900 edition were Pennell's illustrations included.[7] And then, James wrote a brief preface to this edition in which he registered a quiet protest suggesting that his own prose effort was originally intended to be subordinate to Pennell's pictures.[8] Once again, James's picture-text views are echoed.

In 1888 James's essay, "London," was published in *Century*, accompanied by thirteen illustrations by Pennell.[9] As was usually the case when James was illustrated, no active collaboration occurred between the author and his illustrator. Regarding the illustrations for this essay, James wrote Pennell, "I have really nothing to suggest save that you follow your own fancy. If you too are fond of London let that fondness be your guide and you fall in sufficiently with my text. The article from being so general is difficult to illustrate."[10] Then, after making a few suggestions regarding possible subjects (James could not seem to resist the temptation to retain some control) and giving a gentle warning to Pennell that he should be free and fanciful rather than "neat, definite, photographic," James ended his letter with resignation: "But do your own London, and it will be sufficiently mine."[11]

James continued to publish a variety of nonfiction books. The year 1893 saw the issue of some more of his collected travel essays, *Essays in London and Elsewhere*, but it was not illustrated. James's biography, *William Wetmore Story and His Friends*, came out in 1903, but it contained only a photogravure frontispiece portrait of Story. In 1905, James's travel book, *English Hours*, was released, and it was profusely illustrated by Pennell.[12] Perhaps most tellingly, though, James's major book of nonfiction, *The American Scene*, emerged in 1907, and it was unillustrated both in its English and American editions. Indeed, before James traveled to America to gather impressions for this book, Joseph Pennell offered to illustrate it. In his most oblique manner, however, James refused the offer in a letter to Pennell on 23 June 1904: "I can imagine a (pictorial) New York, and a ditto Chicago, and in a manner, a ditto South; but a pictorial Boston eludes, defies, almost infuriates me—and I'm afraid I shan't rise, or fall, to that."[13] Let us recall, of course, that it was during James's visit to America in 1904-05 to make his "American Scene" observations that he met Coburn, and the seed for their collaboration was planted. During this time, James was undoubtedly thinking about the New York Edition and its contents as well as the shape and contents of *The American Scene*. So it is surely no coincidence that the latter was published without illustration.

After the New York Edition was completed, only three additional volumes emerged with illustrations during James's lifetime—*Italian Hours* (1909), *A Small Boy and Others* (1913), and *Notes of a Son and Brother* (1914). (A few serialized short tales were illustrated too.) James seems not to have had much to say regarding the illustration of *Italian Hours*—which, once again, was done by Pennell. But James's comment on what appears to have been the projected but never completed volume on London—also to have been illustrated by Pennell—might best serve as an epitaph for most of the illustrated books he had published. James wrote Coburn in 1909 that Pennell was, "alas," working on illustrations for another of his books.[14]

"Alas," indeed! Not until his memoirs—*A Small Boy and Others* and *Notes of a Son and Brother*—did James again seem to participate happily in the illustration of his work. On these occasions, this was due likely to the fact that the illustrations used were—like the texts themselves—intimately connected with James's life. Reproductions of important personal visual documents, they give evidence of crucial aspects of James's past. As such, they triggered James's memory and stimulated the writing of prose that is especially vivid. A daguerreotype portrait (see figure 32) of James and his father, taken when James was twelve, was used for the frontispiece to *A Small Boy and Others*. Of its meaning, James wrote, "I cherish, to the extent of here reproducing, an old daguerreotype all the circumstances of the taking of which I intensely recall. . . . It documents for me in so welcome and so definite a manner my father's cultivation of my company. It documents at the same time the absurdest little legend of my small boyhood."[15] The illustrations for *Notes of a Son and Brother* are reproductions of artworks originally made by the hand of William James. Included are self-portraits, a sketch of another brother, Wilky James, fragments of two letters, and a painted portrait of Minny Temple, a woman who held a very special place in the memory of James. Once again, James's own words give us insight into the quality of meaning these illustrations held for him. Regarding the sketch of Wilky, James wrote, "William . . . preserved our poor lacerated brother's aspect in a drawing of great and tender truth which

I permit myself to reproduce. It tells for me the double story — I mean both of Wilky's then condition and of the draughtsman's admirable hand."[16] The illustrations found in these memoirs functioned for James both as cherished objects in themselves and as meaning-charged evidence of the past. As such, they are an inextricable part of the memories James was offering.

In the preface to *The Golden Bowl* James most consciously focused on "that question of the general acceptability of illustration" as it specifically pertained to his literature.[17] It is worth repeating what he had to say on the matter, because this preface contains the most complete statement of James's objections to illustration as well as his views regarding how pictures should work with texts. The grafting of "a picture by another hand on my own picture," he asserted, was "a lawless incident," for illustrations that relieved "responsible prose of the duty of being, while placed before us, good enough, interesting enough and . . . pictorial enough . . . [do] it the worst of services."[18] Yet, James welcomed illustration "with the emphatic view that . . . it would quite stand off and on its own feet and thus, as a separate and independent subject of publication, carrying its text in its spirit, just as that text correspondingly carries the plastic possibility, become a still more glorious tribute."[19] Coburn's photographic frontispieces did not "pretend to keep . . . dramatic step with their suggestive matter," nor were they "competitive and obvious."[20] Instead, they were generalized pictures, "symbols . . . of no particular thing in the text, but only of the type or idea of this or that thing."[21] Their purpose was to convey "the aspect of things or the combination of objects that might, by latent virtue in it, speak for its connexion with something in the book, and yet at the same time speak enough for its odd or interesting self."[22] Clearly, James believed that where other efforts at mingling pictures and texts had failed — including his own — the New York Edition enterprise had succeeded.

The perception that competition between picture and text could be a problem was not new, as James realized. His discussions of the work of DuMaurier, Daumier, and Gavarni usually never mentioned the texts those artists decorated, suggested that James believed that the pictures were better than the literature they accompanied. There is, however, an exception to this point that further reveals James's attitude. James wrote an essay, "George DuMaurier," in 1897 after DuMaurier's death. In it, he discussed *Trilby*, a book written *and* illustrated by DuMaurier himself. James noted that he had read the illustrated *Trilby* first; but in preparing his eulogy for DuMaurier, he had reread an unillustrated edition of the novel. Referring to the latter, James remarked, "*Trilby*, at all events, becomes without the illustrations distinctly more serious."[23] Of course, he was repeating — by implication — his often made observation that pictures usually interfered with texts. In this instance, James was suggesting that the pictures had the power to modify the tone implicit in the prose, and so their presence or absence subtly altered the entire literary work.

Regarding Phiz and Cruikshank and the relationship between their pictures and Dickens's texts, James also recognized the imputed qualities of competitiveness and interference. For no matter how vividly James remembered Dickens's prose, he wrote about "Cruikshank's splendid form of the work [of Dickens], of which our own foreground was clear. It perhaps even seemed to me more Cruikshank's than Dickens's; it was a thing of such vividly terrible images."[24] James had obviously recognized that even in Dickens, the illustrations, as J. R. Harvey puts it, "were not confined to the vivid suggestion of character and mood; they could develop a novel's themes subtly, delicately, and powerfully, and in essentially visual terms."[25] To James, this was a usurpation of the function of the novelist and was not to be tolerated in the publication of his own work, in spite of the popularity of illustrated editions. If the writer could not communicate in prose what it was he was trying to convey, he simply failed as a writer. Illustrations, more often than not, were pleasant decorative additions to texts when they did not interfere with the prose; or they were delightful saving features when they were superior to the prose. But when both prose and pictures were good and competed, James was quite disturbed. Consequently, in his New York Edition he sought to achieve the best of both worlds—masterful prose accompanied by beautiful illustrations that enhanced but did not compete with that prose.

The awareness that illustration could interfere with texts was not uniquely Henry James's. During the 1880s and 1890s, the picture-text relation was an important issue for literary and art critics in England and America and was regarded by most as problematic. Some were quite disturbed by the proliferation of illustrated literature, lamenting that the age was one of "over-illustration" and inveighing against "the tyranny of the pictorial." Charles T. Congdon made the former charge in an 1884 issue of *North American Review* but assured readers, "illustration is a fashion, and cannot last. In one sense it is aboriginal and savage, if not childish." He then explained:

Nothing that encourages affectation, or that leads us to be satisfied with the pretty and to forget the great, can promote a real love of art. It is of small use that we admire, though even that is better than to say we admire while knowing nothing about the matter; the main point is, whether an object is worthy of admiration. A man who likes a meretricious picture, and admits his gratification, is so far worthy of praise; but that does nothing for the picture, nor is the man himself less an object of commiseration. Tinsel is tinsel, and fillagree is fillagree, and leather is leather, and prunella is prunella, and will be until the end of time. What good has the picture-card mania (now happily dying out, if not dead)

ever done to any human soul? Chromo-lithography was carried to such an extent that at
last the popular stomach revolted. The same fate awaits over-illustrated, tawdry, and
bright looking books. People will come back to good plain letterpress, to quiet binding
and to mere frontispieces, with a portrait or so to gratify a reasonable curiosity.26

The latter charge was made ten years later, in 1895, by Sidney Fairfield in
Lippincott's Monthly Magazine. "With all this space in our publications
preempted by the pictorial," Fairfield warned, "the gentry who live by
selling what they write must take metaphorically to the woods, for the
reading public has suddenly become picture-mad. The highest thought, the
deepest truth, the most exquisite bit of description, poetry, dialogue, love,
tragedy, humor, realism of any kind, all are subjected by the weeklies and
monthlies to the tyranny of the pictorial."27

Others, however, were not so single minded in their opposition to
illustration, though they usually acknowledged that picture-text "marriages" were not always successful. While to an illustrator such as Joseph
Pennell, illustration was good "so long as it improves the appearance of the
page," to Pennell's contemporary, Holbrook Jackson, decoration could get
out of hand.28 Commenting on abuses in illustration, Jackson drew upon
the work of Aubrey Beardsley as an example. Though he thought
Beardsley's work visually brilliant, Jackson wrote, "None of the books he
illustrated or decorated are decorated in the best sense. His designs over-
power the text — not because they are greater but because they are unappro-
priate, sometimes even impertinent. The diabolical thumb-nail notes in the
'Bon Mot' series have nothing whatever to do with the texts."29 As Jackson
saw it, there were many "artists who were content to illustrate a theme in the
usual nineteenth-century manner without any regard for the appearance of
the printed page. These artists were not concerned with the ultimate balance
and proportion of a book as a work of art; their business was interpretive,
and their medium, pictures, and they considered it an achievement to make
drawings which, whilst serving their immediate illustrative purpose,
remained themselves separate and even independent pictures."30

The issue of proper illustration was also treated by Philip Gilbert
Hamerton, a popular and influential English art critic whose work was
known by James.31 Hamerton wrote a dialogue, "Book Illustration," which
was included in *Portfolio Papers* (1889). The dialogue takes place among a
poet, a scientist, an artist, and a critic. Through these various characters,
Hamerton brought up the various aspects, problems, and attitudes that
were pertinent to the question of book illustration. Hamerton discussed the
idea that literature and pictorial art are separate and that their inclusion
together in a book (at least, in fiction) gives rise to the strong risk of a
rivalry between them. Though the poet in the dialogue asserts that that

rivalry always occurs (to the detriment of good literature, he believes), the artist argues that the decorative value of pictures may be helpful to literature, especially mediocre literature. The main conclusion of the dialogue, though, seems to be that illustration's most valuable use is as an accompaniment to nonfiction texts—implying that its most important function is that of providing visual examples.[32]

It is quite likely that James read Hamerton's dialogue, for James's own dialogue on illustration, "After the Play," first appeared in a June 1889 issue of the *New Review* and might be considered either a response of sorts to Hamerton or else a timely coincidence. At the very least, James was probably familiar with the opinions of others who discussed the subject, despite the fact that he nowhere referred to any essay or dialogue that dealt with illustration. What is certain, though, is that James's work was illustrated in ways that contradicted his mature views about how texts ought to be accompanied by pictures. Generally speaking, the illustrations of his writings appear as attempts at explaining the texts. The pictures, more often than not, are explicit, realistic scenes, peopled by rather undistinctively sketched, occasionally ridiculous looking men and women whose presences are tied to specific scenes in the texts by quotations that serve as captions. In no sense do they conform to James's belief—as expressed in "After the Play"—that illustrations ought to communicate the story's "essence" instead of becoming its "embroidery."[33]

A look at how *Washington Square* is illustrated gives rise to the suspicion that James may not have been fully satisfied even with this picture-text relationship. If that speculation is correct, then we have a possible answer to the question why so little of James's fiction was subsequently illustrated; for if James's valued friend, George DuMaurier, could not satisfactorily illustrate James's work, who could? Of course, James never directly criticized DuMaurier's illustrations for *Washington Square*, but the conclusion that James might not have been fully pleased with these pictures becomes plausible when we consider what James had to say about DuMaurier's art in general. James believed that DuMaurier's highest achievement was found in his social satires.[34] As James wrote in his 1883 essay on the artist, "DuMaurier is full of soft irony."[35] But James added a caveat: if the "fashionable novel" of the 1830s were ever revived, "DuMaurier would be the man to make the pictures. . . . The only trouble would be the superiority of his illustrations to the text."[36] Since James's fiction was definitely not intended to be a revival of the 1830s "fashionable novel," it is possible that James was implying that DuMaurier's style was not suited to accompany his fiction. Certainly, *Washington Square* in particular does not seem to lend itself to being illustrated with caricatures.

Perhaps aware of this, DuMaurier did not create caricatures for the twelve illustrations used in *Washington Square*—though the style of drawing contains some of the lucidly linear sweep of much caricature. The closest any of the sketches come to caricature is in the picture that represents Morris Townsend, Catherine Sloper's suitor (figure 27). Most of his renderings are in the realistic style—despite their distinct DuMaurier quality—and, as such, seem to represent quite specific persons rather than the more generalized, exaggerated types so often found in DuMaurier's *Punch* caricatures (figure 28).[37] The subtle social satire and soft irony are mostly missing in the *Washington Square* illustrations. And it is entirely plausible to suggest that James sensed the lack of just those qualities that he had so admired in the caricaturist's most brilliant work.

A second, more clear cut problem arises concerning DuMaurier's illustrations—that of how they work with James's text. The manner in which they function further corroborates the suspicion that James may not have been fully satisfied with the illustrated *Washington Square*. Most of the pictures are quite specific in their references. And all of the full-page illustrations reproduce explicitly the scenes in the text that they—albeit redundantly—picture. Moreover, quotations from the text act as captions to these pictures so that their textual connection will not be missed by the reader. Working as visual replications of dramatic scenes described by the words, the pictures compete. Because these illustrations are in the dramatic mode, they give more of a literal sense to the work than James might have preferred; but what is worse, they give the reader DuMaurier's exact picture instead of James's. There are, of course, other smaller illustrations which are unaccompanied by captions and which occasionally decorate the beginnings of new chapters. Yet even these tend to depict scenes that subsequently appear in the text, so the sense of their being visual aids is not entirely absent. In only one instance—possibly two—does the illustration in *Washington Square* work in a more generalizing, symbolic way. At the beginning of chapter nineteen, for example, Catherine is shown following her father along a path. [38] This rendering symbolically foreshadows the subtle power that Dr. Sloper will exert over Catherine in order to keep her from marrying Morris Townsend. Obviously, such a use of illustration prefigures James's subsequent approach in the New York Edition, but the symbolic mode never occurs again in James's illustrated fiction until that time.

As already noted, when James' fiction was illustrated, it was mainly illustrated in its serialized form. Unfortunately, none of the subsequent picture-text marriages improved on the *Washington Square* effort. In fact, they were often a good deal worse, because they lacked work by illustrators possessing the ability to George DuMaurier. "Louisa Pallant," serialized in

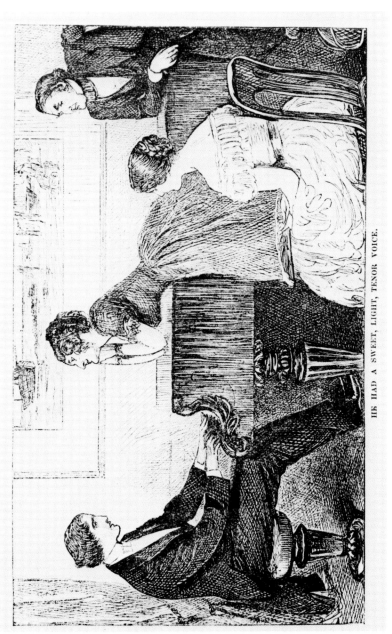

HE HAD A SWEET, LIGHT, TENOR VOICE.

Figure 27.   George DuMaurier, Illustration, in *Washington Square*,
by Henry James (1881).
(Courtesy of Special Collections Department, General
Library, University of New Mexico.)

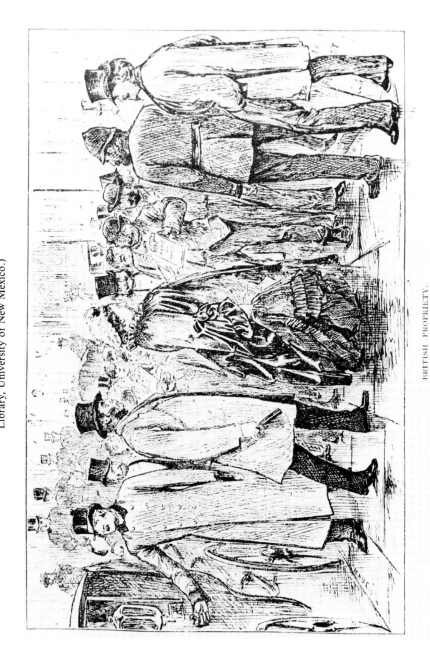

Figure 28. George DuMaurier, Caricature, in *Punch*. (Courtesy of Special Collections Department, General Library, University of New Mexico.)

BRITISH PROPRIETY.

"THE COUPLE WALKED AND WALKED, SLOWLY."

Figure 29.   C.S. Reinhart, Illustration, in "Louisa Pallant," by
Henry James, *Harper's Monthly* (January 1888).
(Courtesy of Special Collections Department, General
Library, University of New Mexico.)

Harper's Monthly of February 1888, is a good example of this.[39] Three illustrations by James's friend C. S. Reinhart accompany the text. They are naturalistic sketches that function clearly as visual aids (figure 29). In the story's layout, they appear close to each of the specific scenes they visually reproduce; and so the dullest reader will not miss the connection, they are each captioned with a particular quotation from the scene in the text that is depicted. Indeed, the caption of one picture baldly instructs the reader, "see page 349" (figure 26). As drawings, the illustrations are not especially unusual. They are skillful, realistic renderings, but they lack the grace and edge of DuMaurier's *Washington Square* illustrations. More important, however, they also lack the grace and wit of James's text. Reading the tale, it quickly becomes evident that these illustrations add nothing to the text. James's prose could just as easily do without them. Still, the pictures do not greatly interfere with the text either, except insofar as they break the reader's concentration by their placement in the layout of the magazine page.

Other examples of James's illustrated serial fiction include "The Real Thing," which appeared in the 16 April 1892 issue of *Black and White*.[40] This story about an illustrator and his models is accompanied by three illustrations made from drawings by Rudolf Blind. Again, the illustrations work as explanatory pictures. The drawings are literal in their representation, and their captions link the pictures with the text. The only difference seems to be in the quality of the renderings. The characters in the illustrations appear stiff, their faces somewhat wooden. Their presence alongside the text adds a disagreeable quality to James's tale. But worse, their stiffness contributes an unintended irony to a story that dwells partly on the married couple whose lack of variety as models, we recall, impeded the success of the illustrator in his attempt to make illustrations based on them. Another story, "Greville Fane," serialized in two September 1892 issues of the *Illustrated London News*, also exemplifies the same literal approach to illustrating texts that exists in "The Real Thing," but in this instance the illustrations by A. Forestier are more skillful than those by Blind.[41] Still another example to consider is James's "The Beldonald Holbein," published in the October 1901 issue of *Harper's Monthly* and accompanied by three illustrations made by Lucius Hitchcock.[42] Just as in "Louisa Pallant," "The Real Thing," and "Greville Fane," the illustrations for "The Beldonald Holbein" work as literal pictures meant to explain the text to readers. The only difference here is that the illustrations are the least competent of all. They are quite unattractive pictures. The artist of the story is depicted as a silly looking man, and the scenes are printed in garish colors (figure 30).

After the New York Edition collaboration was completed, James's serial fiction continued to be illustrated in much the same fashion as

"SO MANY WAYS I MEAN OF BEING ONE"

Figure 30. Lucius Hitchcock, Illustration, in "The Beldonald
Holbein," by Henry James, *Harper's Monthly* (October 1901).
(Courtesy of Special Collections Department, General Library,
University of New Mexico.)

before.⁴³ James could not always escape the hands of illustrators when he submitted his fiction to the magazines. All in all, when we reflect on the results of the entire body of his illustrated fiction, we understand more fully why James disliked being illustrated.

For an artist such as James, the illustration of nonfiction might seem to be a less worrisome issue than the illustration of fiction was. This is partly because nonfiction is usually considered a lesser genre—mere journalism. It is also partly because nonfiction appears on the surface to be objective in terms of its subject and mode of representation, something whose correspondence to the existing world strives to be more literal—a more reportorial and less creative mode of writing. A travel essay, for instance, is not an invention of the imagination but is on its face a description of a place that exists outside of the text. At its deeper levels, however, it is an invention— just as all writing is: it is selective in its details and is concerned not only with what a particular place looks like but also with what that place means to the senses and mind of the reporter. An awareness of that latter point forces us to recognize that there is a subjective element in the most objective appearing report. Of course, some travelers are more sensitive than others to the implications and nuances of places and things, and their creative imaginations and prose styles interpret what they perceive with more fullness, insight, and grace. Consequently, any gifted writer of travel literature might be expected to resent the encroachment of illustration on his texts.

James was no exception to this. Evident in all of James's travel writings are his creative imagination and his complex and subtle prose style. The reader is given more than just a concrete description of the physical place. Atmosphere, texture, style of existence, and meaning were culled from the places, and James's imagination transformed these aspects in his most Jamesian manner. At their best, his travel essays rank with his best efforts in prose—both fiction and nonfiction.⁴⁴ Small wonder, then, that he also often responded negatively to efforts at illustrating his nonfiction, in particular his travel literature.⁴⁵

A look at some examples of how James's travel writings were illustrated indicates that here the approach to picture and text combinations differed somewhat from the approach used in his fiction. James's "London" (1888) was illustrated by Joseph Pennell. As in all of the instances when James was illustrated—excepting the New York Edition—no active collaboration occurred between James and the illustrator.⁴⁶ There are thirteen illustrations in "London," and what is surprising about them is that most of them seem only loosely and generally connected with the text. Rarely do Pennell's pictures tie specifically into the words in the usual explanatory manner (recall James's admonition to Pennell, quoted near the beginning of this chapter). Though they do depict specific places, they often give the reader a view that James did not treat explicitly in the text, something that James mentions briefly but does not describe. For instance, James notes his debarking at Charing Cross Station when he first arrived in London.[47] No description of Charing Cross Station follows. Instead, on the opposite page is found Pennell's illustration, "Charing Cross Station."[48] The text is expanded by Pennell's picture.

Only in one sense do Pennell's illustrations compete with James's text. An important aspect of James's text is his definition and evocation of the atmosphere, texture, and tone of London, and it is these things which Pennell also tries to express in his pictures. Generally, he is not as successful as James, although occasionally the sense of atmosphere is sensitively expressed. James, however, communicates the texture and activity of London far more beautifully, complexly, and richly than do Pennell's illustrations. The latter are somewhat impressionistic in manner, partly vague and partly detailed. They seem to be quick sketches, and as such attempt to communicate the general sense of the place—its atmosphere, tone, texture. But the lack of tonal variety in the drawings undercuts the expression of these qualities. "Piccadilly" (figure 31), for example, attempts to evoke the feeling of a place that James discusses in his text. Yet, like a Rorschach test, the picture is filled with black blotches on a white space, neither giving the reader the exact look of the place nor capturing the subtle qualities James had created in the prose. The effect is indistinct without being atmospheric and does not contribute to the reader's knowledge of London nor does it please his desire to see lovely pictures.[49]

The 1900 edition of *A Little Tour of France* finally included the illustrations originally made by Pennell for the first edition published some years before. This book offers, in James's words, "impressions, immediate, easy, and consciously limited."[50] It contains, as James said, "the perception of surface" rather than "the perception of very complex underlying matters."[51] Pennell's sketches are decorative and, again, impressionistic in manner. The book itself amounts to a charming Baedeker whose text supports Pennell's charming sketches. These vague sketches, in turn, pleasantly generalize some of the places and landscapes described by James. Pictures and text are often closely related in ways that James probably felt were competitive, though their vagueness gives them more charm than reportorial value. James's *English Hours* (1905), also illustrated by Pennell, is somewhat similar in its approach to the picture-text relationship. Pennell's drawings are utilized as explanatory pictures, but their extreme sketchiness works against this purpose. They function more successfully as charming decorations. James's prose is left alone; the illustrations do not noticeably interfere with

PICCADILLY.

Figure 31. Joseph Pennell, Illustration, in "London," by Henry
James, *Century Magazine* (December 1888).
(Courtesy of Special Collections Department, General
Library, University of New Mexico.)

the text. A similar picture-text relation exists in James's last travel book, *Italian Hours* (1909), which once again was illustrated by Pennell.[52] What is notable, however, about each of these three travel books is the number of illustrations to be found. In *A Little Tour of France*, there are forty-three pictures; in *English Hours*, the number increases considerably to ninety-two (including frontispiece); in *Italian Hours*, the number decreases slightly to sixty-four. The sheer numbers of pictures accompanying these texts must have disconcerted James somewhat, though he never mentions the point. So many sketches tend to turn these travel books into the picture books that James and others decried.

Other nonfiction books by James were also illustrated, but in these instances the conflict is minimal, and indeed, in some instances, the inclusion of pictures is useful. James's essay on "DuMaurier and London Society" (1883) used illustration to provide the readers with examples of DuMaurier's work — an altogether reasonable use of pictures.[53] *Picture and Text* (1893) was illustrated in the same way. In these instances, the illustrations work as documents of the art and artists being discussed. Their presence is not only appropriate but necessary for the fullest comprehension of the subject, and I do not for one moment suggest that James resented them as competing with his texts. Finally, as discussed briefly near the beginning of this chapter, James's two memoirs — *A Small Boy and Others* and *Notes of a Son and Brother* — contained illustrations. Again, the illustrations do not interfere in any way. The daguerreotype and the sketches by William James were Henry James's personal artifacts and just as essential to James's memoir as the prose memories they stimulated. As memory-charged documents, their presence is entirely in sympathy with James's words and thus integral to the completeness of the texts themselves.

The illustration of nonfiction writings such as those mentioned above appears to have caused James no difficulty; but the illustration of his fiction and his travel literature clearly posed a problem. James confronted the question of whether or not to illustrate these genres with a mixture of refusal, protest, resigned annoyance, benign neglect, and apology.[54] Whenever possible, he kept illustration out of his literature; when it was not possible, he washed his hands of the affair. Not until he entered into the collaboration with Alvin Langdon Coburn would Henry James welcome the illustration of his own prose and participate in its creation to ensure that it was "responsible" and "subordinate." Before he could do that, however, James not only had to overcome his deep seated aversion to being illustrated; he also had to overcome an aversion to the medium used to illustrate the New York Edition — photography.

Part Three: The Photographic Age

This is just what the Daguerreotype has done. It has fixed the most fleeting of our illusions, that which the apostle and the philosopher and the poet have alike used as the type of instability and unreality. The photograph has completed the triumph, by making a sheet of paper reflect images like a mirror and hold them as a picture.

This triumph of human ingenuity is the most audacious, remote, improbable, incredible . . . of all the discoveries man has made. It has become such an everyday matter with us, that we forget its miraculous nature. . . .

— Dr. Oliver Wendell Holmes, *Atlantic Monthly*

So well understood are the pictorial necessities of modern publication that original photographs obtained . . . are hawked about the big daily and weekly newspaper offices. . . . The descriptive matter to go with them is then produced by some skilful writer. . . .

At least one of the magazines published in New York is almost wholly produced, as to its text, by three or four of its office-men . . . who "write around" the pictures; that is, they supply the reading-matter for somebody's photographs.

— Sidney Fairfield, *Lippincott's Monthly Magazine*

5

The Challenge of Unadorned Realism

There is little dispute that the invention of photography had a pervasive, jarring impact on culture and consciousness during the years following its public announcement in 1839. Nonetheless, by midcentury photography became a ubiquitous phenomenon throughout the Western world. The medium simply could not be ignored. Everything, everybody was being recorded on film. In *A Small Boy and Others*, Henry James noted "the quite sharp reminiscence of my first sitting for my daguerreotype [figure 32]. I repaired with my father on an August day [in 1854] to the great Broadway establishment of Mr. Brady, supreme in that then beautiful art."[1] The daguerreotype taken of the father and son was to be a surprise gift for young Henry's mother, but James's vivid recollection of it had nothing to do with that fact. "Sharp, again," James continued, "is my sense of not being so adequately dressed as I should have taken thought for had I foreseen my exposure. . . . The main resource of a small New York boy in this line at that time was the little sheathlike jacket, tight to the body, closed at the neck and adorned in front with a single row of brass buttons."[2] Sometime before the daguerreotype was made, William Makepeace Thackeray was in New York for a lecture, and he visited the Jameses. While there, the English novelist glimpsed young Henry standing in the doorway dressed in the very jacket that would be worn later for the daguerreotype portrait. Thackeray responded instantly with what an older James recalled were "formidable words," and these words as well as the youthful Henry's reaction to them remained fixed in James's memory sixty years after their utterance:

"Come here, little boy, and show me your extraordinary jacket!" My sense of my jacket became from that hour a heavy one. . . . I was to know later on why he had been so amused and why, after asking me if this were the common uniform of my age and class, he remarked that in England, were I to go there, I should be addressed as "Buttons." It had been revealed to me thus in a flash that we were somehow *queer*, and though never exactly crushed by it I became aware that I at least felt so as I stood with my head in Mr. Brady's vise. Beautiful most decidedly the lost art of the daguerreotype; I remember the

Figure 32. Mathew Brady, Daguerreotype of Henry James, Sr.,
and Henry James, Jr., (1854).
(By permission of Houghton Library, Harvard University.)

"exposure" as on this occasion interminably long, yet with the result of a facial anguish far less harshly reproduced than my suffered snapshots of a later age.[3]

Clothed in the symbol of his oddness, the youth was caught and "exposed" through the common nineteenth-century rite of being photographed; and Thackeray's "formidable" observation — felt so intensely by young Henry at the time of the picture making — merged inextricably with the daguerreotype image from the moment of its making. No matter how lovely the daguerreotypist's art, the "exposure" would be a vivid, permanent revelation of the memory of a humiliating moment. The image, in short, was a piece of embarrassing evidence.

The nineteenth century seemed to be an age preoccupied with observation and with collecting and reporting data. For a number of complex and ambiguous reasons, people were becoming obsessed with facts and details found in the world. And this mind-set called forth, among other things, a more empirically rooted science (notably biology), mass journalism, realist and naturalist art, a proliferation of world expositions, and the invention of photography. That the camera itself was an instrument perfectly suited to this consciousness is evidenced by explorer Meriwether Lewis's expression of frustrated desire found in the *Journals of the Lewis and Clark Expedition*. After a vain attempt to sketch a magnificent landscape scene encountered during the expedition, he lamented, "I most sincerely regreted [sic] that I had not brought a crimee [camera] obscura with me by the assistance of which even I could have hoped to have done better but alas this was also out of my reach; I therefore . . . indeavoured [sic] to trace some of the stronger features of this seen [sic] . . . to give to the world some faint idea of an object which at this moment fills me with such pleasure and astonishment."[4] What Lewis really needed — indeed, seemed half consciously to long for — was a device that would do the drawing for him, and it is important to recognize that he was not alone in his desire.[5] Not surprisingly, the invention of photography finally burst upon the scene in 1839 and began to flourish in its use and acceptance.

As historians of photography have made clear, the medium was not really invented in 1839.[6] Rather, that was the year that its invention was announced to the world. The principles and material elements that make up photography were sporadically and disparately discovered over a period of hundreds of years. The *camera obscura* — the "darkened room" device illustrating the physical principles of the path of light rays as they travel through a small hole in one side of the box and produce an upsidedown image on the opposite wall — had been known by the Greeks. During the Renaissance, it became used by artists to help them perfect their renderings of three-dimensional objects on flat surfaces. The *camera obscura* and the phenomenon it illustrated were truly amazing, and it is no wonder that individuals eventually tried to find a means of capturing permanently the images thrown on its back wall. Experiments to discover some way of doing this began to take place at least one hundred years before photography's public debut. Johann Heinrich Schulze is the scientist generally credited with having made the important initial breakthrough with his 1727 discovery that silver salts are light sensitive and that light rays could burn an image onto a flat surface covered with these salts. But he could not learn how to stop the burning action—that is, to fix the image permanently. When the picture continued to be exposed to light, the image disappeared as all the salts turned uniformly black. Not until experimenters found out how to stop the light sensitivity of their chemicals could images be viewed in direct light.

This was achieved by at least six individuals, most of whom worked separately between 1816 and 1839.[7] Two inventors, Louis Jacques Mandé Daguerre, a French painter and creator of dioramas, and William Henry Fox Talbot, an English scientist, mathematician, and linguistic scholar, announced the discoveries of their quite different photographic processes to the world in the same year. Talbot's process, called the calotype, was basically the negative-positive process we are so familiar with today. It was announced before a meeting of the Royal Society in London on 31 January 1839. Daguerre's process—the exquisite daguerreotype that James called a "lost art," and Dr. Oliver Wendell Holmes termed, "the mirror with a memory"[8]—was a direct positive process wherein each image made was unique. Its invention was made public nearly six months after the calotype by French scientist François Arago when he explained its details and potential uses at a joint meeting of the Academy of Sciences and the Academy of Fine Arts on 19 August 1839 in Paris. Almost immediately, Daguerre's process became the most widely used—except in England—because the French government purchased it and bequeathed its use to the world. In contrast, Talbot patented his calotype in 1841 (when it was finally perfected) and limited its use to those who would pay him a royalty.[9]

The manual describing the daguerreotype process, *Histoire et description du procédé nomme de Daguerréotype* (1839), was immediately translated into several languages and disseminated in over thirty different kinds of editions and summaries. The news and information pertaining to the process reached America on 20 September 1839, a month after its announcement in Paris, and its practice was instantly taken up by men such as the painter and inventor Samuel F. B. Morse.[10] America, according to Beaumont Newhall, "adopted the daguerreotype with the most enthusiasm, and excelled in its practice."[11] And between the time of its introduction in the United States and the Civil War, Richard Rudisill asserts, "the daguerre-otype . . . produced more visual images in America than almost any other medium."[12] Certainly, part of the medium's popularity can be explained by its main use: though the extraordinarily beautiful daguerreotype was used for recording all sorts of things, its widest early use was in portraiture. For the first time in history, large numbers of people could obtain their own likenesses, obtaining a visual family history for themselves and their heirs. The process became so accessible and popular in America that, Robert Taft notes, "In 1853, the New York *Daily Tribune* estimated that three million daguerreotypes were being produced annually and, judging from the known number of daguerreotypists, this does not seen unreasonable."[13] Of course, by this time, other types of images were being made too (cityscapes and landscapes, for example). As photography became simplified and thus cheaper and easier to use through the invention of new processes and improvements, the practice of making images other than portraits would become increasingly widespread.[14]

The daguerreotype was indeed a popular process, yet it (along with the calotype) was soon replaced by the collodion wetplate process invented in 1851. Though other processes were also invented at about the same time (for example, the ambrotype [1854] and the tintype [1856], two cheaper variations on the daguerreotype), the collodion process triumphed because it was the fastest and cheapest. Also, as a glass negative/paper positive process, it could produce theoretically an unlimited number of prints. Wetplate photography continued to be used until the 1870s when it was replaced by the dryplate process, a method of picture making that was even cheaper and easier. Inevitably, the medium continued to grow in popularity, both in terms of its use and its product. Finally, when the handheld detec-tive camera was developed and roll film was perfected (by 1888), photogra-phy was ready to become truly an amateur mass medium. Alongside pho-tography's evolution as a medium in its own right, we should remember that photographic processes for making periodical and book illustrations were beginning to be invented and used by the 1860s, and that the perfection of the halftone process by the 1890s would result in a proliferation of photo-graphic illustrations in newspapers, magazines, and books.[15]

Cheapness, ease of use, and a capacity for mass reproducibility and wide dissemination were among the essential ingredients that made photog-raphy the first "democratic art."[16] Before the nineteenth century ended, photography would be used for many different purposes — science, art, social reform, evidence, record keeping, entertainment, commerce, per-sonal pleasure; and the products of the medium — portraits, *cartes de visite*, stereographs, cabinet photographs, lantern slides, snapshots, picture postcards, photographic illustrations, indeed even cameras—would become common household objects. By the time James was daguerreotyped by Brady in the mid-1850s, use of that elusive, exquisite, mirror imaged medium had already begun to fade, and it was on the brink of becoming a "lost art." As far as we know, Henry James was never daguerreotyped again; but as he has already pointed out, he often "suffered snapshots" afterwards.

Many years after James recorded the vivid memory of his daguerreotyping, Paul Valéry commemorated the one hundredth birthday of photography. He remarked that with its announcement in 1839, "A marked revision occurred in all standards of visual knowledge. Man's way of seeing began to change, and even his way of living felt the repercussions of this novelty, which immediately passed from the laboratory into everyday use, creating new need and hitherto unimagined customs."[17] Just one year before Valéry made his observation, Robert Taft posed a question in his book *Photography and the American Scene* (1938), that suggests the magnitude of Valéry's point. Taft asked, "How would you describe a photograph if you had never seen one before and were totally unfamiliar with its appearance?"[18] Obviously, none of us can lift ourselves out of our historical context, with its image saturated experience, and answer that question. But we can sense its import, as well as begin to understand Valéry's insight, if we examine some of the responses of people who experienced photography freshly at the time the medium was introduced and during the years thereafter when it was still a new phenomenon.

On the day in 1912 that the Brady daguerreotype triggered his recollection of Thackeray's pointed remark, James experienced the power of the photographic image to make people look at themselves, and be looked at, in an entirely new way.[19] "Daguerreotypes," Richard Rudisill writes (and by implication, this includes all photographs), "were deliberately wrought images to which people responded at the level of personal feeling. At times they responded more directly to the images than to the subjects themselves . . . [and] the value attached to the subject of a picture was often transferred to the picture itself in a way that allowed the picture not only to reflect attitudes or feelings but to affect what people saw and how they saw it."[20] To the James who looked at his daguerreotype some sixty years after its making, the image was a permanent embodiment of Thackeray's observation. This photograph expressed a past moment that James had once actually experienced, a moment that gave rise to an emotional feeling that instantly merged with the experience itself and the object of that experience—the small boy in his "odd" jacket. The daguerreotype of the small boy in his "odd" jacket was a record offering the perpetual presence of the past experience with its inherent emotional meaning, and James could escape neither the fact nor the emotion fixed by the picture.

As the medium that most perfectly reproduces the material world in front of the lens, photography has always made it difficult for individuals to separate themselves from their images of themselves. The two become quite easily merged. This suggests that the quality of the photograph's incredible realism is perhaps the key element for an understanding of the impact and meaning of the photograph as well as of the responses it has engendered.[21] Beginning with the daguerreotype, all photographic images tended to be read not as an image of something, a miniature representation, but instead as the world itself. During the nineteenth century, photographs tended to function as unconscious substitutes for the material reality appearing in them. People responded not by consciously thinking, "This is only a representation, an interpretation of, say, an Egyptian pyramid that once existed before a photographer's lens in a particular place, at a particular time." Rather, they thought, "This *is* an Egyptian pyramid itself." They somehow were transported to Egypt by the image, and they often unconsciously responded as though they were there. As Valéry suggested, "photography laid down a real pictorial record of the social life."[22] and of the natural phenomena found in the world, and its nineteenth-century audience tended to take the images literally, confusing the image with the world itself.

Much of the recorded response to the infant medium was favorable. People were amazed, delighted, and in some instances disquieted by photography's objectivity, inclusiveness, integrity, and ability to arrest time—in short, its nearly perfect mimesis. Yet, though the nineteenth-century mind was ready for the invention of this extraordinary medium and eagerly devoured its seemingly magical products, it was not quite prepared for some of the implications of the miniature, colorless, detailed frames of arrested time and space.

Not surprisingly, painters were among the first to comment. Upon first viewing a daguerreotype, Paul Delaroche, the French painter, is said to have remarked, "Painting is dead from this day!"[23] Then, after some reflection on the matter, he qualified his rash outburst:

M. Daguerre's process completely satisfies art's every need, as the results prove. It carries some of its basic qualities to such perfection that it will become for even the most skillful painters a subject for observation and study. The drawings obtained by this means are at once remarkable for the perfection of details and for the richness and harmony of the whole. Nature is reproduced in them not only with truth, but with art. The correctness of line, the precision of form, is as complete as possible, and yet, at the same time, broad energetic modeling is to be found in them as well as a total impression equally rich in tone and in effect. The rules of aerial perspective are as scrupulously observed as those of linear perspective. Color is translated with so much truth that its absence is forgotten.

The painter, therefore, will find this technique a rapid way of making collections of studies which he could otherwise obtain only with much time and trouble and, what ever his talents might be, in a far less perfect manner.24

In America, when Samuel F. B. Morse first saw daguerreotypes in 1839, he responded immediately with an amazement that equalled Delaroche's. Morse called them, "Rembrandt perfected."25 Morse also reflected on their likely impact on the art world in a lecture delivered before a meeting of the National Academy of Design. The daguerreotype, Morse argued, "will ease the artist's task of providing him with facsimile sketches of nature, buildings, landscapes, groups of figures . . . not copies of nature, but portions of nature itself . . . [and] the public would become acquainted through photography with correctness of perspective and proportion, and thus be better qualified to see the difference between professional and less well-trained work."26 Other painters such as Delacroix (one of James's favorite painters) viewed the daguerreotype similarly, though with perhaps less enthusiasm. It was, he explained, "the mirror of the object," something from which he believed he had learned "to read—and I learn far more by looking than the inventions of any scribbler could ever teach me."27 Turner, on the other hand, is reported to have responded more like Delaroche, exclaiming, "This is the end of Art. I am glad I have had my day."28

Response came also from literary artists. Edgar Allan Poe wrote in the 15 January 1840 issue of *Alexander's Weekly Messenger* that the daguerreotype "must undoubtedly be regarded as the most extraordinary triumph of modern science." He continued by explaining why:

For, in truth, the daguerreotyped plate . . . is *infinitely* more accurate in its representation than painting by human hands. If we examine a work of ordinary art, by means of a powerful microscope, all traces of resemblance to nature will disappear—but the closest scrutiny of the photographic drawing discloses only a more absolute truth, a more perfect identity of aspect with the thing represented. The variations of shade, the gradations of both linear and aerial perspective are those of truth itself in the supremeness of its perfection.29

Henry David Thoreau was equally impressed with the daguerreotype, though he sensed—as few others apparently did—that the human insight of the photographer determined the quality and depth of the result. "Nature is readily made to repeat herself in a thousand forms," Thoreau wrote in 1841, "and in the daguerreotype her own light is amanuensis, and the picture too has more than a surface significance,—a depth equal to the prospect,—so that the microscope may be applied to the one as the spyglass to the other. Thus we may easily multiply the forms of the outward; but to give the within outwardness, that is not easy."30 Thoreau's insight that the daguerreotypist could "give the within outwardness" later became utilized in Nathanniel Hawthorne's *The House of the Seven Gables* (1851), except there Hawthorne suggested that this power belonged inherently to the medium itself: "While we give it [the daguerreotype] credit only for depicting the merest surface," the daguerreotypist hero, Holgrave, says, "it actually brings out the secret character with the truth that no painter would ever venture upon, even could he detect it."[31]

Ralph Waldo Emerson reflected on the new medium, too. In 1841, he wrote in his *Journal* that, "The daguerreotype is good for its authenticity. No man quarrels with his shadow, nor will he with his miniature when the sun was the painter."[32] Several pages later, Emerson returned to his ruminations on the new invention and its meaning:

> Were you ever daguerreotyped, O immortal man? And did you look with all vigor at the lens of the camera, or rather, by the direction of the operator, at the brass peg a little below it, to give the picture the full benefit of your expanded and flashing eye? and in your zeal not to blur the image, did you keep every finger in its place with such energy that your hands became clenched as for fight or despair, and in your resolution to keep your face still, did you feel every muscle becoming every moment more rigid; the brows contracted into a Tartarian frown, and the eyes fixed as they are fixed in a fit, in madness, or in death? And when, at last you are relieved of your dismal duties, did you find the curtain drawn perfectly, and the coat perfectly, and the hands true, clenched for combat, and the shape of the face and head? — but, unhappily, the total expression escaped from the face and the portrait of a mask instead of a man? Could you not by grasping it very tight hold the stream of a river, or of a small brook, and prevent it from flowing?[33]

Like so many others of his day, Emerson disliked being daguerreotyped, because he felt his likenesses were not very good. Yet, at a deeper level, he seemed disturbed by daguerreotype portraits. They suggested madness or, worse, death; they took time out of its natural flow, offering arrested moments to a generation that was not accustomed to seeing a world in a fragmented, disembodied, discontinuous form. Still, Emerson acknowledged, "the Daguerreotype is the true Republican style of painting. The artist stands aside and lets you paint yourself."[34]

Unlike Emerson, Dr. Oliver Wendell Holmes expressed unqualified enthusiasm for the young medium. He published three extensive essays in the *Atlantic Monthly* on photography — one each in the years 1859, 1861, and 1863.[35] To Holmes, photography was the "most remarkable material product of human skill,"[36] offering the viewer "a copy of nature in all her sweet gradations and harmonies and contrasts."[37] In his essays, Holmes spared no compliment and made several extraordinarily perspicacious observations about the meaning and implications of photographic images. Photography's realism was the subject of one of the essays. Holmes was contemplating the power and meaning of some Civil War stereographs. They are, he wrote, "terrible momentos," for they possess a "fidelity . . . which the truthful sunbeam has delineated in all their dread reality." Holmes continued:

> Let him who wishes to know what war is look at this series of illustrations. These wrecks of manhood thrown together in careless heaps or ranged in ghastly rows for burial were alive but yesterday. . . . Many people would not look through this series. Many, having seen it and dreamed of its horrors, would lock it up in some sweet drawer, that it might not thrill or revolt those whose soul sickens at such sights. It was so nearly like visiting the battlefield to look over these views, that all the emotions excited by the actual sight of the stained and sordid scene, strewed with rags and wrecks, came back to us, and we buried them in the recesses of our cabinet as we would have buried the mutilated remains of the dead they too vividly represented.[38]

In another of the essays, Holmes went beyond the issue of photography's realism to touch upon a characteristic of the medium that would not receive a name until the following century—photography's inherent surrealism. With the photograph, Holmes emphasized, *"Form is henceforth divorced from matter.* In fact, matter as a visible object is of no great use any longer, except as a mould on which form is shaped. Give us a few negatives of a thing worth seeing, taken from different points of view, and that is all we want of it."[39] Again, the perception emerged that an image is linked in the mind with the thing itself, but this time it was accompanied by the observation that the thing itself was no longer important. To Holmes, photography was better than material reality; it was a substitute for the world as well as an incomparable delight, an education, and an art.

To Charles Baudelaire, however, photography was an abomination. Reviewing the Paris Salon of 1859 (the same time Holmes was writing), the great French poet construed photography to be a potential threat to art. In his review, he fumed:

> As the photographic industry was the refuge of every would-be painter, every painter too ill-endowed or too lazy to complete his studies, this universal infatuation bore not only the mark of a blindness, an imbecility, but had also the air of a vengence [sic]. I do not believe, or at least I do not wish to believe, in the absolute success of such a brutish conspiracy, in which, as in all others, one finds both fools and knaves; but I am convinced that the ill-applied developments of photography, like all other purely material developments of progress, have contributed much to the impoverishment of the French artistic genius, which is already so scarce. . . . If photography is allowed to supplement art in some of its functions, it will soon have supplanted or corrupted it altogether, thanks to the stupidity of the multitude which is its natural ally. It is time, then, for it to return to its true duty, which is to be the servant of the sciences and arts—but the very humble servent [sic], like printing or short-hand, which have neither created nor supplemented literature.[40]

Baudelaire's angry outburst summed up an attitude that had been implicit in many of the responses of others before him—even those who had welcomed photography's appearance on the historical scene. Delacroix, for instance, believed that "the daguerreotype should be considered only as a translator entrusted to initiate us farther into the secrets of nature."[41] Millet, the Barbizon painter, said: "Photographs are like casts from nature, which never can be as good as a good statue. No mechanism can be substituted for genius."[42] And Thomas Cole, the American painter of landscapes and grand allegories such as "The Voyage of Life" series, had argued, "the art of painting is creative, as well as an imitative art, and it is in no danger of being superseded by any mechanical contrivance."[43]

Nonetheless, painters used photography in spite of its presumed mechanical quality. Delacroix, Ingres, Corot, Courbet, and other highly regarded painters used photographs as aids in their painting.[44] Subsequently, the pre-Raphaelite painters, such as Rossetti and Millais, used photographs, too, actually striving for the realism and detail that in the end only betrayed the anachronism implicit in their subject matter. Though it was not always acknowledged—perhaps, even, not clearly understood—the new medium was influencing painting in discernible ways. Art historians such as Van Deren Coke and Aaron Scharf have argued persuasively that photography had a major impact on painting styles during the nineteenth and early twentieth centuries, specifically on Impressionism and post-Impressionism. Despite the fact that their views regarding the direct influence of photographs on painters have recently been disputed, it still seems reasonable to conclude and fully acknowledge that photographic style is pre-eminent in many Impressionist and post-Impressionist paintings.[45]

Photography also influenced writing, though in ways that are just beginning to be analyzed. In Valéry's view, "the moment that photography appeared, the descriptive genre began to invade Letters. In verse as in prose, the decor and the exterior aspects of life took an almost excessive place. . . . With photography . . . realism pronounces itself in our Literature."[46] The medium certainly offered writers another subject to use in their art (as in Hawthorne's *The House of the Seven Gables* [1851] and in Cuthbert Bede's *Photographic Pleasures* [1855]). More important, the spatial/temporal form of the modernist novel, emerging as early as 1857 in Flaubert's *Madame Bovary*, may have been suggested by photography.[47]

Yet, no matter how useful a tool or how wide its influence, the medium of photography was in no sense universally esteemed as an art. On the contrary, it was often rejected for its presumed artlessness. One of the results of this rejection was the growth of a conscious movement to practice art photography, called pictorialism. Beaumont Newhall introduces his discussion of the beginnings of pictorial photography with a question posited by English critic C. Jabez Hughes in 1861, a question that underlies the consciousness of the fledgling movement. Hughes wrote, "Hitherto photography has been principally content with representing truth. Can its sphere not be enlarged? And may it not aspire to delineate Beauty, too?"[48] Many painters and not a few of the important literati had already said no to this question. But from the beginning, photography had been much too close in its relation to painting to be easily rejected by artists. After all, Daguerre was a painter, and Fox Talbot undertook his experiments to discover photography when he failed to produce an adequate sketch of a beautiful landscape at Lake Como in Italy.[49] Moreover, after photography burst forth on the scene, many artists, in the words of Coke, "took up the camera. They therefore thought of themselves as artist-photographers and were billed as such in their advertisements."[50]

Initially, photography was accepted or rejected as an art on the basis that it was simply what it was — photography. During the early years, there was little attempt to make it imitate the surface effects of other artistic media. Of course, at the outset photography was compared with existing pictorial art, particularly with the work of Rembrandt. The generally accepted academic rules of pictorial art were also applied to photography, and many photographers respected these painting conventions, seeing no conflict between their application and photography's realism. Not surprisingly, photographers also adopted the subject matter and genres used in painting — for example, portraiture, still life, and landscape. Unfortunately for photographers, though, many artists felt there was a conflict between painting's conventions and photography's realism, so questions began to be raised about whether photography was an art.[51]

As already noted, much of the photographic imagery taken during the early decades was portraiture. Unquestionably, some of the most beautiful nineteenth-century photographs made were portraits. During the 1840s, 1850s, and 1860s there emerged several portrait photographers who created photographs that seem to us to be fine art at its most lovely. Calotypists D. O. Hill and Robert Adamson worked in Scotland during the 1840s, leaving a stunning photographic record of many of their contemporaries that included not only dignitaries but ordinary Newhaven fishermen and their wives. At the same time in America, masterful work was created by two Boston daguerreotypists, Albert Sands Southworth and Josiah Johnson Hawes. Mathew Brady also began his work in New York in 1843. The Frenchman, Nadar, friend of painters and writers and the man who gave the Impressionists space for their revolutionary exhibition in 1874, brilliantly practiced portrait photography during the 1850s and 1860s in Paris. And

Julia Margaret Cameron, perhaps the most gifted nineteenth-century portrait photographer, began working in England during the 1860s, photographing such persons as Thomas Carlyle, Sir John Herschel, Alfred Lord Tennyson, and the future Mrs. Leslie Stephen.[52]

Other kinds of images were made by photographers, too, and these were often created with the self-conscious intention that they be viewed as art. Both Daguerre and Talbot made cityscapes, landscapes, and still lifes that were consciously artful. Englishman John Edwin Mayall created ten daguerreotypes in 1843 as illustrations of the Lord's Prayer.[53] When he subsequently showed them in his London studio, Beaumont Newhall notes, "they were acclaimed by the British art press."[54] Later, in 1851, what is believed to have been the first large public photographic exhibition was held in the London Crystal Palace during the Great Exhibition, and medals were awarded to photographers. Among the many images shown were a beautiful series of eight daguerreotypes made by two Americans, Charles Fontayne and William Southgate Porter. Each plate was 12 inches by 10 inches, and side by side the eight daguerreotypes measured eight feet, giving viewers a dramatic, panoramic view of Cincinnati's waterfront.[55]

These were among the kinds of straightforward photographic images that Dr. Holmes praised as being "admirable" artistic "specimens."[56] Still, Holmes's — and the *Atlantic's* — seal of approval was not enough to settle the matter of photography's legitimacy as an art. The controversy arose not only because of the medium's unprecedented realism, but for other reasons as well. Since anyone intelligent enough to master the medium's chemistry and technique could practice the "art," all established notions of what comprised and certified artistic competence and craft were challenged and undermined. Photographs were made for all sorts of purposes, unartistic as well as artistic ones; and, in Alan Thomas's words, it was not "easy to distinguish the products of one intention — to record the visible world — from the products of the other — to create beautiful pictures."[57]

A medium that catches and fixes within an arbitrarily shaped frame the fragments of a world that, to the human eye and mind, is constantly in flux was a unique phenomenon in the nineteenth century. People were not accustomed to seeing framed, stopped time. Nor were they used to seeing most things at any but conventional eyelevel vantage points. And because the camera's frame isolates the world's details as they exist before the lens in sufficient light to be burned onto film at a particular moment, new and often disconcerting formal relationships began to appear in pictures. Despite the fact that early photographers usually sought to arrange their compositions according to their understanding of the academic painting rules of the day, they did not always succeed. Ineptitude, artistic ignorance, mistakes and accidents, unconcern, and the lack of premeditation inherent in increasingly instantaneous picture making resulted in chaotic, unbalanced, "inartistic" photographs. Odd points of view, people and things cut off by the frame, tipped picture planes, people and things caught off balance or in awkward spatial relationships with each other, unexpected and unwanted details, blurs — these and other aesthetic "errors" found their way into photographic images by midcentury. Of course, there was also the colorless aspect of photography: it was dreamlike and put particular emphasis on the qualities of light, texture, abstract form, and radical spatial organization. In the eye of the nineteenth-century beholder, the world took on new shape and structure through photographs and not everyone was pleased — nor were they willing to believe such a phenomenon artful. Hence, from the beginning, the medium itself offended many conservative artists and critics.

Another aspect must be briefly considered, too. During the infancy and adolescence of photography, as Valéry suggested, artists were becoming interested in depicting common objects, ordinary people, and scenes taken directly from life. Writers and painters, as well as photographers, were gleaning their subject matter from what they observed, and they sought to treat the slices of life they collected with unprecedented democratic objectivity. They were inventing realist art and, as a consequence, were also threatening established aesthetic attitudes — particularly that which required artists to idealize their subject matter. Not surprisingly, photography was often asserted to be an abettor of this corrupting activity because of its extraordinary inclusiveness and "extreme pictorial objectivity,"[58] and the accusation cast a further aspersion on the possible artfulness of the medium.

Beginning in the 1850s, the issue of whether or not photography was a fine art was beginning to be widely debated, and the debates gave rise to two divergent responses among the photographic community. The first response held tenaciously to the idea that photography could be an art by remaining photographic and producing, without any manipulation, straight images taken directly from nature. Holmes supported this view. Another proponent, American photographer Marcus Aurelius Root, wrote a book called *The Camera and the Pencil* in 1864, in which he argued for, and explained, the straight photographic approach to picture making.[59] In effect, writers such as Root and Holmes were urging that, as Richard Rudisill puts it, photography's "basis of artistic merit" lay in "the fact that it was factual and symbolic in its effect on the viewer."[60]

The other camp, however, believed that the new medium should emulate painting and prove that photography was not merely a mechanical recording device.[61] Their means ranged from the simple method of carefully posing scenes and retouching finished images to the extreme one of constructing single images from several separately made negatives. Their goals were to soften the harsh realism and to get rid of messy details and inharmonious forms, infusing spirit, imagination, artistic order, and beauty into their images. Two of the leading practitioners of this school were Oscar Rejlander, who created his allegorical "Two Ways of Life" (1857) from thirty separately made negatives, and Henry Peach Robinson, who created his famous composite photograph, "Fading Away" (1858), from seven negatives.[62] In 1869, Robinson also published a book, *Pictorial Effect in Photography*, in which he urged photographers to become aware of the rules of composition that were based on painting conventions. He further exhorted photographers to pose people carefully in scenes and manipulate the print in any way "to avoid the mean, the bare and the ugly, and to aim to elevate" the subject depicted.[63] Robinson's influence on art-photographers was pervasive and often dubious in result. Though the gifted Julia Margaret Cameron had been utilizing "Rembrandt lighting" to achieve her brilliantly dramatic but otherwise straight photographic portraits, she fell under the influence of Robinson during the 1870s, tending more and more to photograph subjects dressed anachronistically in clothing from the past and posed melodramatically in scenes similar to those found in pre-Raphaelite painting.[64] Unlike her portraits, these photographs appear bathetic.

Writing nearly one hundred years later, Robert Doty suggests that the "sham means of producing tableaux which would appeal to the popular desires for the superficial aspects of beauty were the dominant factors in what was gradually becoming known as 'pictorial photography,' that is photographs which were intended to be beautiful, or tell a story, and which appealed directly to the emotions of the viewer."[65] The images that these art-photographers created were very popular, indeed, but despite the best intentions, they did not succeed in impressing art critics sufficiently to win for photographers a respected place inside the palace of art. Their failure is bluntly evidenced by the response of an anonymous reviewer of the photographic sections at the Philadelphia Exhibition of 1876. Speaking of the exhibition as a whole, the reviewer wrote, "To begin with, it is to be remembered that it exhibits the productions of an inartistic age. One of the most decided proofs of this is the place occupied by photography, which has a large pavilion of its own. The real value of photography for likenesses lies in its being the imprint of life; it is not and never can become an art . . . it should be kept within its proper limits."[66] Then, turning the discussion to the work of Julia Margaret Cameron (her *Idylls of the King* series made under the influence of Robinson), the reviewer went on the attack.

Cameron's photographs, he wrote, are "absurd, blurred groups. . . . The attempt at artistic and dramatic effect is enormous; the result is merely a series of very poor photographs of ill-dressed actors and actresses in exaggerated attitudes."[67] It is clear that the reviewer regretted them, for he acknowledged that Mrs. Cameron's portraits of the 1860s were striking. Finally, though, he proclaimed that, "The best American as well as English photographs [found in the exhibition] are those of natural scenery," and ended the matter on that note.[68]

At the turn of the century, pictorial photography was still widely practiced and exhibitions were fairly common in intellectual and artistic centers like London, New York, and Paris. By the same token, the prejudice against art photography had become very widespread among critics and artists. Photography, even in its softened, pictorial form, was still deemed a serious threat to art and good taste. Discussing "Style" in 1889, P. G. Hamerton asserted, "It requires great skill to paint like a well-coloured photograph, yet such painting would be remarkable only for the complete absence of style."[69] A few years later, Joseph Pennell devoted an entire essay to the subject, "Is Photography among the Fine Arts?"[70] Pennell's piece was an extended diatribe that made Baudelaire's complaint seem reserved. Pennell began, "For some years photographers have been assuring us that photography is a fine art, and that they themselves are artists," and then added, "It seems to me, therefore, high time to investigate their claim."[71] He next explained that, if photography was to be included among the fine arts, it had to be judged by the same standards as painting, something rarely, if ever, done by critics. Using two photographic exhibitions in London as a pretext for his attack, Pennell proceeded to assess "critically" photography's claim to be a fine art. At bottom, Pennell saw "no reason . . . why a mechanical contrivance should be called artistic, and those who make use of it artists. It would be pleasant, no doubt, for photographers to obtain the same social and financial recognition as artists; it would be pleasant, too, if the Italian with his hurdy-gurdy could win for himself the reputation and fortune of Paderewski."[72] What disturbed Pennell—deeply, given the tone of his essay—was that photography was so easy. It was practiced by amateurs off on a holiday, individuals for whom photographing was a mere pastime, an "amusement," a "relaxation."[73]

"And who does the work? who makes the picture?" queried Pennell. Answering quickly, he asserted, the photographer

pushes the button, and a picture is the result. Until lately he was the mute inglorious Milton; now he has discovered a machine to make his masterpiece for him. No wonder he laughs at the poor artist who must humbly toil to create beauty, which a camera manufactures for him at once. What a farce it is to think of Titian and Velasquez and

Rembrandt actually studying and working, puzzling their brains over subtleties of drawing and modelling, of light and atmosphere and colour, when the modern master has but
to step into a shop, buy a camera, play a few tricks with gum chromate — I believe it is
called — to turn you out a finished masterpiece which is far more like the real thing, he
says, than any mere hand-made picture ever could be.[74]

Photographers were simply not serious. And as if that were not enough,
they were not honest, either. "The art of the photographer," Pennell continued, "is to make his photographs as much like something that they are not
as he can. . . . The revolutionary photograph is one that bears upon the
surface a vague resemblance to a poor photograph of a charcoal, a sepia, or
a wash drawing, to an aquatint or a water-colour. The photographer plays
with his print, until it is neither the photograph it ought to be, nor the
drawing he would like it to be. But his one ambition is to have you forget
that his photograph is a photograph."[75] Pennell then snidely dismissed the
notion that photography "has made the artist more accurate" with a rhetori-
cal question: "I wonder how much more accurate Van Eyck would have
been had he had a kodak."[76]

Pennell finally concluded that, "unless a man can draw with his own
unaided hand he is not an artist," and ended his inquiry on a confident but
odd note: "just as margarine has never superseded butter, or chalk and
water milk, or been put in equal rank with it, so photography, even at its
best and in the hands of artists, will never destroy art, will never be considered one of the fine arts."[77] Photography was an imitation only, equivalent
to the inexpensive spread, and there the matter rested. But unfortunately
for Pennell, the matter would not be allowed to rest for long. This attitude
would begin to be challenged head-on by a new generation of pictorialists,
one that was led by the tireless, ingenious photographer and promoter,
Alfred Stieglitz, and that included the talented art-photographer, Alvin
Langdon Coburn.

"But has photography accomplished anything?" asked Pennell before ending his attack. "Yes, it has cheapened art greatly . . . . In the beginning of
the century England was celebrated for its beautifully illustrated books, in
which the greatest artists, engravers, and printers collaborated to produce a
perfect whole. To-day, the place of these books has been taken by the
Strand Magazine and the *Sketch*, thanks to the services of photography
. . . . Now, the process-block makers are mostly photographers, who are
killing each other in the race for cheapness."[78] Pennell, of course, was
referring to the triumph of the halftone photomechanical process which he
bluntly felt was supplanting the demand for hand drawn illustration and
artists such as himself. The halftone process — one that made it possible to

reproduce photographs and words on a single press at the same time — was first demonstrated successfully by Stephen Horgan in the 4 March 1880 issue of the *New York Daily Graphic*.[79] Though a process with extraordinary implications for mass journalism, it needed further development and began to be used only gradually, first by periodical and book publishers and then by newspapers. By 1897, it was capable of being used on the high speed presses newspapers were being printed on and thus became the dominant picture reproduction method in the publication industry. Not only were halftone photographs replacing hand illustration, but as Sidney Fairfield noted in his 1895 *Lippincott's* article, they were also taking over the realm of literature:

> So well understood are the pictorial necessities of modern publication that original photographs obtained . . . are hawked about the big daily and weekly newspaper offices and sold on their merits. The descriptive matter to go with them is then produced by some skilful writer, with the assistance of the library or the newspaper "graveyard." At least one of the magazines published in New York is almost wholly produced, as to its text, by three or four of its office-men, who work over pen-names now more or less familiar from repetition on the title-page, and who "write around" the pictures; that is, they supply the reading-matter for somebody's photographs. Very few of the readers of this magazine are clever enough to detect this little trick in magazine-making: they fancy that whatever is published in a magazine, on calendered paper, with an illuminated cover and with half-tones judiciously sprinkled in to make the best showing, is necessarily high-class reading-matter. And, while we may deplore this Cheap-John literature masquerading in the guise of the best and highest, we cannot but admire the business intuition of those publishers who recognize the selling value of mere pictures. Of course this subordination of what is literary to what is pictorial is particularly hard on the man dependent on his pen, now more numerous than ever before; but he is rapidly learning to take his medicine uncomplainingly, and he either has a camera or is facile enough with pen or pencil to produce a rough sketch which some professional sketch-artist can make over into a genuine masterpiece and affix his own name to with fitting artistic indistinctness.[80]

The halftone process was the result of efforts to develop effective and, ultimately, more efficient, cheaper photomechanical processes that had begun when photography was introduced to the world in 1839.[81] As early as 1840, a method had been perfected for turning a daguerreotype plate into a printing plate for making aquatints. This was followed by the development of a photomechanical process called photoglyphic etching, invented by Fox Talbot in 1852. By the 1860s, beautiful but expensive and slow processes such as the woodburytype, the collotype, and the photogravure were invented and used. The invention of these different photomechanical processes was very important, not only because they made it possible to reproduce photographs in books and, eventually, in large circulation magazines and newspapers, but also because they could be used to reproduce hand drawn pictures and paintings. Of course, the first widespread use of photomechanical reproduction technology was as an aid to the making of wood engravings for illustrations. From the 1860s onwards, photographs of all kinds of pictures were printed directly on wood blocks, so engravers could carve the block for printing. This saved time, since the slow intermediate step of having to draw another's picture on the block was eliminated. Not until the perfection of the halftone process, however, would photographs themselves be utilized widely as illustrations.[82]

Beginning in the 1840s, photographs were used to illustrate books and as models for making the wood engravings that appeared in the important illustrated weeklies. The latter use, according to Beaumont Newhall, first began in 1842.[83] Thereafter, it was not uncommon to see the phrase, "From a daguerreotype," or a reference to a particular photographer printed beneath a wood engraved illustration. The former use occurred just as early, though it is a bit difficult to attribute the first book to use photographs as illustration. In 1840, the first part of a travel view series, *Excursions daguerriennes*, was published in Paris; the series was completed in 1844. Though technically aquatints made from daguerreotype plates, these printed views were photographic in their exactitude, as the *Edinburgh Review* noted in a January 1843 unsigned essay discussing the new photographic processes.[84] The first book to use a real photograph as an illustration—a tipped-in frontispiece—was a pamphlet, *Record of the Death Bed of C. M. W.*, written in 1844 by John Walter, Jr., in memory of his sister. Of much more significance, however, is Fox Talbot's *The Pencil of Nature*, a beautiful and revolutionary book published in six installments between 1844 and 1846. Talbot created a picture-text book that used twenty-four original, tipped-in calotypes. His intention was to illustrate the potential uses of the calotype process. Each photograph exemplified a specific use of the new medium, from scientific to artistic, and Talbot's text perspicuously explained the use being illustrated. Other books using photographs followed—for example, *The Talbotype Applied to Hieroglyphics* (1846), and *Talbotype Illustrations to the Annals of the Artists of Spain* (1847)—but none rivaled *The Pencil of Nature* in importance or quality.[85]

More use was made of photographs as illustrations in books during the 1850s and 1860s, though by no means were photographic images per se used extensively. When used, though, their primary function seemed to be informational, providing visual details of the world for readers. John L. Stephen used photographically assisted illustrations in his *Incidents of Travel in Yucatan*, published by Harper in 1843. John Ruskin used illustration based on daguerreotypes in his *The Seven Lamps of Architecture* (1849) and, subsequently, even considered using actual photographs in *The Stones of Venice* (1851).[86] Piazzi Smyth's *Teneriffe, an Astronomer's Experiment*

(1858) used stereographic illustrations, and Charles Darwin's *The Expression of Emotions in Man and Animals* (1872) was illustrated with photographs originally made by the popular pictorialist, Oscar Rejlander. Novels also began to be illustrated with photographs, a practice that may first have occurred with the "extra-illustration" of books published by the German, Bernhard Tauchnitz.[87] This firm published English and American editions for the European market, and booksellers often engaged in the practice of adding photographic illustrations to them (thus "extra-illustrating" them). Hence the original hand drawn illustrations became mingled with photographs of places; and these books apparently became popular as travel guides. Among the Tauchnitz "extra-illustrated" editions was Nathaniel Hawthorne's *Transformations; or, The Romance of Monte Beni*, appearing in 1860 with mounted photographs.[88] George Eliot's *Romolo* also emerged in an "extra-illustrated" Tauchnitz edition in 1863, mixing photographs with the original illustrations by Frederic Leighton.[89] Others issued volumes of fiction and poetry that were illustrated with photographs, too. Sir Walter Scott's *The Lady of the Lake* was published in 1869 by an Edinburgh firm, Adam and Charles Black, using photographic illustrations.[90]

Quite commonly, the photographic images included in these works were topographical scenes, giving a travelogue quality to the novels they accompanied. Occasionally, however, another type of use was attempted. Julia Margaret Cameron's illustrations for Tennyson's *Idylls of the King* (1875) were dramatic in mode, seeking to capture the spirit and tone of Tennyson's work through theatrically posed images of actors and actresses dressed in historical costumes. These were the *tableaux vivants* so disliked by the reviewer of the photographic display at the Philadelphia Exhibition of 1876.[91] A problem, however, often emerged whenever photographic illustration was used, as Betsy Jablow puts it, "to illustrate a prephotographic subject. Is the credibility of the reader stretched too far when he or she looks at images of nineteenth-century Florence inserted in an historical fiction set in the fifteenth century or at Cameron's prints of Lancelot and Guinevere?"[92] Too much specificity, too direct veracity interfered with imaginative literature. No such interference occurred when photographs were used in travel books, in scientific tracts, or in reportorial accounts such as John Thomson's and Adolphe Smith's *Street Life in London* (1877) or Jacob Riis's *How the Other Half Lives* (1890). In these instances, photographic realism supported the purposes of the texts' authors by offering contemporary visual descriptions of the phenomena that the words alone could only denote more indirectly.[93]

With imaginative literature, however, specificity could and did damage or destroy the qualities that fiction writers and poets were trying to convey through words. A case in point is an 1899 edition of Mark Twain's *Pudd'nhead Wilson*, containing a photographic frontispiece that pictures Twain's heroine, Roxana.[94] The photograph unwittingly reveals much more about the racist attitudes of the day than it does about the Roxana described by Twain. This frontispiece presents a very unattractive, very dark looking woman — the classic stereotype of the black mammy. As such, it directly contradicts Twain's verbal picture of Roxana as a very light (she is an octaroon), quite beautiful woman who could have passed for white. The photograph's distorted specificity utterly interferes with the writer's carefully wrought verbal picture. Another, less disconcerting example may be found in W. D. Howells's *Their Silver Wedding Journey* (1899).[95] In this novel, both photographs and hand drawn pictures illustrate the text throughout. The harsh realism of the halftone reproductions of photographs contrasts bluntly with the softened, romanticised realism of Howells's text as well as with W. T. Smedley's picturesque, idealized sketches. A tension is set up that could not likely have been resolved, even had Howells been given an opportunity to do so.[96]

Though photographic illustration came to be more and more in demand, it tended to be used most often alongside nonfiction. Pick up any illustrated periodical published between 1890 and 1910 — particularly the American ones such as *Harper's Monthly*, *Century*, or *Collier's* — and leaf through its pages. The overwhelming likelihood is that you will find the fiction illustrated by hand drawn pictures and the nonfiction illustrated with halftone photographs. In the former case, the illustrations will be in the dramatic mode; in the latter, they will be informational. Though I have not made a systematic study of this phenomenon, I suspect that the use of photographic illustration increased when the magazine's editorial staff chose to appeal to a mass market. For instance, recall that the *Atlantic Monthly*, always an elite literary and intellectual journal, never used illustrations of any variety and often featured articles decrying the overuse of pictures in books, magazines, and newspapers. Yet, photographs dominated the pages of mass-oriented magazines such as *Ladies' Home Journal* and *Success*, magazines that published more nonfiction than fiction.[97]

Reaction to the use of photographs for illustrating literature was just as negative as the prevalent attitudes regarding the acceptance of photography as a fine art; and, as might be expected, attitudes ranged from mild to complete disapproval of the practice. Preferring hand drawn illustration to photographs, William Cullen Bryant asserted, "Photographs lack the spirit and personal quality which the accomplished painter or draughtsman infuses into his work."[98] But P. G. Hamerton, in his dialogue on "Book Illustration" had his critic declare flatly, "a pure photograph from nature is out of place in any book whatever."[99] Such prejudices seemed to become more and more widespread as the nineteenth century approached its end, for the number of discussions pertaining to the appropriateness of using photography as an illustrative medium in books of fiction and poetry increased. An 1891 *Atlantic* reviewer centered most of his review of "Holiday Books" on the subject, and he declared the use of photographs to be a complete interference with the spirit of writers such as Hawthorne, Eliot, and Wordsworth. Finally, commenting on a Wordsworth volume that contained hand drawn illustration, this reviewer wrote with obvious relief: "No one can feast his eyes on these lovely pastoral pictures, and call to mind what the same book would be illustrated by the most faithful photographs of Westmoreland and Cumberland, without perceiving that as Wordsworth's sonnets are not a guidebook, so Mr. Parson's pictures are not photographic reports."[100] Even as late as 1906, James John Hissey, in *Untravelled England*, felt that he needed to apologize to the reader for using photographs as illustrations: "My next apology is for the illustrations," he wrote. "These are reproductions of some of my photographs taken on the journey under varying conditions of time and weather. Drawings sympathetically engraved on wood would have pleased me vastly better, but the sympathetic engraver has to be discovered. The photographs, however, possess the merit of being faithful representations of places and scenes we came upon, without any artistic embellishment."[101]

Despite his need to apologize for using photographs in his book, Hissey seemed to value accuracy more than charming decoration (though what he may really have valued most of all was the book's potential marketability). Whatever Hissey's real motives were for using photographic illustration, his declared preference suggests a reason why photomechanical reproduction gradually replaced hand drawn illustration in the mass-publication industry: its exactitude, a quality that happily for publishers was eventually accompanied by those of efficiency and cheapness.

When the photography-on-the-block process began to be used in the 1860s, it was welcomed because of its accuracy in replicating the artist's original drawing. Engravers prided themselves on their responsibility to be accurate in the carving of the printing blocks, and by 1880 many could agree that photography had been a distinct benefit to them in the practice of their profession.[102] "Just here came in the assistance of photography, by which the paintings or drawings on canvas or on paper were transferred directly to the wood," said engraver John P. Davies, in "A Symposium of Wood-Engravers," appearing in the February 1880 issue of *Harper's New Monthly Magazine*. "The art of wood engraving," he continued, "received in consequence a fresh impulse and entered into a new liberty, the possibilities of which it is yet too soon to estimate."[103] Another engraver, Frederick Juengling, agreed, lauding "the perfect placing of the drawing by means of photography, thereby insuring a degree of accuracy not easily obtainable in other arts of this class."[104] And though these engravers recognized that photography had some disadvantages, it was generally declared "a powerful auxiliary" in making wood engravings.[105] Illustrators, too, were often pleased by the innovation, for many of them resented what they deemed to be the encroachment of the engraver's interpretation on their own; and the use of photography-on-the-block could prevent this.[106] But they were also wary of the risks of using photographs (even as aids to drawing), because of the medium's realism and its supposed mechanicalness. Critic Walter Crane summed up the dangers of photography's impact on illustration. Though he found photography an important, somewhat positive influence on book and periodical production, he nonetheless declared it to be of "doubtful advantage" in terms of its stylistic influence. It had led, in Crane's view, to the deterioration of "inventive design. . . having concentrated artistic interest on the literal realization of certain aspects of superficial facts, and instantaneous impressions instead of ideas, and the abstract treatment of form and line."[107] To the extent that photography had been merely a tool for artists—in P. G. Hamerton's words, "a wonderfully obedient slave for the collecting of memoranda"[108]—it had been helpful. But by the 1890s, photography had become more than just a tool for illustrators; in the minds of critics, it had influenced the quality and style of illustration, and—as Pennell made so clear in his 1897 diatribe—it threatened to replace hand drawn illustration entirely.

Intellectual historian, Neil Harris, argues that, "in a period of ten or fifteen years the whole system of packaging visual information was transformed, made more appealing and persuadable, and assumed a form and adopted conventions that have persisted right through the present," and he terms it "an iconographical revolution of the first order. . . . The single generation of Americans (and certainly English and Europeans, too) living between 1885 and 1910 went through an experience of visual reorientation that had few earlier precedents, although it would be matched by some twentieth-century experiences."[109] Though I would move the first date back to 1839 (in order to include the invention of photography and its rapid, widespread acceptance), I believe that Harris is correct. Among those most profoundly affected were the members of the artistic and intellectual community that was beginning to take shape in the Western world. The outbursts of Delaroche, Baudelaire, Pennell, Fairfield, and others suggest the hostility this pictorial revolution gave rise to as well as some of the reasons for such vehement responses. The halftone was the culmination of efforts to develop photomechanical processes that had begun with the public announcement of photography. The impact of the halftone's triumph was very threatening to intellectuals and artists who had an ideological (and sometimes pecuniary) stake in nineteenth-century notions of art and creative genius. Art in the Victorian world was an elite activity, and anything that seemed to undercut its elitist aura was deemed pernicious. Knowledge of the tradition, training of the senses, acquisition of the skills, the practice of hand craft, the exercise of individual imagination, and the creation of the unique art object were all essential elements if literary and pictorial art was to be certified Art.

The artist and the work of art became threatened at the outset of what Walter Benjamin called, "the age of mechanical reproduction."[110] As an easy, democratic, popular medium, photography was perceived as corrupting; so, too, was the proliferation of the illustrated press; and finally, photomechanical reproduction emerged to administer the last blow. In an effort to appeal to a mass readership, mechanical pictures were being used in place of words and pictures made by individual artistic geniuses, and the members of the elite intellectual and artistic culture that valued Art was disturbed. The new processes were inevitably linked to profit making, for the mechanization of picture publishing made it possible to appeal to a mass popular market by diminishing (at least, in the view of the members of the elite culture) the quality of the product to appeal to the largest number of people—hence, reducing it to the lowest common denominator. The quality of the products of the new processes and the layouts used to display pictures and words were indeed different. Halftone reproduction did transfer more information than earlier processes, but it was less attractive than photogravure, collotype, woodburytype, or for that matter, wood engraving. The halftone lacked the richness and the light to dark gradations of tone that the more difficult, expensive processes reproduced. Finally, photography and the new photomechanical technique contained a real economic threat: it replaced many of the hand artists and the engravers who once made illustrations—it threw them out of jobs. It also threatened writers by demanding that they supply suitable texts for the picture press or cease to place their writings with publishers.[111]

Mechanism, mindlessness, and ease were perceived as becoming substitutes for artistic imagination and skill and an established artistic tradition. Machines were replacing individuals, the real was replacing the ideal, mass-produced art was replacing the unique Art object, and mass taste was being flaunted just outside the palace of art. So its custodians were fighting back vehemently, trying to make themselves heard above the noise of the vulgar crowd.[112] "The childish view, so to speak, 'is on top,' " cried out a *Nation* writer in 1893.[113] His lament would be repeated over and over again as intellectual attacks on the emerging mass culture continued into the twentieth century.[114] What was at stake was the Victorian idea of high art, the dominance of concepts like individual genius, craft, the unique artwork, and cultivated taste. In short, the hegemony of a class-based culture that ruled from the art academies and the elite magazines and book publishing houses was being challenged. To this group, it seemed as though a kind of Gresham's law of aesthetics was at work, and this reprehensible state of affairs was perceived as having been abetted in no small measure by the invention and proliferation of photography.

6

The Real Thing: Photography, Literary Realism, and James's Art

In a 1904 *Atlantic* essay dwelling extensively on the use of photographs to illustrate literature, an anonymous reviewer concluded:

> In some . . . modern stories illustrations are legitimate, especially in realistic fiction, which is so perplexingly unreal. I should like to own an illustrated edition of Henry James for my wife and children. The vague, interthreaded abstractions would, under the touch of a really great illustrator, solidify into visual actualities which any child could apperceive. . . . The style is so easy to write, but difficult to read. . . . The illustrator who could depict James's women probably does not exist. If he could be found, what a benefactor would he be of his race and generation.[1]

It is entirely possible that Henry James saw this review, since he usually kept abreast of current literary matters, and the *Atlantic* was among the most important literary and cultural journals of his day. If he did, he doubtless was deeply annoyed, probably angered, by it. Though James had always sought a large readership, even a mass readership, he refused to pander to readers either by simplifying his style or giving them pleasing endings.[2] Instead, he often used popular forms such as romance and melodrama but always treated them ironically or gave them unexpected twists; and beginning in the mid-1890s, he consciously moved toward a profoundly difficult, complex style, one that required great concentration and effort on the part of the reader.[3] Consequently, his audience diminished over the years.

Of course, criticism such as that made by the above quoted reviewer was not new to James, nor would it cease during his lifetime. His brother, William James, repeated it on different occasions in letters. "I read your *Golden Bowl* a month or more ago," wrote William in 1905, "and it put me, as most of your recenter long stories have put me, in a very puzzled state of mind. . . . But why won't you, just to please Brother, sit down and write a new book, with no twilight or mustiness in the plot, with great vigor and decisiveness in the action, no fencing in the dialogue, no psychological commentaries, and absolute straightness in the style?"[4] In 1907, William wrote again, this time in reference to *The American Scene* (1907):

> You know how opposed your whole "third manner" of execution is to the literary ideals which animate my crude and Orson-like breast, mine being to say a thing in one sentence as straight and explicit as it can be made, and then to drop it forever; yours being to avoid naming it straight, but by dint of breathing and sighing all round and round it, to arouse in the reader who may have had a similar perception already . . . the illusion of a solid object, made . . . out of impalpable materials, air, and the prismatic interferences of light, ingeniously focussed by mirrors upon empty space. . . . In this crowded and hurried reading age, pages that require such close attention remain unread and neglected.[5]

Though such comments were characteristic of a widespread misunderstanding of Henry James's prose, they nonetheless reflect in an oddly accurate way the stylistic change that had occurred in his writing between the time James first became an author in the 1870s and the turn of the century. James began as part of an emerging nineteenth-century literary movement termed — often pejoratively — realism. And despite the fact that his art eventually became quite distinct from the work of realist writers such as Zola, Turgenev, Tolstoy, and Howells, James clearly had once shared with them many of the same aesthetic tenets and artistic strategies. He participated energetically in the numerous debates over literary realism, and he forcefully defended the movement as well as the work of its adherents. His style, however, gradually evolved beyond realism into what has been termed a "subjective-objective" mode of narration.[6] As the *Atlantic* reviewer aptly though negatively noted, James's late phase did indeed exhibit an abstracted realism that was "perplexingly unreal." By 1904, James had become a modernist.

What has any of this to do with photography, in general, and with James's collaboration with Coburn, in particular? Much, I suggest. The paradox of the collaboration is not explained simply by showing that photography was an illustrative medium that James could direct and control. It is true that James discovered a medium that enabled him to share decisively in the "cultivation" of the "garden" of illustrations that now accompany his New York Edition prose. Through the camera, he became — partially, at least — his own illustrator. But that explanation is incomplete, not merely because of the status of photography as an art, but also because of James's own attitudes toward the medium.

On the face of the evidence, it appears that James took sides with those who rejected photography as a fine art. Yet, if he was in agreement with photography's critics, it was tacit — one almost of benign neglect. All James's writings indicate that he was either unaware of, or unconcerned with, the fact that there was an art movement in photography. Not until after the turn of the century, when he was reflecting on the possibility of collaborating with Coburn, is there any evidence that he ever attended a photographic exhibition or thought about photography as an artform.[7]

Still, as is bluntly confirmed by his vivid recollection of the incident surrounding his 1854 daguerreotype portrait (figure 32) James was fully cognizant of the existence of the medium. It early became a part of his life—pervasively so, he noted sardonically regarding his "suffered snapshots of a later age" (figure 33).[8] Indeed, James recalled in *A Small Boy and Others*, his brother William once practiced "photography in the room I for a while shared with him at Boulogne, with every stern reality of big umbrous camera, prolonged exposure, exposure mostly of myself, darkened development, also interminable, and ubiquitous brown blot."[9] On sparse occasions in his letters home, James also spoke of photographs, though nearly always in a utilitarian sense. To William, he once wrote, "I will try to have a photograph taken" of the house at Rye.[10] But such instances, when read alone, tell us little else than that James was aware of photography in a rather offhanded way.

More to the point of assessing James's attitudes toward photography are the responses to photographs that crop up in his various nonfictional writings throughout his life. To some degree, these responses manifest the psychological impact on photography on James's conscious mind. The first instance of this was, again, the 1854 daguerreotype—a symbolic reminder of an embarrassment. A later circumstance concerned a snapshot of a close friend of James, Wolcott Balestier, who had died while a young man. James wrote Balestier's mother in 1900: "His [Balestier's] photograph hangs here beside me as I write—and he looks down at me, as if he knew I am speaking of him. My memory, my affection, thank heaven, holds him fast."[11] For a moment, James sensed, "he looks down at me," again indicating the power of the photograph's realism over the conscious mind. Another similar episode appears in another letter by James, one written to Mrs. Frank Mathews in 1902. She had sent James a photograph, and he responded:

> The photographer has *retouched* the impression rather too freely, especially the eyes (if one could but keep their hands off!) but the image has a pleasing ghostliness, as out of the far past, and affects me pathetically as if it were of the dead—of one who died young and innocent. Well, so he did, and I can speak of him or admire him, poor charming slightly mawkish youth, quite as I would another. I remember (it now all comes back to me) when (and where) I was so taken: at the age of *20*, though I look younger, and at a time when I had had an accident (an injury to my back,) and was rather sick and sorry. I look rather as if I wanted propping up. But you have propped me up, now, handsomely for all time, and I feel that I shall go down so to the remotest posterity.[12]

Figure 33. Anonymous, Snapshot of Henry James and Alice
James (ca. 1904–05).
(By permission of Houghton Library, Harvard University.)

There was pleasantness, humor, and perhaps a little pain in this reminiscence, caused by the photograph that took him back to his own youth for a moment. Clearly, photographs exerted a power over James as a stimulus to memory and emotional feeling or, on occasion, as a substitute for the person depicted.

Of course, photographs did not always produce the same reaction. In *Notes of a Son and Brother*, James recalled his cousin, Minny Temple, whom he cared for deeply but who died a young woman in 1870. The photograph of her, James wrote, is only "helpful to memory — so that I am moved to reproduce it only till I feel again how the fondness of memory must strike the light for apprehension."[13] And in an 1893 letter to his good friend, Robert Louis Stevenson, James noted the inadequacy of a photograph to evoke a desired presence. More annoyed than moved, James wrote, "I have a most charming and interesting letter, and a photographic representation of your fine head. . . . The portrait has its points as a momento, but they are not fine points as a likeness. I remember, I think of you, I evoke you, much more plastically."[14] Photographic likenesses were not always satisfying replacements for the thing itself, especially when it came to personal matters.

When it came to public matters, however, photographs often evinced a strong response from James. In 1914, James wrote to Edith Wharton about receiving "an immensely revealing small photograph of one of the outraged aspects of the outraged cathedral [Rheims], the vividest picture of the irreparable outrage."[15] During the same year, James also wrote of Abraham Lincoln's assassination, an event symbolized for him by an intensely recalled, but undescribed photograph: "it was open to us to waver at shop windows exposing the new photograph, exposing that is, *the* photograph, and ask ourselves what we had been guilty of as a people, when all was said, to deserve the infliction of that form."[16] In all these instances, likeness underlay the responses James had to photographs. They were good or bad, powerful or weak depictions of aspects or persons that once existed in the real world. At best, they were cherished documents; at worst inflictions.

Documents were one thing, but art was another. On only a few occasions did James ever link art with photographs in his writings. When he did — as occasionally happened in some of his critical pieces — the implication was clear: photography was not art. Two instances worth noting pertain to using photography in reference to literature; two others are in reference to painting; all occur early in James's writing career. In 1864, in an unsigned review of Nassau W. Senior's *Essays on Fiction*, James noted, "even the most photographically disposed novels address pre-eminently the imagination."[17] A year later, reviewing Anthony Trollope's *Miss Mackenzie*,

James was more explicit regarding what he meant by the term, "photographically disposed novels." Trollope, James wrote, "is an excellent observer; and such an one may accomplish much. But why does he not observe great things as well as little ones?" Trollope's problem, James felt, was that he "deals wholly in small effects. . . . Nothing . . . is omitted; but, alas! nothing is infused. The scene possesses no interest but such as resides in the crude facts . . . the picture is clever, it is faithful, it is even horrible, but it is not interesting." Trollope's "virtues are all virtues of detail: the virtues of the photography. The photograph lacks the supreme virtue of possessing a character. It is the detail alone that distinguishes one photograph from another."[18] Twelve years later, James still expressed the same viewpoint. This time, writing about painters who used photographs, James remarked that a M. Heilbuth "is very real . . . his pictures have to an inordinate degree that deplorable look of being based on photographs, which is the fame of so much of the clever painting of our day. The painters have used photographs so much in their work that the result is tainted by that hideous inexpressiveness of the mechanical document. You see that the picture has been painted by a short cut."[19] And still later, in his review of "Honoré Daumier," James wrote (with evident relief): "The caricaturist of that day had not the help of the ubiquitous photograph."[20]

To James, then, photographs were likenesses embodying memories or serving as substitutes for the subjects themselves, yet their only virtues were "virtues of detail." They lacked "character," were "ubiquitous," and too often exuded "hideous inexpressiveness." Such qualities were not congenial to good literature or painting. Art could not afford to keep company with such a medium — or so Henry James seemed to believe.

James also made references to photography and photographs several times in his fiction. In some instances, these were incidental, helping to describe characters, offering insights into their perceptions and consciousness, or simply adding to the "realistic" social texture of the novel or tale. Occasionally, however, references to the medium served as important devices — moving a plot along or providing a central metaphor that gave meaning to the work. In most of these usages, James affirmed his apparent lack of respect for photography. Never once did he suggest that the medium might be an art.

During the early years of its practice, photography was notorious for the difficulties encountered in getting good likenesses.[21] This shared piece of knowledge was used to provide a descriptive simile in *The American* (1877). At one place in the novel, James's hero Christopher Newman is talking with Madame de Cintré, the woman whose hand he is seeking. Newman tells her, "you've a high spirit, a high standard; but with you it's all natural and unaffected: you don't seem to have stuck your head in a vise, as if you were sitting for the photograph of propriety."[22] James understood that his audience would recognize this allusion, that such an image would help them form precisely the picture he wished to convey regarding his heroine.

In a subsequent work, James again made reference to the photograph, this time in conjunction with other mass media related phenomena. In *The Aspern Papers* (1888), James's unnamed narrator relates his experience of attempting to get hold of some extent literary papers once belonging to a famous dead poet, Jeffrey Aspern. He had gone to Venice, he explains, to talk with Aspern's surviving mistress, a Miss Bordereau. The narrator had learned of her whereabouts through a friend, and he notes his "wonder that we had not found her out sooner, and the substance of our explanation was that she had kept so quiet. The poor lady on the whole had had reason for doing so. But it was a revelation to us that self-effacement on such a scale had been possible in the latter half of the nineteenth century—the age of newspapers and telegrams and photographs and interviewers."[23] The manner of James's usage here clearly linked him with the nineteenth-century intellectual and artistic elite's concern over the emerging technological, mass culture. Along with the other terms listed, the word photograph characterized a new age in which few persons would be able to retain any vestige of privacy. The photograph (as well as newspapers, telegrams, and interviewers) symbolized the cheapening of the quality of life and culture that artists and intellectuals like James felt was taking place during the late nineteenth century.[24]

Another allusion to photographs, though, reveals that James could use the medium more complexly—in a way other than as a device to denote a negative implication. In *What Maisie Knew* (1897), James utilized the medium to introduce readers to one of the most important characters in the book—Sir Claude. This time, no particular value judgment is embodied in the usage. Maisie, the book's young heroine, is shown a package by Miss Overmore, her governess. The package contains "a 'cabinet' photograph of Sir Claude and Maisie lost herself in admiration of the fair smooth face, the regular features, the kind eyes, the amiable air, the general glossiness and smartness of her prospective stepfather."[25] Maisie is then described as holding "the photograph and Sir Claude," and though it goes against her previous training in manners, she asks for it and is given its "possession" by Miss Overmore.[26] In this instance, James used the photograph in a way that indicates how people—James himself included—often responded to photographic images, and it is clear that James fully understood this common response. The photograph is just that—a photograph of Sir Claude; yet it begins to become Sir Claude in the minds of the viewers, particularly

Maisie. Through this external detail, James revealed Maisie's deep-seated psychological need for a parent and a stable family life. Later in the book, the merger between the photographic image and the person depicted occurs again during Sir Claude's brief absence: "Without Sir Claude's photograph, however, the place would have been, as he said, as dull as a cold dinner."27

James's most extensive literary use of photography occurred in "The Real Thing," the tale about an illustrator and his models. In this story (published in 1893, four years before *What Maisie Knew* and the emergence of James's "late manner" style), James once again exposed his negative attitudes toward photography—only this time in a more complete sense. In "The Real Thing," James utilized photography in a way that came much closer to Hawthorne's use of it in *The House of the Seven Gables*, but James stood Hawthorne's insight regarding the capacity of the medium on its head. James's allusions to photography in "The Real Thing" give readers an insight into two of the story's characters, and it is precisely the photographic aspect of the characters that provides the story with its narrative twists. When these two characters, Major and Mrs. Monarch (once well-off, we recall, but now destitute), ask the artist-narrator to use them as models for his illustrations, the artist remarks that people such as themselves would get tired modeling. Still, he pursues the matter, asking them if they have had any experience. Mrs. Monarch replies, "We've been photographed, immensely."28 It is after this conversation that the artist hires them.

So far, no clear attitude regarding photography has been betrayed by James, though the tone is a touch sardonic; the reference to the medium seems to be merely a detail adding realism to the portrayal of the couple. Later, however, the reference to photography appears again. This time, it takes on central importance, for it is used to expose a deep-seated flaw in Mrs. Monarch's character and experience and subtly criticize her class. Ultimately, readers are led to recognize, it is this flaw that dictates the tale's inexorable movement toward its unsettling end. Mrs. Monarch is modeling one day, and James's artist-narrator describes the scene:

> She sat with great intensity, giving the whole of her mind to it, and was capable of remaining for an hour almost as motionless as if she were before a photographer's lens. I could see that she had been photographed often, but somehow the very habit that made her good for that purpose unfitted her for mine. At first I was extremely pleased with her lady-like air, and it was a satisfaction, on coming to follow her lines, to see how good they were and how far they could lead the pencil. But after a few times I began to find her too insurmountably stiff; do what I would with it my drawing looked like a photograph or a copy of a photograph. Her figure had no variety of expression—she herself had no sense of variety.29

Subsequently, Mr. Monarch exhibits the same flaw. He too has "no sense of variety," and because of their lack, both he and Mrs. Monarch—desperately in need of work—become the servants, making and pouring tea for the artist and his new models, Oronte and Miss Churm—the two characters who had originally been the artist's servants.

Not only did James expose the flaw in the Monarchs' artificial character through equating it with static photographic portraiture, but he also commented on the relationship between the photograph and the other arts in the process. As he had argued in his review on painting, discussed above, photography was not useful to the painter. By the 1890s, James's position seemed clear regarding the photograph's artfulness: he not only dismissed the medium as stiff and lifeless, as inexpressive and utterly without character, and as notable only for its detail, but went even further than critics such as Baudelaire, saying bluntly that photography could not even be considered as a useful handmaiden to the arts. It impeded the "interesting." Yet, between that time and the start of the New York Edition collaboration, James would change his mind and decide that photography might be capable of being used in an artful way after all.[30]

James's reasons for using such negative literary references to photography are not hard to surmise. As we have already seen, he had often derogated the medium in his nonfiction writings, and we may fairly conclude that this was an honest expression of his regard for the medium. Moreover, James was a writer whose fiction drew upon the social life surrounding him, using whatever sources would best serve his meanings and purposes as an artist. Always an acute observer, James certainly knew that his audience would comprehend the meanings implicit in his use of photography as literary material. He could also be certain that this would be equally true of his literary peers. None of them misunderstood James's "photographic" references' meanings, and most of them were surely in agreement with his treatment of the medium. Indeed, photographic analogies had been making their appearance in literary circles as terms of critical derision since approximately midcentury.[31] Not surprisingly, use of such analogies occurred alongside the rise of, and as a part of the debate over literary realism.

With the appearance of writers such as Balzac, Stendhal, Dickens, and George Eliot, traditional literary aesthetics began to be threatened.[32] As realists—or, at the very least, precursors of realism—those writers introduced into their fiction characters, scenes, and plots that were often considered by readers to be common, vulgar, and undramatic. Their's was too factual a depiction of life, too close a replication of the details found in the everyday world for conventional tastes. Their narrative strategy was to allow new worlds to enter onto the page without the appearance of authorial mediation: it was a mode that sought objectivity in the presentation of things, persons, and actions. The victims of this perceived attack on literary conventions were Beauty, Truth, and the Idealization of Nature — all artistic requisites of the two ruling art movements, Romanticism and Classicism. Of course, Beauty, Truth, and the Idealization of life did not disappear immediately from literature when realist writers began publishing, nor did the author become completely invisible in all novels and tales — even those of writers like Balzac or Eliot. Realist writers were, after all, partly schooled in the literary tradition of their predecessors. Nonetheless, they were also schooled in the emerging worldview of their age — an empirical worldview that emphasized close observation of the world's details and permitted only the drawing of tentative conclusions — truths instead of Truth — from these observations. Despite opposition, realist art gradually attracted practitioners and adherents, and realism became a central aesthetic battleground during the second half of the nineteenth century — in America as well as in Europe.[33]

Because of photography's uncanny mimetic accuracy, it was perhaps inevitable that it would become a major symbol representing realist art. For many, recall, the photograph reproduced only a surface truth; its value lay in its detail and nothing else. Literature, on the other hand, had the obligation of going beyond the rendering of surface details. In the view of critic T. S. Perry, expounded in the *North American Review* in 1872, a writer shirked his duty if he imagined "that the simple rehersal of the barrenest external phenomena of life and nature . . . can be of any real interest to the reader. . . . It is the bane of realism . . . to forget that it represents only one important side of truth."[34] Perry continued, "In the true novel the scene, the incidents, are subordinated to the sufferings, actions, and qualities of the characters. . . . The geology, the botany, the ethnography, may be accurate to date, the reader may be in perpetual shivers from the urgency of the dangers that threaten every one in the novel, but the real story lies beneath the hats and bonnets of those concerned, not in the distant cataracts that wet them, nor the bullets that scar them."[35] Perry ended his essay with the assertion that novels usually "fail from their dulness [*sic*], whether caused by their photographic accuracy, or by the sluggish imagination of the author," and he admonished to the novelist to "be a poet . . . look at life, not as the statistician, not as the census-taker, nor yet as the newspaper reporter, but with an eye that sees . . . the animating principles, good or bad, that direct human existence. . . . The idealizing novelist will be the real novelist. All truth does not lie in facts."[36]

In an 1878 *Atlantic* essay, another writer reflected on "*realism*: If we are to have nothing else in literature and painting, would it not be well to drop the terms *fiction* and *art* entirely?"[37] Great art, in this critic's opinion, had always been "essentially ideal, and it is with the ideal that the true artist has to deal. It is in this respect that his work differs from that of the photographer and the newspaper reporter. We care not where he procures his materials, whether from the field of life or the yet more fertile one of the imagination; they must be remolded and adapted to this ideal world."[38] Still another, friendlier reviewer of realist writing examined "The novels of Mr. Howells" in an 1880 issue of *Nation*, and noted that "Realism can never successfully substitute photographic detail for this short-cut to truth, and the greatest realists do not attempt it."[39] Perhaps the fullest and harshest attack against realism, though, appeared in 1883 when writer and critic Charles Dudley Warner wrote in the pages of the *Atlantic*:

> One of the worst characteristics of modern fiction is its so-called truth to nature. For fiction is an art, as painting is, as sculpture is, as acting is. A photograph of a natural object is not art; nor is the plaster cast of a man's face, nor is the bare setting on the stage of an actual occurrence. Art requires an idealization of nature. . . .
>
> However our jargon of criticism may confound terms, we do not need to be reminded that art and nature are distinct; that art, though dependent on nature, is a separate creation; that art is selection and idealization, with a view to impressing the mind with human or even higher than human, sentiments and ideas. . . .
>
> When we praise our recent fiction for its photographic fidelity to nature we condemn it, for we deny to it the art which would give it value. We forget that the creation of the novel should be, to a certain extent, a synthetic process, and impart to human actions that ideal quality which we demand in practice.[40]

The argument was powerful as well as common, and realism's adherents often found themselves in the position of having to explain why the best realist works were not merely "photographic" but instead went beyond the mere reproduction of surface details and mechanicalness to exhibit the qualities of imagination and beauty of individual expression. Emile Zola, for example, felt compelled to answer this charge in his book, *The Experimental Novel* (1880):

> But see how things begin to clear up when you take the position of the experimental method in the novel, with all the scientific rigor of the physical sciences. A stupid reproach made against us naturalist writers is that we wish to be merely photographers. In vain have we asserted that we accept temperament and personal expression; people go right on answering us with imbecile arguments about the impossibility of the strictly true, about the necessity of arrangement of facts to make any work of art whatever. Well, with the application of the experimental method to the novel all argument comes to an end. The idea of experiment carries with it the idea of modification. We begin certainly with true facts which are our indestructible base; but to show the mechanism of the facts, we have to produce and direct the phenomena; that is our part of invention and genius in the work.[41]

Despite such defenses, the reproaches were repeated again and again. And realist and naturalist writers continued to respond to them. "It is curious to notice," Frank Norris wrote in the 27 June 1896 San Francisco *Wave*, "how persistently M. Zola is misunderstood. How strangely he is misinterpreted even by those who conscientiously admire the novels of 'man of the iron pen.' For most people Naturalism has a vague meaning. It is a sort of inner circle of realism—a kind of diametric opposite of romanticism, a theory of fiction wherein things are represented 'as they really are,' inexorably, with the truthfulness of a camera. This idea can be shown to be far from right."[42]

Of course, not all defenders of literary realism denied the aptness of the photography analogy nor did they think that it was a damning criticism. In an 1884 interview, Mark Twain, referring to "Howells' newspaper man [Bartley Hubbard] who is brought before the public a second time in 'Silas Lapham,'" said: "He is a wonderful creation, a photograph of many such men who do exist, not a cheerful, nice sort of man to sit at a communion table perhaps, but still a strong, living man."[43] Hamlin Garland approvingly quoted another critic, Grant Allen: "The modern American novel . . . *is the real realism, the natural naturalism*; it depends for its effects upon the faithful, almost photographic delineation of actual life."[44] And W. D. Howells himself made the same point in an essay on Frank Norris: "by and by he will achieve something of the impartial fidelity of the photograph."[45]

Henry James understood completely the terms and ideas used in the battles that were being waged over literary realism. As noted earlier, he had used the pejorative critical reference to photography on more than one occasion in his own literary and art reviews. And though I have not discovered any reference to James's fiction as being "photographic," his work was widely considered to be part of the realist school.[46] Indeed, it was sometimes attacked with words to that effect: James was a "realist—he copies life; and realism in literature, although not so plainly a disappointment as in art, is quite as unsatisfactory."[47] Even his supporters, such as Horace E. Scudder, praised him in realist terms, noting defensively that it was through "the nice portrayal of surfaces, by which an undercurrent of moving life is now revealed, now concealed, that the highest art is disclosed,"[48] and then crediting James with having achieved such a level of attainment because he "gives us a picture of human life as it passes before the spectator, who might himself be a part of it, and at the same time offers an interpretation of that life."[49]

The war over whether literary realism was or was not an art was expressed in arguments quite similar to those used by critics who attacked photography's status as art. When the conflict over realism began, photography's struggle had already been going on for some time and was widely enough known to contribute the epithet "photographic" to the debate over the legitimacy of realism in literature. The irony implicit in both battles was that photography's detractors misunderstood both phenomena. They believed that the medium of photography and the style of realism were indistinguishable from the material world, being either at one with it or mere reproductions of it: in either case, both were incapable of revealing the truths that lay beneath the surfaces of things because of their literal quality, their unmediated presence. Literalism seemed to eschew the act of interpretation. Furthermore, the presumed mechanicalness of reproducing the world's surfaces on paper denied the act of creative imagination and the quality of individual genius. Both photography and literary realism were regarded as mindless acts by elite nineteenth-century critics.

But those holding this view were wrong. Neither photographs nor realist art are the world itself put before us by mindless reproductive acts. On the contrary, both are modes of representing the world and possess particular codes, strategies, and style. During the nineteenth century, few evidently understood that, as E. H. Gombrich cogently argues, "All art originates in the human mind, in our reactions to the world rather than in the visible world itself, and it is precisely because all art is 'conceptual' that all representations are recognized by their style."[50] The nineteenth-century critics notwithstanding, photography and literary realism were just as much results of deliberate responses of human minds to the world—hence "conceptual" and thus acts of representation—as were paintings or writings embodying the styles of Romanticism or Classicism.

Realism's (and photography's) problem was its transparency, its presumed literalness and lack of style. Yet, those are qualities that in part denoted its style and interpretative strategy. "Realism," Catherine Belsey argues, "is plausible not because it reflects the world, but because it is constructed out of what is (discursively) familiar."[51] Now, this "familiarity does not mean that realism can never surprise us. . . . It can do so through unexpected juxtapositions and complexities. But it assembles these juxtapositions and complexities out of what we already know, and it is for this reason that we experience it as realistic."[52] "Realism offers itself as transparent," and though it is now considered "a predominately conservative form" (for our "experience of reading a realist text is ultimately reassuring, however harrowing the events of the story, because the world evoked in the fiction, its patterns of cause and effect, of social relationships and moral values, largely confirm the patterns of the world we seem to know"), it was by no means considered a conservative form during the mid and late nineteenth century.[53] At its inception, realism—photography, too—offered unfamiliar qualities to patrons of the arts. Art had to be "an idealization of nature," as Warner put it, and not the apparently unaltered world itself.[54] People expected their representations to contain particular codes and structures that they had been used to seeing and reading in conventional works of art. All else was ugliness, chaos — inartistic. The introduction of an unadorned world into artworks was too much for most nineteenth-century art lovers. Realism and photography were simply too direct and too ubiquitous for cultivated tastes.

If Henry James was a vigorous supporter of literary realism and if realism and photography had so much in common, why did he join the critics of photography who dismissed the medium as art? The simplest answer is because James did not consider the best realist works to be merely photographic. Realism, as Scudder noted regarding James's own fiction, had to go beyond representing surfaces and interpret life. It was an important, modern literary mode for a writer like James who sought to experiment and create new kinds of fiction. But, as always, the simple answer has its depths and complexities: it is impossible to pin down James the author to any one literary movement, because he never ceased to change and evolve as a novelist. Though he may be said to have begun as a kind of realist, he ended a modernist. He grew up reading Dickens and Balzac and loved their work. He became an admirer, too, of the work of George Eliot. As a young aspiring writer in Paris, he came to know Turgenev and admire the latter's fiction. Though he began writing in a world that was still mostly wedded either to a decorative but empty Classicism or to a melodramatized, sentimentalized Romanticism, the writers he respected were those who were attempting to break from these forms and chart new directions. James joined them and became one of the master navigators.

As might be expected of a writer caught in a transitional period, James's literature contained remnants of the dominant literary modes, particularly that of Romanticism. Yet James was never suffocated by this, for he learned to use romantic elements to achieve new and often successful artistic effects.[55] The romantic ideal, for example, was utilized in *Roderick Hudson* (1875) to provide an important element in the work's conflict. Though on one level James began and developed as a literary realist, he was always after more than just accurate surface renderings. He was always concerned with representing the psychological aspects of his characters, their own evolving consciousnesses and the subtleties of their social relationships.[56] In his creation of the experimental novel of consciousness, with its subtly shifting points of view, its unfolding ambiguity and complexity, and its Bergsonian sense of time, James went well beyond literary realism and became, along with Proust and Joyce, one of the founders of the modernist novel.

To romantic artists, art was a spiritual thing, and it was discussed in terms which were often vague but nonetheless evoked the ideal. Beauty, Truth, the Ideal, and Art were almost always written with capital letters, and the goals usually sought by romantic artists were the higher sublime Truths. "Were I called on to define, *very* briefly, the term 'Art,'" wrote Edgar Allan Poe, "I should call it 'the reproduction of what the senses perceive in Nature through the veil of the soul.' The mere imitation, however accurate, of what *is* in Nature, entitles no man to the sacred name of 'Artist.'"[57] Another romantic, Emerson, agreed, urging that "in our fine arts, not imitation but creation is the aim. In landscapes the painter should give the suggestion of a fairer creation than we know. The details, the prose of nature he should omit and give us only the spirit and splendor."[58] Observation and experience were important to the romantics, but what they discovered was far from ordinary; and their creations idealized and spiritualized their findings dramatically in order to uplift their audience in some way.

Observation and experience were also at the base of literary realism, the movement that most directly challenged Romanticism. But according to realist aesthetics, art needed to be true to life, though — and this is an important distinction — not be taken for life itself.[59] The tendency of realism was to emphasize the experience of ordinary people. It was concerned, in Harold Kolb's words, with "what people are rather than what they ought to be."[60] Realist writers tended to place persons in situations that held different possibilities for them, but which possibilities were grasped depended on the characters' psychology, immediate perceptions, and fortuitous experiences.[61] Characters were not mere puppets whose lives were obviously manipulated by the writer. On the contrary, the illusion of objectivity existed, where the characters appeared to be engaged in the process of testing life and choosing among its offerings.

Realism as seen by the realists, then, was not just a slice of raw life, but instead was a life and experience refined and given form through the imagination of the artist; it was an interpretation of life, given meaning without diminishing the plausibility of the created illusion. Idealized lives, spiritual essences, and absolute truths were usually avoided. Replacing those things were the often unpleasant, multiple, complex and highly tentative truths that were thought to reside in real human psychology and sociology. The new truths rarely provided uplifting ideals but instead often led to a critical view of conventional social values and behavior. Truths that were so precarious, relative, and pragmatically achieved, seldom made audiences comfortable.

Authorial intrusion was radically diminished in realist literary works, forcing the reader to rely on the often conflicting perceptions of the characters and their relations with each other. No longer could the reader be all-knowing regarding the lives of the fictional characters, and often the reader's uncertainty was further exacerbated by the realist work's tendency to be open-ended. But uncertainty was a part of the human condition as seen by the realists, and they interpreted reality as they believed it to be, forging a new sense of artistic truth that challenged romantic Truth.

Beauty was another apparent victim of literary realism. In the romantic world view, ordinary lives and situations were not in themselves beautiful — they were, quite simply, ordinary. To the realist, however, those things were often capable of revealing a new kind of truth and beauty. Common lives were seen by realists as often containing uncommon aspects or as exhibiting moments of acute insight into ordinary reality. In this manner, the reader was led to make significant discoveries about life. Common themes, moreover, could be rendered with insight and given uncommon form, texture, atmosphere, and meaning.

All in all, it is not difficult to see why literary realists either rejected the photography analogy altogether or simply saw it as having only a partial relation to the literature they were creating.

Though by no means all of James's fiction fits neatly into the category of literary realism, James nonetheless always shared in many of realism's aesthetic assumptions and methods. Realism's approach to experience was a well ingrained habit in James's life from the earliest years. As James wrote of his youth,

> I had but one success, always — that of endlessly supposing, wondering, admiring: I was sunk in that luxury, which had never yet been so great, and it might well make up for anything. It made up perfectly, and more particularly as the stopgap as which I have already defined it, for the scantness of the period immediately round us; since how could I have wanted richer when the limits of reality, as I advanced upon them, seemed ever to recede and recede?[62]

When he became a young adult, his fascination with observing life persisted. For himself when a young man, James wrote, "The world immediately round about us at any rate bristled with . . . 'things seen' and felt. . . . I think I fairly cultivated the perceiving of it all, so that nothing of it, under some face or other, shouldn't brush my sense and add to my impression."[63] James was a confirmed observer who, like the photographer, took in all the aspects of experience he could perceive. This manner of responding to the world carried over into James's approach to fiction. In a letter to the Deerfield Summer School — he had been invited to speak there during the summer of 1889 — he wrote,

There are no tendencies worth anything but to see the actual or the imaginative, which is just as visible, and to paint it. I have only two little words for the matter remotely approaching to rule or doctrine; one is life and the other freedom. Tell the ladies and gentlemen, the ingenious inquirers, to consider life directly and closely, and not to be put off with mean and puerile falsities, and be conscientious about it. It is infinitely large, various and comprehensive.[64]

Just as he advised, James took his artistic subjects from life. As R. P. Blackmur puts it, "Often a single fact reported at a dinner-table was enough for James to seize on and plant in the warm bed of his imagination."[65] James expressed his aesthetics most completely, perhaps, in his essay "The Art of Fiction" (1888) and in his prefaces to the New York Edition (1907–09). In these it becomes quite clear that James believed that life was the source for art. In "The Art of Fiction," he wrote, "A novel is in its broadest definition a personal, a direct impression of life: that, to begin with, constitutes its value, which is greater or less according to the intensity of the impression."[66] To James, the writer had to strike "the note of life."[67] James believed that there existed "no impression of life, no manner of seeing it and feeling it, to which the paean of the novelist may not offer place."[68] Later, he added, "No themes are so human as those that reflect for us, out of the confusion of bliss and bale, of the things that help with the things that hurt."[69]

But life merely reproduced was not sufficient for James's art. Art was not life, it was art. Consequently, realist fiction was not life but "the illusion of life."[70] Art derived from life. "Experience," in James's view, was "an immense sensibility, a kind of huge spider web of the finest silken threads suspended in the chamber of consciousness . . . the very atmosphere of the mind; and when the mind is imaginative — much more when it happens to be that of a man of genius — it takes to itself the faintest hints of life, it converts the very pulses of the air into revelations."[71] Thus, as was the case with most realists, the world was the basis of art, but it had to be given form and meaning by the artist in order for it to reveal anything. As James expressed it in a letter written near the end of his life, "It is art that *makes* life, makes interest, makes importance, for our consideration and application of these things and I know of no substitute whatever for the force and beauty of its process."[72] And, to James, it was imagination that transformed existence into those things.[73]

Though James was an artist who drew from the world, transforming its found moments through imagination, there is a quality in his life and fiction of spiritualization and idealization of the real world.[74] As a reviewer wrote of James in 1894, his "characters talk too uniformly well for dramatic truth; they are framed, the fine and the vulgar, in a setting of culture which is sometimes too rich for realism."[75] James seems to have recognized this tendency in himself, for at one point, he described his own upbringing as one bathed before "the footlights of a familiar idealism."[76] Moreover, an example of its deeply ingrained presence is present in his response to the death of his beloved cousin Minny Temple: "I think of her gladly," wrote James to his mother in 1870, "as undrained from suffering and embalmed forever in all our hearts and lives. Twenty years hence what a pure eloquent vision she will be."[77]

Not only is there a quality of idealization in James's responses to life, but there is the accompanying one of romanticism. Regarding James's fiction, W. D. Howells noted in 1882, his "best efforts seem to me those of romance; his best types have an ideal development."[78] Later, in 1890, Horace E. Scudder noted the same quality but perspicuously recognized that James utilized romantic devices in inventive, fresh ways: "The triumph of the novelist, in our judgment, lies in the fact that he can hold the careless reader to the close, cajoling him with the notion that he is in for the matrimonial hunt of the conventional novel, while at the same time he slowly opens to the student of life a singular interesting relation of the progress of human souls, each moving toward its determination by choice and the gravitation of nature, and presenting constantly fresh examples of the problems of which they are themselves only now and then distinctly conscious."[79] As mentioned earlier, James often stood popular forms on their head, making them serve his artistic purposes and thereby exposing their shallowness and falseness.[80] He also used idealization somewhat similarly, infusing it into characters like Isabel Archer, in *The Portrait of a Lady* (1881), and Milly Theale, in *The Wings of the Dove* (1902), in order to enable the reader to examine the possibilities and realities of lives lived in the world. Consequently, though both the qualities of idealization and romanticism appear in James's works, their use was such that it gave the reader an unidealized, unromantic vision of life. Simply put, James often debunked unthinking idealism and romanticism.

Overriding—and underlying—all other aspects in James's art is the question of the working relationship between the artist's selecting and shaping imagination and the raw, unrefined life that was the source of art. That question was brilliantly explored in "The Real Thing," the fascinating 1893 tale by James that has already helped bring into focus some of the important issues with which this book is concerned. Besides revealing James's attitudes about illustration and photography, "The Real Thing" presents a subtle discourse on the nature of the artist's perception of reality and its relation to the world itself. Lying hidden at the base of this relation is the question of whether living, breathing reality is only what appears on the surface. Recall that the genteel, shabby Monarchs represent themselves to the artist as "the real thing" in order to pursuade him that they will be perfect as models for the illustrations of ladies and gentlemen. Implicit in their assertion is that the artist need only copy the "real thing" in order to convey the truth. Yet, though the Monarchs appear on the surface to be the "real thing" they believe themselves to be, the artist sees beneath their surfaces. To the artist, James wrote in his notebooks, the Monarchs "could only *show* themselves,"[81] and what they show is their superficiality, stiffness, and lack of variety. They are people who have spent their lives developing only a surface for people to see, and like a photograph—the Monarchs, recall, had "been photographed immensely"—they have no depths, no complexity: they possess only the "hideous inexpressiveness of the mechanical document."[82] The artist, of course, sees more than others. The "real thing," in this instance, is not sufficient for the artist, for the Monarchs' limited actuality is in no way useful to his purpose—indeed, impedes it. Had he been asked to paint their portraits, he would have been able to do them brilliantly. As the artist says, "I had immediately *seen* them. I had seized their type—I had already settled what I would do with it. Something that wouldn't absolutely have pleased them, I afterwards reflected."[83] Obviously, he would have revealed what lay beneath the Monarchs' surfaces, interpreting the Monarchs' facades as being just that—shells covering emptiness.

As models for illustrations of fictional characters who did possess interesting qualities, the Monarchs fail. No matter how hard the artist tries, he cannot create the illustrations he needs based on these "real" types, so ironically, the artist turns to the Italian immigrant Oronte and the working class Cockney Miss Churm for his needed models, because even though not the "real thing," they nonetheless have the capacity to express the varieties and complexities of character the artist must have as a guide for the creation of the illustrations. Oronte and Churm, like artists, instinctively know that surfaces alone are insufficient; these must be given life and interpreted if meaning is to be rendered fully. Their art is to be able to dramatize the "real thing." Through acts of imagination, Oronte and Churm become more "real" than the Monarchs who, despite thinking themselves the "real thing," understand nothing about what the "real thing" contains. The interpretation of the "real thing"—that is, art—results in more reality than does the "real thing" in the raw, unaided by imagination.

James's "The Real Thing" was an answer to the vulgar critical belief—usually put forth as a accusation—that literary realism meant only that art imitates life, and the Monarchs were sardonic parodies of the opposite, Wildean view, "life imitates art." James was suggesting that, in themselves, the surfaces of life are meaningless. Life requires probing and imagination if it is to take on meaning. While James would certainly have conceeded that life is important as a source of art, central to his story's meaning is the view that it cannot become art by itself. The particular life to be used as a source initially had to be interesting and offer possibilities to the artist; then it remained for the artist to render it convincingly and give it meaning through his shaping imagination. Life itself might "exist" without imagination. But art definitely could not.

If for James, as Leon Edel puts it, "The 'real thing' was simply itself, photographic," whereas "Art transfigured reality,"[84] how is it that James could have changed his mind so drastically and welcomed the photography of Coburn into the pages of the New York Edition? Part of the answer lies in the quality of James's perceptual/conceptual approach to the world and the literary results of this approach. American painter John La Farge once attributed to Henry James "a painter's eye," yet it is more accurate to say that James possessed a photographer's eye and perception of the world and that his literature, beginning with the late phase, embodied a photographic/ cinematic style and structure.[85] James was born into, and grew up during, the time I have called the "the photographic age," and it was in that cultural atmosphere — with its peculiar perceptual/conceptual codes — that he developed his own perceiving/conceiving consciousness.[86]

In his writings, James gave abundant evidence of just how exceedingly photographic this consciousness was. In *A Small Boy and Others*, he described his first recollection of a visual experience. It was in Paris in 1845, and he wrote, "I had been there for a short time in the second year of my life, and I was to communicate to my parents later on that as a baby . . . I had been impressed with a view, framed by the clear window of the vehicle as we passed, of a great stately square surrounded with high roofed houses and having in its center a tall and glorious column."[87] It was the Place Vendôme that James had mentally photographed; and he kept this along with many other images in the album of his memory: "I have but to close my eyes in order to open them inwardly again," James explained.[88] As an adult, James continued to perceive in this fashion. In *Notes of a Son and Brother*, he extolled the "wondrous opportunity of vision, that is *appreciation of the thing seen* . . . I longed to live by my eyes."[89] He continued to live, as it were, by his eyes. Recalling Liverpool in *The Middle Years*, James recorded "the impression, the damp and darksome light washed in from the steep, black bricky street."[90] In this last memoir, he continued to write of the whole experience of England as if it was a series of photographs placed in an album. He could not, he explained, "resist the individual *vivid* image of the past wherever encountered, these images have always such terms of their own, such subtle secrets and insidious arts for keeping us in relation with them, for bribing us by the beauty, the authority, the wonder of their saved intensity."[91] James understood that the world was before his eyes, to be seen photographically, "sifting and changing . . . always there, to be looked at when you please, and to be most easily and comfortably ignored when you don't."[92]

James's language is revealing. Words—"images," "impressions"—and phrases—"impressed with a view, framed by the clear window," "saved intensity," "individual *vivid* image," "experience consists of impressions"— suggest photographs and photographic vision.[93] These recur with a great deal of consistency in James's writings and connote a distinct perceptual/ conceptual approach to experience, one that James shared not only with the Impressionist and post-Impressionist painters but also with writers like Gustave Flaubert, Anton Chekhov, Stephen Crane, and Marcel Proust. "Impression" and "image," in particular, were words commonly used during the nineteenth century both to name a specific kind of perception (instantaneous seeing and its "effect, especially a strong effect, produced on the intellect, conscience, or feelings."[94]) *and* to refer to photographs. Such language communicates not a self-contained world in repose but instead one of fragments, immediately and vividly present yet constantly changing, grasped from the flow of experience and recreated in the instantaneous forms in which they first appeared to the senses.

James was always exact in, and supremely conscious of, his use of language; and it seems clear that by the time his late phase was emerging, he was also fully aware of the temporal/spatial implications of his perceptual/ conceptual approach: "Not to be denied also, over and above this," James wrote, "is the downright pleasure of the illusion yet again created, the *apparent* transfer from the past to the present of the particular combination of things that did at its hour ever so directly operate and that isn't after all then drained of virtue, wholly wasted and lost, for sensation, for participation in the act of life, in the attesting sights, sounds, smells, the illusion, as I say, of the recording senses."[95]

James possessed another trait that linked him to photography, and it was this habit that surely contributed to the photographic aspect of his consciousness and prose. He was a Baudelaireian *flâneur* who explored the streets ceaselessly in order to observe all they contained and thereby acquire direct impressions of places and people. He began this as a child in Paris, London, and New York and continued the practice throughout his life. For example, James recalled that as a small boy, the London streets "had much to build out for us. I see again that we but endlessly daubed, and that our walks, with an obsession of their own, constantly abetted our daubing."[96]

And of his early years in New York, he wrote, "I see myself moreover as somehow always alone . . . and feel how the sense of my being so, being at any rate master of my short steps, such as they were, through all the beguiling streets, was probably the very savour of each of my chance feasts."[97] For James, it was important

> just to *be* somewhere — almost anywhere would do — and somehow receive an impression or an accession, feel a relation or a vibration. He [the small boy] was to go without many things, ever so many — as all persons do in whom contemplation takes so much the place of action; but everywhere, in the years that came soon after, and that in fact continued long, in the streets of great towns . . . he was to enjoy more than anything the far from showy practice of wandering and dawdling and gaping: he was really, I think, much to profit by it.[98]

This practice of walking, directly observing the world's details, and taking mental impressions of what caught his eye was of utmost importance to James's method of literary creation. Consider, for example, his explanation of the origin of *The Princess Casamassima* (1886). The book, James wrote,

> proceeded quite directly, during the first year of a long residence in London, from the habit and interest in walking the streets. I walked a great deal . . . and to do this was to receive many impressions, so the impressions worked and sought an issue, so the book after a time was born. It is a fact that, as I look back, the attentive exploration of London, the assault directly made by the great city upon an imagination quick to react, fully explains a large part of it. One walked of course with one's eyes greatly open . . . and to a mind curious, before the human scene, of meanings and revelations the great grey Babylon easily becomes, on its face, a garden bristling with an immense illustrative flora. Possible stories, presentable figures, rise from the thick jungle as the observer moves, fluttering up like startled game, and before he knows it indeed he has fairly to guard against the brush of importunate wings.[99]

James gathered materials for his art exactly as do some of the world's great instantaneous photographers. So it was entirely apt for James's New York Edition collaborator, Alvin Langdon Coburn, to remark years after the collaboration took place, "Henry James must have had sensitive plates in his brain on which to record his impressions."[100]

In an essay on the relation of photography to realism in the pictorial arts, Robert A. Sobieszek observes, "it was the unmitigated acceptance of natural and social phenomena which is found in both the theories and practice of the Realists as well as in the aesthetics and the pictures of photography. Both Realism and photography jointly contributed to a corpus of visual material with the same or similar subject matter, an almost identical fascination in the material appearance of reality, and a distinct contemporaneity of the pictorial image."[101] Though literary realism and naturalism are in certain respects different from realism in the pictorial arts, Sobieszek's point is as valid for the former as it is for the latter. Both literary realists and naturalists as well as "realist" painters (Courbet, for example) utilized "natural and social phenomena" found in the contemporary, everyday world and replicated the "material appearance" of these in their art. Their mode of representation was mimetic, that is realistic in the sense that they sought to reproduce as exactly as possible the look of the world before the eyes. But so too had been the representations of so many artists preceeding them. Use of mimetic representation began hundreds of years before in Western culture and has been practiced by artists throughout the ages—writers like Homer, Cervantes, Smollett, Austin, Balzac, and painters like Rembrandt, Vermeer, Hogarth, Ingres, Delacroix, Courbet, Manet. In the nineteenth century, realism became identified with more than just mimetic representation of subject matter. It included that characteristic, but it also denoted a new attitude toward subject matter and style and it is this new attitude I have been treating in this chapter. The fascination with the contemporary, commonplace—even vulgar—world was an important ingredient in nineteenth-century realism. The ability to find drama and meaning—even a kind of beauty—in such a world was shared by realist writers and painters. It was a distinct attitude toward the world, then, that identified and linked most realists, but it is important to note that their interest in ordinary lives did not mean that they accepted such a world uncritically. On the contrary, one of the purposes of artists like Courbet, Balzac, Dickens, Howells, and Henry James was critical. Literary realists and naturalists, in particular, used fragments from the world as a means to test and criticize characters' and societies' values and behavior. It was this practice that contributed to the displeasure of nineteenth-century audiences. The rising bourgeoisie preferred optimistic art, art that entertained them at the same time that it affirmed their lives and the society they lived in—not art that challenged their cultural hegemony or suggested alternatives to their world.[102]

Photography, as I have argued, symbolized the threat of realism in the minds of many nineteenth-century observers. But photography and its nineteenth-century manner of practice and presentation exhibited another quality that is pertinent to this discussion. This characteristic was less understood and less directly challenging, though it was important nonetheless. Like other artists, photographers mediate experience and structure the world for us, transfiguring it in particular ways. Straight photography, unlike painting or writing, mediates and structures the world in a peculiar temporal/spatial way, and it was this quality that, in part, gave rise to the recognition of photographic style noted by so many of the art and literary critics of the nineteenth century. Photographic style was not only distinguishable by its emphasis on ordinary details reproduced directly from the social and natural world but also for the often disconcertingly awkward, chaotic arrangement of those details in relation to each other—i.e. the *mise-en-scène*. To many, such radical composition appeared to repudiate order and conscious artistic effort; yet some artists saw that it best represented a world in flux, and they began to adopt the new compositional style and explore its possibilities. Photographic style was an extreme manifestation of the way the world was being seen and represented by the most radical nineteenth-century artists.[103]

One of the aspects of that style has been termed "freeze frame." This temporal/spatial quality appears in Impressionist painting (recall Egbert's comment that the Impressionists thought "that a picture should be a record of a moment"[104]). It also appears in the texts of many nineteenth-century writers. Emerson, for example, believed that, "To the attentive eye, each moment of the year has its own beauty, and in the same field, it beholds, every hour, a picture which was never seen before, and which shall never be seen again," and many of his verbal images were attempts to capture such fleeting qualities: "The leafless trees become spires of flame in the sunset, with the blue east for their background, and the stars of the dead calices of flowers, and every withered stem and stubble rimed with frost, contribute something to the mute music."[105] Whitman also wrote poetry in "stop-time":

> The negro holds firmly the reins of his four horses, the
>   block swags underneath on its tied-over chain,
> The negro that drives the long dray of the stone-yard,
>   steady and tall he stands pois'd on one leg on the
>   string-piece,
> His blue shirt exposes his ample neck and breast and loosens
>   over his hip-band,
> His glance is calm and commanding, he tosses the slouch of
>   his hat away from his forehead,
> The sun falls on his crispy hair and mustache, falls on the
>   black of his polish'd and perfect limbs.
>
> I behold the picturesque giant and love him, and I do not
>   stop there,
> I go with the team also.[106]

In these examples, two photographic characteristics are present: close attention is given to the recording of ordinary details; and the picture is a moment lifted from the flux of time, it is a moment suspended and given a spatial dimension—as in a photograph.[107]

This second aspect of photographic style began to appear frequently in late nineteenth-century art and literature, and a new ordering principle began to be displayed. Wylie Sypher, in *From Rococo to Cubism*, reminds us that "no two cameras can take the same photograph of a scene. As man changes his point of view, reality changes its nature for him."[108] Of course, the artistic expression of this idea occurred most notably and completely in the cubist experiments of Picasso and Braque and in the cinematic discoveries of Griffith, Eisenstein, and Vertov. Yet, the idea was implicit both in certain formats displaying photographs and in the scientific and journalistic images that were published at the time.[109] The putting together in albums or magazines of numerous single photographs, often of the same people in different poses, presented viewers with several temporal/spatial moments that were given a larger, discontinuous spatial unity though their accidental or arbitrary contiguity. The format of uncut *cartes de visite* created the same effect. Such common nineteenth-century formats are not dissimilar to the multiple imagery made and published by Muybridge during the 1880s (figure 34). Nor, for that matter, are they unlike sequential photographs made by landscape photographers like Timothy O'Sullivan and published as stereographs. Of course, painters were experimenting along these lines too — notably Monet, in his series of Rouen Cathedral paintings, and Degas, in his extraordinary painting, "Dancer Tying her Slipper" (1883?).[110] And like experimental photographers and painters, certain writers were beginning to recognize that reality was constantly changing and shifting and thus multiple in its manifestations. Because they too wished to explore reality's multiplicity more deeply and represent it more accurately in their art, they sought methods of incorporating this phenomenon in their literature. Narrative structure changed. Beginnings, middles, and ends no longer necessarily appeared in that order, nor were they always clearly distinguishable from one another.[111]

In his seminal essay, "Spatial Form in Modern Literature," Joseph Frank argues that "modern literature, as exemplified by such writers as T.S. Eliot, Ezra Pound, Marcel Proust, and Jame Joyce, is moving in the direction of spatial form. . . . All these writers ideally intend the reader to apprehend their work spatially, in a moment of time, rather than as a sequence."[112] Sypher argues similarly and links this phenomenon to the movies: "The changing perspectives on which we build our existence appear in the cinema, a modern form of illusion that related motion, time, and space in a new kind of composition. It may well be that according to the law of technical primacy — the theory that in each era all the arts fall under the influence of one of the arts — the cinema has technical primacy during the years between the rise of cubism and the present."[113] Sypher, however, goes on to make a distinction between the relative importance of film and pho-

Figure 34.   Eadweard Muybridge, Photograph, in *Animal Locomotion* (1887).
(Courtesy of University Art Museum, University of New Mexico.)

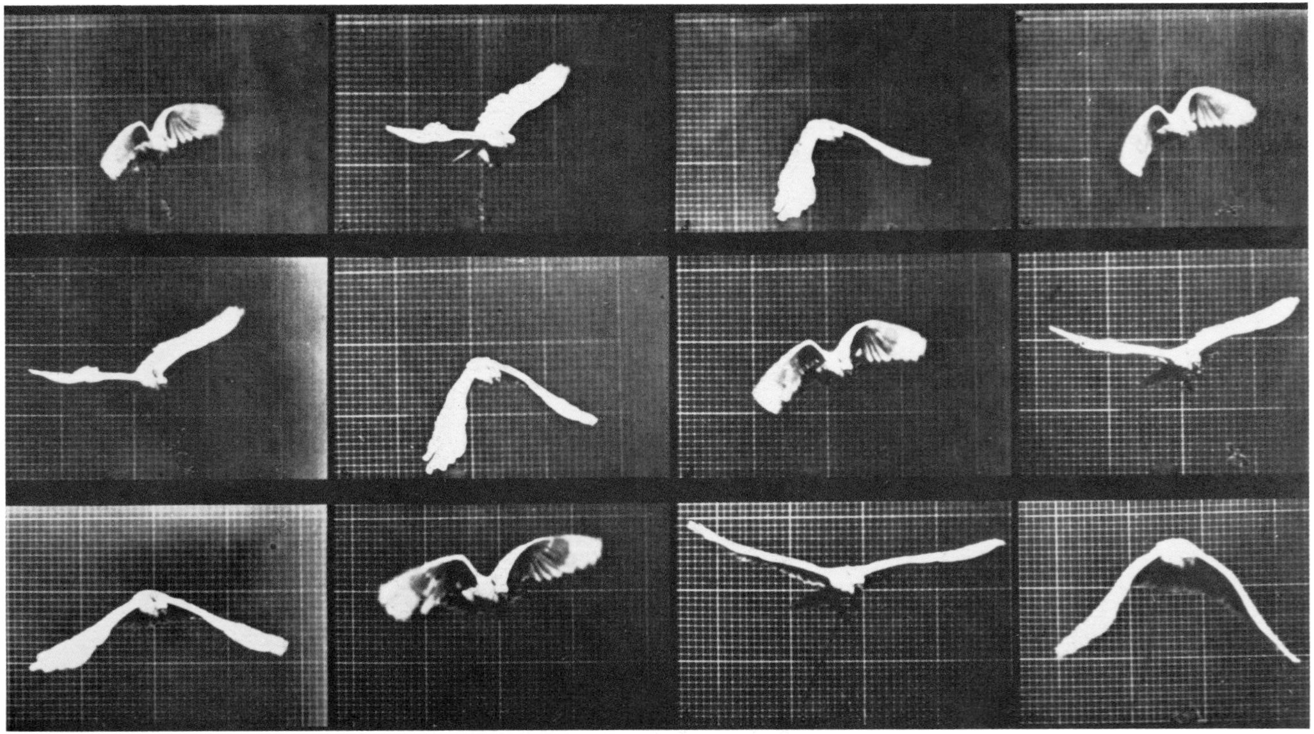

tography, urging that photography did not revolutionize art until it became film. Contrary to Sypher, I would argue that photography did contradict the traditional visual and narrative modes before it finally "became the cinema"[114] — and it did so because of its unique temporal/spatial format. Still photography might be said to have had technical primacy during the nineteenth century, because — to borrow Sypher's words — it also was "a modern form of illusion that related motion, time, and space in a new kind of composition." It suggested "the problems of changing appearances in time and space"[115] — well before the 1890s when the movie camera was being perfected and used. The cinema itself was an extension of still photography and the implicit, revolutionary aesthetic qualities of that radical invention.

Although neither Frank nor Sypher include James among the modernists who spatialized time in their fictions, Henry James belongs there. For he was one of the earliest novelists to experiment with "photographic" imagery and "cinematic" narrative techniques. In his late phase works, James often created descriptive "freeze-frames" and combined them in ways that defy the clear, progressive flow of time. Leon Edel has attributed the inception of this late stylistic characteristic to James's experience with the theater during the mid-1890s. Beginning with *The Spoils of Poynton* (1896), Edel argues, James ceased to utilize clear narrative and instead presented characters who emerge as though on a stage, moved by "the skeletal structure of drama."[116] Elsewhere, however, Edel describes James's mature style in words that suggest not theatrical but photographic and cinematic analogies. "Characters are glimpsed," Edel writes, "from different angles: the pictures are framed. Early in the novel [he is discussing *The Ambassadors* (1903)] we are given the feeling that we have access to a series of cameras — and James is writing long before the modern cinema": point of view shifts as "he keeps his camera moving."[117] In his essay, "Novel and Camera," Edel notes James's attendance at the cinema and again suggests the relation of cinema to James's prose style:

> Henry James was writing at the threshhold of the cinema. He went to see the primitive bioscope inventions, yet it never occurred to him that they might involve any threat to the verbal art — so safe did the Edwardians feel in their citadel of words, so authoritative, so ensconsed for the future. James did recognize the appeal of cinematic technique; he described one such image in his late tale "Crapy Cornelia" [1909], where at a given moment the character White-Mason looks at a woman's head "crowned with a little sparsely feathered black hat," and it "grew and grew, came nearer and nearer while it met his eyes, after the manner of images in the cinematograph."[118]

Though James himself never used the terms photography and cinema to explain what it was he was trying to do in his prose, he nonetheless made statements that suggest the relationship of his prose experiments to these phenomena.[119] In the New York Edition preface to his first novel, *Roderick Hudson*, James wrote a comment that suggests his awareness of the need for the artist to find a method of catching hold of the fleeting world in the attempt to create verbal pictures: "Really, universally, [human] relations stop nowhere, and the exquisite problem of the artist is eternally but to draw, by a geometry of his own, the circle within which they shall happily *appear* to do so. He is in the perpetual predicament that the continuity of things is the whole matter . . . that this continuity is never, by the space of an instant or an inch, broken."[120] In the preface to *The Portrait of a Lady*, James asserted, "The house of fiction has . . . not one window, but a million . . . . These apertures, of dissimilar shape and size, hang so, all together, over the human scene . . . [which] is 'the choice of subject'; the pierced aperture, either broad or balconied or slit-like and low-browed, is the 'literary form'."[121] The problem facing the artist, James explained, "resides in the fact that, though the relations of a human figure or a social occurrence are what make such objects interesting, they also make them, to the same tune, difficult to isolate, to surround with the sharp black line, to frame in the square, the circle, the charming oval, that helps any arrangement of objects to become a picture."[122] But this difficulty could be overcome, as James noted in reference to his conception of Milly Theale in *The Wings of the Dove*: it was problematic, requiring "discrete and ingenious" expression and demanding "a reflection that fortunately grew and grew, however, in proportion as I focused my image."[123] One had, in short, to frame and focus one's images in order to isolate and clarify them for the reader's attention; yet, one had to do so in a manner that did not distort the fact that these images were a part of the rush of ongoing life in a world of extraordinary complexity and multiplicity.

In James's late phase prose, the center of consciousness works as a kind of camera. Like the camera, it admits only the light that is reflected through its lens, cutting everything else out of the picture's frame. And when the point of view is changed—and this is often—a new and different image is framed. James's centers of consciousness, in Viola Winner's words, brought "into focus the otherwise inchoate external world."[124] But they also enabled James to do more than just represent a multiplicity of surfaces of life in his fiction. We see surfaces, but we see them as they are focused on and internalized and interpreted by characters. The world is not just objectively offered in James's fiction; its objective presence is rendered subjectively through the characters' perceptions and comprehensions of it. And these, in turn, are themselves constantly shifting and changing. This is what H. Peter Stowell means when he characterizes James as a "subjective-objective" writer. This explains why James's fiction moved beyond realism into what

Stowell argues is literary impressionism and Alan Spiegel, Leon Edel, and I suggest is literary cinema.[125]

Whether the stylistic and structural qualities of James's late phase writing be called literary impressionism or cinema or even cubism, however, does not really matter. Nor is it important to this study to establish once and for all that photography and cinema caused literary realism and modernism. What is essential to my argument, instead, is the recognition that some of the central traits exhibited in literary impressionism (or cinema or cubism) are characteristics that were inherent in the revolutionary media and practice of photography and cinema. I have sought to show that certain qualities were present both in photography and in the literary movements that James's fiction fits into. These were part of the intellectual environment of James's age. Without question, James's perceptual/conceptual approach to the world was "photographic"; so too was his working method as a writer. And finally, his late phase prose explored what Sypher calls, "The changing perspectives on which we build our existence," and related "time, motion, and space in a new kind of composition."[126] Hence, it was "cinematic." It was this "new kind of composition" that so bewildered and frustrated Henry James's brother, William, when he complained about Henry's propensity to create the "illusion of a solid object, made . . . out of impalpable materials, air, and the prismatic interferences of light, ingeniously focussed by mirrors upon empty space."[127] It was a radically experimental prose style that made a contemporary critic bemoan James's "vague, interthreaded abstractions," and caused an anonymous reader of *The American Scene* to remark, "A strange, very difficult book to master. . . . Like a prism, he [James] breaks up the white light but only the longer wavelengths and infra-red seem best refracted."[128]

Because of his "photographic" and "cinematic" perceptual/conceptual approach to encountering and observing the world and to making literature, James was not as alien to photography as his frequent verbal attacks suggest. Inherent in his mindset was a propensity for someday finding out that photography might be a compatible, useful medium. What remained for him to recognize was what that use might be and what sort of photography would fit his needs.

Part Four: Pictures as Texts

To be at all critically, or as we have been fond of calling it, analytically, minded—over and beyond an inherent love of the general many colored picture of things—is to be subject to the superstition that objects and places, coherently grouped, disposed for human use and addressed to it, must have a sense of their own, a mystic meaning proper to themselves to give out: to give out, that is, to the participant at once so interested and so detached as to be moved to a report of the matter.

—Henry James, *The American Scene*

Although not literally a photographer, I believe that Henry James must have had sensitive plates on his brain on which to record his impressions! He always knew exactly what he wanted, although many of the pictures were but images in his mind and imagination, and what we did was to browse diligently until we found such a subject.

—Alvin Langdon Coburn,
Alvin Langdon Coburn, Photographer

7

The Writer and the Photographer: Coburn, Art-Photography, and James's Choice

If James's perceptual/conceptual approach to living and writing was indeed "photographic" and "cinematic," why throughout much of his life did he denigrate photography as an essentially artless medium? Why did he disdain and ignore photography's potential as an art? Finally, why did he seem to turn about completely and use photographic frontispieces in his New York Edition? An important part of the answer to these questions lies in the kind of photography—that is, forms and stylistic approaches—James was used to seeing. Evidence culled from his life and thought indicates that James's experience with photography had to do mainly with portraiture, both in its carefully posed and in its snapshot forms. And, except for his early encounter with the daguerreotype, he knew the medium mostly through commercially made or amateur-snapped paper prints. The approach of such photography was generally straightforward in its replication of the world, avoiding radical alterations of the image while at the same time either posing the subjects theatrically or catching them off guard in a playful manner. When an image was altered—through retouchnig, for example—it was seldom changed with the skill or artistic imagination necessary to make it convincing; usually, the alteration blatantly contradicted the unaltered realism of the rest of the image, making it hopelessly artless—neither a good photograph nor a beautiful picture. Snapshooters, too, usually avoided altering their pictures, trying instead to capture as "good" a likeness as their eyes and skill could manage. Altered or not, formal or informal, many nineteenth-century photographs exhibited either a stiffness that eschewed naturalness and grace or a looseness and awkwardness that defied a sense of control. The former trait, of course, prompted James to utilize photography as a metaphor in works like *The American* and "The Real Thing."

It is quite possible that James also saw some of the pre-Raphaelite influenced art-photography that was practiced widely during the 1870s and 1880s, since this form was quite popular in Victorian England. Perhaps

James saw examples of this kind of work in the studios of some of the pre-Raphaelite artists he knew as well as in the homes of his friends. Whatever the case, James never discussed it. Since by 1877 James had real reservations about pre-Raphaelite painting itself, it is very likely that their approach to subject matter—often allegorical, always highly dramatized—would have been even more repugnant to him if encountered in a medium so direct as photography.[1] Indeed, had he seen this sort of art-photography and chosen to discuss it, he would likely have ridiculed its blatant tendency to melodramatize and sentimentalize. It is also probable that James looked at other sorts of straight images such as landscape photographs and cityscapes—all of which were widely available in stereograph form. If he did, he probably enjoyed them, was amused by them. But, like the reviewer of the photographic exhibition at the Philadelphia Exposition of 1876 quoted earlier, he certainly would not have taken them seriously as art.

It could be said that there were two impulses at work during the nineteenth century—the aesthetic and the documentary. The aesthetic, of course, was concerned with beauty, with generalizing and idealizing nature and was a mystifying process. The documentary, on the other hand, was concerned with facts, with particularizing nature, and thus was an anti-idealizing, demystifying impulse.[2] Of course, both were present in realist literature and art and in photography. But as modes of discourse, the dominance of one in a style or medium seemed to negate the presence of the other. James himself exhibited both tendencies, but for James the aesthetic was essential to his reason for being. Facts were important, but not for their own sake and not in raw form. There were seeds to be planted in the soil of one's artistic imagination, to be watered and nurtured to see what sort of art they might grow into.[3] The consequence of this cultivation was a lush garden, art—the aesthetic. Clearly, though he used a documentary method of gathering materials, James saw himself a proponant of the aesthetic mode of discourse. And since the photography he knew seemed an inherently documentary phenomenon, superficial and characterless, James understandably dismissed it as "artless." Yet, despite their seeming contradictory natures, both modes intermingled in the art of the nineteenth century—even in James's art. That is why so many critics treated realism as merely "photographic" literature and why so many realists either denied this or tried to explain how it was that their writing did more than just document life.

Photography was inherently caught up in this dichotomy. Since, as Max Kozloff puts it, photography "allows the most explicit record of the visual world we have," it was read as a documentary medium.[4] So when art-photographers tried to make it into art, they usually tried to obliterate the medium's documentary qualities. Yet, it was difficult to do, and even when a photographer like Julia Margaret Cameron succeeded in softening, dramatizing, and thus generalizing her imagery, she still courted criticism that derived from the recognition that her's was a documentary medium.

The directness of photography — its documentary aspect — is certainly a characteristic that led to James's early rejection of it as art. A medium that recorded surfaces so exactly, he concluded, was mechanical and allowed the artist no room for imaginative interpretation. Photography's ubiquitousness put off James, too, for what it recorded and framed were pictures that most people were not accustomed to taking seriously as art. Though James exhibited no reluctance toward accepting common subjects as fit for an artist's attention, photography's directness and lack of character were damning. A hideously inexpressive medium, its products were either too stiff or too casual. Ugly or ordinary subject matter was not the problem. James respected, for example, the work of the painter Winslow Homer: though he found Homer's subjects dull and homely, he believed Homer saved them by choosing "the best pictorial features," and seeing naturally "everything at one with its envelope of light and air . . . not in lines but in masses."⁵ Homer's brilliant selectivity and technique saved him, in James's view, from his uninteresting subject matter.

A medium that was as direct and haphazard as nineteenth-century photography could not have appealed to an artist such as James, for he valued subtlety, indirection, atmosphere, ambiguity, ordered complexity, and richness of textures and shades. Moreover, he insisted that subjects not only be rendered in the manner that would express those qualities but that the subjects themselves be made to bristle with meanings. The impression of life needed to be just that — an impression of reality that was refined and given order and meaning through the mediation of the artist's shaping imagination. The main question for the artist was, as James noted,

> To give the image and the sense of certain things while still keeping them subordinate to his plan, keeping them in relation to matters more immediate and apparent, to give all the sense, in a work, without all the substance or all the surface, and so to summarize and foreshorten, so to make values both rich and sharp, *that the mere procession of items and profiles is not only, for the occasion, superseded*, but it, for essential quality, almost "compromised" — such a case of delicacy proposes itself at every turn to the painter of life who wishes both to treat his chosen subject and confine his necessary picture. It is only by positively doing such things that art becomes exquisite, and it is only by positively becoming exquisite that it keeps clear of becoming vulgar, repudiates the coarse industries that masquerade in its name.⁶

Obviously, in order for James to take photography seriously as art, the medium had to obviate its flaws and demonstrate its capacity to achieve the qualities James demanded from art. Only then would James reconsider its value.

James's views on the visual arts are as important an ingredient for an understanding of his aesthetics as are his views regarding literature. James not only evolved radically as a writer but also changed enormously with regard to his opinions on visual art. These changes of opinion are instructive. Viola Winner, reviewing James's art criticism, argues that though James's "aesthetic had its roots in the Victorian morality, his modification of former views reveals an unexpected flexibility. . . . By the last years of the century, he came to stress the importance of design over content and even came close to conceiving of art as an annexation rather than a representation of life."[7] Winner is correct, for James began his art appreciation early in his youth as an admirer of mimetic, but often highly idealized art, such as expressed in the work of the pre-Raphaelites and the historical painting of Paul Delaroche.[8] As time passed, however, James grew to understand and love the greater, often more painterly artists such as Delacroix, Tintoretto, Titian, and Turner. And though he passionately came to love painting that exhibited the "grand manner" of the Renaissance, he was still capable of seeing genius in a painter like Winslow Homer. Ultimately, James even learned to accept Impressionist painting as beautiful in spite of his initial public opposition to it.[9] It ought not be surprising that a man with such tastes in visual art would find photography by and large not only uninteresting but artless.

It is important to emphasize that though James had definite tastes and aesthetic views, he could and did change his mind. He exhibited flexibility regarding his tastes, he was receptive to new possibilities. Indeed, that James was not absolute even in his view of photography as inherently artless is suggested by his reference to the daguerreotype as a beautiful "lost art." What he saw afterwards, though, led him to conclude that photography was artless. Still, he could change his mind about it, just as he changed his mind about Impressionism. But before James could do that, he had to discover work that he could respect, work that would make him reconsider the potential of the medium. Alvin Langdon Coburn's work did just that—it was the catalyst that made James rethink his attitudes regarding photography. Coburn's photographs demonstrated to James that photography, in the hands of a genius, could be a fine art, that photographic images could produce many of the artistic effects that James admired and sought to infuse into his own literature. Of course, James did not come to this conclusion immediately. Recall that James decided to use Coburn's art only after experiencing a successful portrait session in New York, then seeing Coburn's London exhibition, and finally testing Coburn by having him make some images that might be suitable for inclusion in the Edition. It was all like a perfect Jamesian donnée. The germ for the collaboration came to James fortuitously in 1905, when he was worrying about the details of the New York Edition. Seemingly out of nowhere, the gifted Coburn contacted James and introduced himself and his art. Of course, like all the seeds for James's novels and tales, this one had to germinate in James's fertile imagination. But after reflecting on the qualities he saw in Coburn's work, recognizing an artistry in this work that was entirely compatible with his own, and discovering that photography's objectivity and inclusiveness were perfectly suited to his needs, James embraced Coburn's art, embarked on the collaborative enterprise, and proceeded to become, as it were, his own illustrator.

In 1900, a reviewer wrote in *Photograms of the Year: 1900* that:

> the American school [of photography], in the restricted modern sense, represents, if we read its works aright, a protest against the niggling detail, the factual accuracy of sharp all-over ordinary photography. That wealth of trivial detail which was admired in photography's early days and which is still loved by the great general public whose best praise of a photogram is that it is "so clear," has gone out of fashion with advanced workers on both sides of the Atlantic. Concentration, strength, massing of light and shade, breadth of effect are the highly prized virtues.[10]

The essayist was referring to work shown at the Royal Photographic Society in an exhibition held in London in late 1900 — one which was ponderously entitled, "an exhibition of prints by the new School of American Photography, supplemented by an additional collection of one hundred examples of the work of F. Holland Day, of Boston, U.S.A."[11] Organized by F. Holland Day, the show was extremely well received; but more important for our consideration, it included work by Alvin Langdon Coburn, who was then only eighteen years old.[12]

By the turn of the century, art-photography's proponents were well along in their efforts to revitalize, reform, and promote photography as a fine art. Their task was not an easy one, for they had to do battle on two fronts. The first front was with the artists and critics outside the medium, exemplified most vociferously by Joseph Pennell and his 1897 diatribe against art-photography: "Is Photography among the Fine Arts?" Recall the haughtiness of Pennell's attack, as he rhetorically inquired "why a mechanical contrivance should be called artistic, and those who make use of it artists. It would be pleasant, no doubt, for photographers to obtain the same social and financial recognition as artists; it would be pleasant, too, if the Italian with his hurdy-gurdy could win himself the reputation and fortune of Paderewski."[13] Unfortunately for Pennell and his compatriots, the leadership of the new movement in art-photography was not made up of people like Pennell's "Italian with his hurdy-gurdy"; on the contrary, the generals of the new movement were often men and women of considerable means and education. Most of them possessed the passion, energy, and intelligence to help raise the practice of the art-photography to new levels of aesthetic sophistication and promote their artworks with stubborn vigor, perceptive intelligence, and sometimes groundbreaking taste.

The second front was waged within the international photography community itself. By 1890, art-photography was overwhelmingly being practiced by amateurs, and though they made all kinds of images and used a variety of techniques, a large portion of their photographs illustrated two obstacles that had to be overcome. Katheryn Staley explained one of these in a sympathetic article on "Photography as a Fine Art," appearing in an 1896 issue of *Munsey's Magazine.* "So valuable has the camera become," she asserted,

> to medical men, to astronomers, and to students of various other branches of science, that opticians find it difficult to satisfy their demands in the manufacture of a lens that will give the most minute detail upon every square millimeter of the plate . . . . Painful efforts to include as much unnecessary detail in each photograph as some realists place in their novels, are noticeable at every exhibition. In spite of its limitations, the art has varied possibilities of realism and impressionism.14

Staley believed that there was "necessarily a certain opposition between artistic and scientific photography," and in her illustrated article, she proceeded to describe the work of photographers whom she felt were successful at producing artistic effects.15 Yet, ironically, a number of the examples Staley used unintentionally illustrate the second obstacle to photography's acceptance as a fine art. They are imitations of bad painting (genre or anecdotal paintings) or contain figures who appear like classical statues that have been photographed against dark backdrops. Though "unnecessary detail" has been eliminated from the images, they nonetheless possess a photographic directness that heightens the artificiality of the subject matter. They are either stiff and without character or insipid and sentimental (figures 35 and 36). For the most part, their composition is conventional—not incompetent but simply uninteresting. The approach to the subjects betrays the Victorian proclivity toward capturing an obvious picturesqueness or creating an idealized, noble, uplifting essence. This kind of photography is aptly summed up by the art historian, Thomas Craven, in a 1944 interview with Alfred Stieglitz: "cheap, arty stuff . . . vague nudes retouched into formless nymphs, portraits in a 'Rembrandt lighting,' and landscapes bathed in fog."16 It is doubtful that James would have admired them.

Despite these obstacles—indeed, perhaps because of them—the fine art

"A Reverie"

From a photograph by Miss Mary E. Martin.

Figure 35.   Mary E. Martin, *A Reverie*
Munsey's Magazine, January 1896.
(Courtesy of Amelia Gayle Gorgas Library,
University of Alabama.)

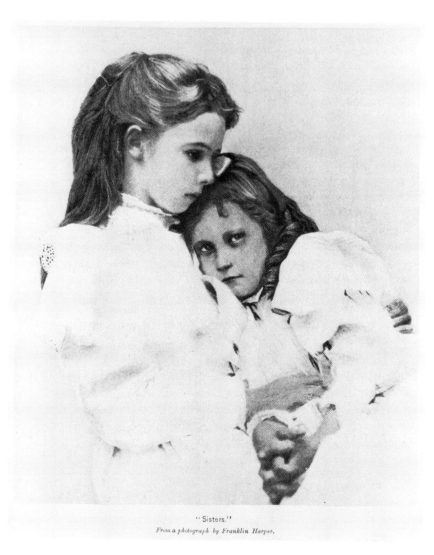

" Sisters."
From a photograph by Franklin Harper.

Figure 36. Franklin Harper, *Sisters*
Munsey's Magazine, January 1896.
(Courtesy of Amelia Gayle Gorgas Library,
University of Alabama.)

of photography evolved during the late nineteenth century and was tirelessly promoted. Various amateur photographic societies had sprung up and continued to thrive in Europe and America during the 1880s and 1890s. In Germany, Dr. Hermann Wilhelm Vogel, an important professor of photochemistry at the Technische Hochschule in Charlottenburg, helped found the Deutsche Gesellschaft von Freunden der Photographie in 1887, which mounted its first exhibition in 1889.[17] In Vienna, the Club der Amateur-Photographien was formed, and beginning in 1891, they held an annual show of art-photography that was very innovative and influential. In England, The Photographic Society of Great Britain already existed, but because it was so conservative, a group of photographers seceded and formed what became the most important art-photography club in England, the Brotherhood of the Linked Ring. This group was formed by Alfred Maskell and others, and it put on annual art-photography salons in London between 1893 and 1909. Their international salons were carefully juried and included only the most outstanding work submitted. They accepted either straight or manipulated imagery by both amateurs and professionals but insisted on showing only art-photography and stressed the fact that they were exhibiting photography as fine art. Their exhibition design was quite modern, and they published portfolios in conjunction with their annual salons. A similar event occurred in Paris in 1894, when a group of French photographers seceded from the staid Société Français de Photographie and formed the Photo-Club de Paris. Other groups formed elsewhere, and annual exhibitions began being held not only in cities like Paris, Vienna, and London, but in Hamburg, Brussels, The Hague, Munich, and Glasgow.

The art-photography movement was emerging in America, too, led from the 1890s onward by Alfred Stieglitz. Stieglitz had studied in Germany under Dr. Vogel, and began making art-photographs in the mid-1880s. In 1887, he entered one of his images, "A Good Joke," in a contest sponsored by *The Amateur Photographer*. This image won a silver medal and had been selected by none other than the important English art-photographer and writer, P. H. Emerson.[18] Eventually, Stieglitz returned to New York and, after a few years of indecision regarding what career to pursue, settled on becoming a photographer and an art promoter. He began his vocation as a crusader for art-photography by assuming the editorship of *The American Amateur Photographer* in 1893.[19] During his editorship, he disseminated and explicated the ideas of the two most important English Pictorialists, P. H. Emerson and H. P. Robinson, and introduced Americans to the work of major European art-photographers. Then in 1896, Stieglitz helped reorganize two foundering camera clubs in New York City. The new club was called the Camera Club of New York, and Stieglitz was selected as its vice president. Shortly afterwards, in 1897, he started the club periodical, *Camera Notes*, which only published work by the most outstanding photographers to be found throughout the world. The club also held frequent lectures and exhibits at its headquarters. As a result of these activities, Stieglitz quickly became one of the most important figures in the American art-photography movement. Through his efforts, the Camera Club of New York earned international respect. In the process, Stieglitz also helped organize and rejuvenate the American Pictorial photography movement and brought to the attention of the world the work of American photographers like Frances Benjamin Johnston, Rudolf Eickemeyer, Jr., and F. Holland Day. By 1899, a young journalist and aspiring fiction writer, Theodore Dreiser, could feature Stieglitz in Orison Swett Marden's popular magazine, *Success*. "There is one man among the master photographers," Dreiser wrote, "who so towers above his followers that there is no longer any dispute as to his leadership. His name is Alfred Stieglitz, and it has become very widely known. His work is so esteemed the world over among those who love art in photographs, and who love to study and emulate superior and original methods, that it has come to have a high market value."[20] Stieglitz not only had become noted within the international art-photography community, but like Thomas Edison (about whom Dreiser also wrote in *Success*) and Teddy Roosevelt, he was touted as a celebrity in America's emerging popular press.

Despite his growing celebrity, however, Stieglitz did not deny others an important place in the movement. On the contrary, Stieglitz attracted and encouraged the involvement of talented, committed individuals. He promoted the photography of others, often neglecting his own work in the process. He invited a number of intelligent, discerning people to write for *Camera Notes*—individuals who would become important figures in the movement: F. Holland Day, Sadakichi Hartmann, Joseph T. Keiley, Charles H. Caffin, and the French photographer and aesthetician Robert Demachy.[21] Yet, because Stieglitz and his colleagues had definite views about art-photography, conflicts eventually developed within the American photography movement. By 1900, William Inness Homer argues, the issue facing the Americans "was no longer whether photography was an art; now the issue was what sort of an art it should be."[22] Stieglitz and his *Camera Notes* comrades believed that the answer lay in the work of the *fin de siècle* photographers that included Frank Eugene, Joseph T. Keiley, F. Holland Day, Gertrude Käsebier, Clarence White, and Eduard Steichen (figures 37 and 38). Though *Camera Notes* did not initially set forth a particular aesthetic canon, distinct principles and stylistic approaches eventually emerged, and these formed a kind of loose definition of what F. Holland

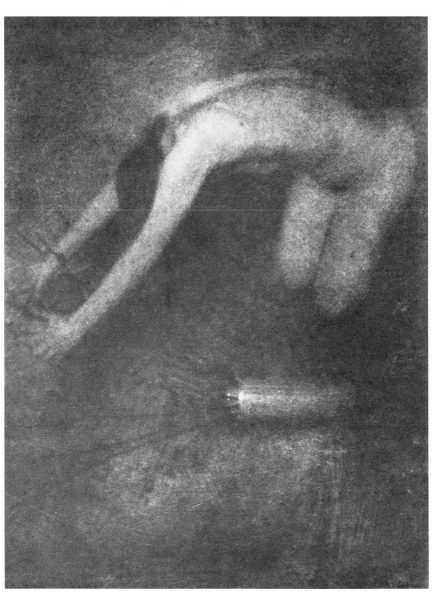

Figure 37.   Eduard J. Steichen, *Dawn-flowers*
Camera Work, April 1903.
(Courtesy of University Art Museum, University of New Mexico.)

Figure 38.   Clarence H. White, *The Orchard*
Camera Work, January 1905.
(Courtesy of University Art Museum, University of New Mexico.)

Day first termed the "New School of American Photography." By 1900, the work of members of this school was characterized by a London *Times* reviewer as exhibiting the "all pervading tendency toward the mysterious and the bizarre; all outlines and detail are in many cases so suppressed and lost in delicate shadow that their meaning and intention are hard to discover."[23]

Insofar as this style can be attributed to anyone, Homer suggests, it can be credited to F. Holland Day.[24] Day, in turn, was influenced by masters of painting such as Rembrandt, Velázquez, and Titian (painters, recall, who were admired by James). Day's own work, in Homer's words, exhibited a "murky, low-keyed tonality, with an accompanying sense of mystery, elegant linear rhythms and tasteful compositional arrangement, and a reliance of the evocation of mood and enigma rather than explicit narratives."[25] His photographs showed him to be "an absolute master of light, and in the 1890s, he far outstripped Stieglitz in the variety and subtlety of effects he was able to obtain. "Indeed," Homer goes on to assert, "Stieglitz's work before 1900 — with a few major exceptions — seemed to lack the sophisticated visual elegance and poetic refinement of Day's photographs."[26]

For various complex, ambiguous reasons, a conflict began to arise between Day and Stieglitz.[27] Day, a wealthy Bostonian, seemed to be attracting a following that threatened to form what Homer calls "the Day-Boston axis" of the American art-photography movement, and Stieglitz evidently viewed this as a challenge to his own power and influence. In any event, Day and Stieglitz vied for leadership, and in the midst of their restrained competition, Day organized the photographic exhibition that became the "New School of American Photography." Day visited London in the company of Fanny Coburn and Alvin Langdon Coburn, his young cousin and student, and persuaded the Royal Photographic Society to sponsor this show. Held in London between 10 October and 8 November 1900, the salon was quite popular in spite of the fact that it apparently shocked viewers with what was thought to be unconventional imagery. Day then took the exhibition to Paris, where it received even more favorable response. All this, of course, surprised and disconcerted Stieglitz and, in Homer's view, probably "laid the groundwork for the Photo-Secession."[28]

Meanwhile, an annual photographic salon had been established in 1898 in Philadelphia, sponsored by the Pennsylvania Academy of Fine Arts and the Philadelphia Photographic Society.[29] Stieglitz had been hoping for some time that such an exhibition would eventually be mounted, and so he had given it his support. Though it was a juried international show, the first year's selections had not been entirely to Stieglitz's satisfaction. But the situation had improved in 1899, and that year's show was notable for introducing the work of a young unknown Milwaukee photographer, Eduard Steichen. These annual exhibitions continued through the turn of the century, though the selections always seemed to everyone involved compromises at best. Not surprisingly, a conflict eventually emerged within the Philadelphia Society itself for control, and it was won by a conservative antiart-photography faction which proceeded to dictate the contents of the 1901 exhibition. When Stieglitz learned of this, he and his friends boycotted the salon. Out of their protest was born the "American Pictorial Photography" show, the "Photo-Secession" movement, and *Camera Work*, all in 1902, and finally, in 1905, one of the most important early photography and art galleries in the world, Stieglitz's "291." These—with Stieglitz playing a leading role—would become major forces not only in the battle to establish photography as a fine art but also in the introduction of modern European art to American audiences.

The "American Pictorial Photography" exhibition was a crucial event in the history of the art-photography movement. Put on by Stieglitz and his "photo-secessionist" compatriots in March 1902 at the National Arts Club in New York, it helped reestablish Stieglitz as the foremost American leader in the art-photography movement and featured the work of most of the important American art-photographers of the day—including photographs by Stieglitz *and* his recent rival F. Holland Day.[30] Later that same year, Stieglitz called together a number of his fellow artists, and they formed a loose organization called the "Photo-Secession." The purpose of the group was to promote pictorial photography, give American art-photographers an opportunity to engage in mutual support, and mount exhibitions of the best work available anywhere in the world. Stieglitz was named head of this organization, and he proceeded to carry out its purposes with incredible energy and intelligence. Moreover, having just resigned as editor of *Camera Notes*, Stieglitz was in a position to begin a new independent photography journal. In 1902, he drew up plans for *Camera Work*, a periodical that would achieve the distinction of being one of the most important and beautifully produced art journals ever to appear in America.[31] Of course, Stieglitz initially saw *Camera Work* as "the mouthpiece of the Photo-Secession," but maintained that it would always be an independent organ.[32] Over the years, he not only included the work of important contemporary pictorial photographers but also presented work by historically important image makers like Hill and Adamson and Julia Margaret Cameron. He featured criticism by Sadakichi Hartmann, Charles H. Caffin, and introduced Gertrude Stein to readers by publishing her early critical sketches on Matisse and Picasso. He also featured nonphotographic art: exquisite reproductions of water colors by Rodin and sketches by Picasso, Matisse, and others. During the years of its existence between the first 1903 issue and the last, appearing in 1917, *Camera Work* always maintained the highest standards of production quality and sought to break new ground in the art world by introducing the work of talented, experimental photographers, painters, and sculptors. Finally, in addition to leading the progressive American art-photography movement and publishing *Camera Work*, Stieglitz founded the first of his art galleries: the "Little Galleries of the Photo-Secession," better known as "291."[33] Under Stieglitz's directorship, "291" initially exhibited and promoted the art-photography of the Photo-Secessionists as well as new photographers; but later Stieglitz broadened his offerings to include shows of African art, children's art, and most importantly, work by some of the major European and American post-Impressionist painters and sculptors.

By 1905, Stieglitz was one of the most important and powerful avant-garde art promoters and taste makers in America, and in 1910 he would celebrate the final victory in the battle for the acceptance of photography as a fine art by mounting the first art-photography exhibition ever held at an art museum.[34] In that year, the Albright Art Gallery in Buffalo, New York, played host to the "International Exhibition of Pictorial Photography," not only exhibiting art-photographs but becoming the first art museum to buy art-photographs for its permanent collection. The war was won.

According to William Innes Homer, Alvin Langdon Coburn was "an important catalyst in prodding Cornelia Sage [then acting director of the Albright] . . . into proceeding with the International Exhibition of Pictorial Photography of 1910."[35] By this time, Coburn was an admired, well established member of Stieglitz's "inner circle."[36] His rise to a position of prominance in the Photo-Secession and in the international art-photography movement was rapid. Recall that he was only eighteen when his work was included in Day's 1900 London exhibition of the American pictorialists. Also that same year, during their trip to London and Paris, Coburn was introduced by Day to important photographers like Eduard Steichen, Frederick Evans, Frank Eugene, and Robert Demachy. Coburn's artistry developed so precociously and his work became so well regarded that he would be selected for membership in both the Photo-Secession and the Linked Ring before he reached the age of twenty-one.[37]

Born into an elite, prosperous Boston family in 1882, Coburn took up photography as a child of eight when he acquired his first Kodak.[38] He met his older cousin, F. Holland Day, in 1898, and showed Day a portfolio of his work. Day was sufficiently impressed to invite Coburn to become his student, take him and his mother to Europe, and include his photographs in an international exhibition. Subsequently, Coburn returned to America and, in 1902, he moved to New York City and established a studio. There he became reacquainted with Steichen and met Stieglitz and Gertrude Käsebier. Käsebier became Coburn's teacher during this period, and Stieglitz became his mentor and promoter. Coburn was elected to the Photo-Secession in late 1902 and was given his first one-person exhibition at the Camera Club of New York in 1903. In the latter year, he was also elected to membership in the Linked Ring.

While in America, Coburn also studied with Arthur Wesley Dow at the latter's summer school. Dow was an influential teacher, who numbered among his students Georgia O'Keeffe and Max Weber.[39] Dow himself was apparently influenced by the Japanese mode of design (so important to the Impressionists during the late nineteenth century), and in Barbara Rose's words, "taught that art resides in harmonious spaces."[40] Coburn's work had already exhibited a strong formal sense, and so not surprisingly he absorbed Dow's lessons and continued to create photographs that sought to embody and perfect this principle (figure 39). That he was succeeding marvelously is not only attested to be the fact that he was given an exhibition at the Camera Club of New York in 1903, but also because a selection of his photographs appeared both in *Photo Era* and *Camera Work* in 1903 and 1904 respectively. More important, the critical commentary accompanying Coburn's photographs was filled with thoughtful admiration and insight regarding his artistry. Reviewing Coburn's 1903 show, Thomas Harrison Cummings suggested that the young artist had reached "the highest levels in artistic photography," and Cummings said he admired not only the "aesthetic intelligence" displayed by the images but their technical qualities.[41] Critic Charles H. Caffin, in the more important periodical *Camera Work*, described Coburn's printing technique and discussed Coburn's "feeling for the significance of form and structure."[42] Though Caffin noted that Coburn occasionally failed to regulate satisfactorily the tonal values in his prints, he asserted that most of Coburn's images nonetheless contained a "delicacy of expression as well as robustness. . . . For the vision of an artist and more than usual command of craftsmanship are apparent in all of them, and underlying these qualities an evident reverence for beauty."[43] By early 1904, Coburn was a significant camera artist whose work was worthy of the most serious attention and criticism.

Coburn returned to London in 1904, and except for visits to America and elsewhere, he lived there for much of the rest of his long life. He continued to be active both in the Linked Ring and in the Photo-Secession, but his interests led him into other circles and activities too. Securing a commission from *Metropolitan Magazine*, Coburn embarked on a project to photograph a number of well known English writers and artists. He began by contacting George Bernard Shaw. Shaw, who was immensely

Figure 39. A.L. Coburn, *The Dumping Ground, Boston*, 1900.
(By permission of the International Museum of
Photography at George Eastman House.)

interested in photography both as an amateur and critic, invited Coburn to visit him and make his portrait. Out of this meeting grew a lifelong friendship between the two men (figure 40). Shaw, of course, was not only charmed by Coburn but admired his work enough to write the critical preface to Coburn's one-person London exhibition of 1906 — the very show Henry James visited. Coburn continued over the years to make portraits of writers and artists — Alfred Stieglitz, August Rodin, G.K. Chesterton, George Meredith, Gertrude Stein, among others — and established a reputation for the unusual quality of his portraiture (figures 41 and 42). Of Coburn's portraits, Shaw wrote in his 1906 catalogue preface:

> It is Mr. Coburn's vision and susceptibility that make him interesting. . . . Look at his portrait of Mr. Gilbert Chesterton . . . Coburn has represented him as swelling off the plate in the very act of being photographed, and blurring his own outlines in the process . . . but Chesterton is right; and a right impression of Chesterton is what Mr. Coburn was driving at. . . . Look at the portrait of Mr. Bernard Partridge! There is no lack of vigour in that image: it is deliberately weighted by comparative underexposure . . . and the result is a powerfully characteristic likeness. Look again at the profile portrait of myself "en penseur" a mere strip of my head. Here the exposure is precisely right, and the definition exquisite without the least hardness. These three portraits were all taken with the same lens in the same camera, under the same circumstances. But there is no reduction of three different subjects to a common technical denominator.[44]

A year later, critic Sadakichi Hartmann would note this individuality of style and its impact: "At the recent One-Print Exhibition of the Professional Photographers' Society of New York, I was greatly astonished to find several prints . . . that reminded me — there was no getting away from it — of Coburn's peculiar method of portraying celebrities."[45] Of course, by then Coburn had published many of his portraits in *Metropolitan*, *Century*, and *Camera Work*, and he would later collect them in two books whose photogravure plates would be made by his own hand: *Men of Mark* (1913) and *More Men of Mark* (1922). Unquestionably, the year Coburn met Henry James for the first time and photographed him (1905), the young man of twenty-three was already an established artist among his peers and the critics.

As Robert Doty sums it up in his book *Photo-Secession*, pictorialist photographers,

> worked toward a photography that went beyond commonplace record, to expressions of beauty and spirit. Technique, once mastered, became unimportant, and the result had to be more than just an image on paper. Composition, massing of light and shade, correct rendition of tonal qualities, arrangement of lines, development of curves, were the means. With them they sought values, textures, character, any aspect that would appeal to the emotions of the viewer. Gradually there emerged a style which depended upon the relation of light and color, the softening of sharp lines, and particularly the suppression of details to obtain an impression. . . . It was quite frankly patterned after the styles of the currently venerated painters, especially Whistler, Corot, and the members of the Barbizon school, Millet in particular. These painters softened their brush work to achieve

Figure 40.   G.B. Shaw, *Portrait of Alvin Langdon Coburn*
Camera Work, July 1906.
(Courtesy of University Art Museum, University of
New Mexico.)

Figure 41.   A.L. Coburn, *George Bernard Shaw*
Camera Work, January 1908.
(Courtesy of University Art Museum, University of
New Mexico.)

Figure 42. A.L. Coburn, *Alfred Stieglitz, Esq.*
Camera Work, January 1908.
(Courtesy of University Art Museum, University of
New Mexico.)

atmospheric effects of an almost scientific kind. Indeed, much of pictorial photography was a conscious emulation of pictures made by the brush, the pencil, or the etcher's burning. Because of the general criticism that photography was made by a machine, the pictorialists felt compelled to prove their work was similar to those graphic arts done by the hand. Hence, they adopted extreme techniques to achieve surface effects comparble to the textured quality distinguishing handwork.46

Though Coburn was very much a part of the pictorialist movement, he believed that photography would only "achieve victory by virtue of its own merits — by the unique subtlety of its tonal range and its capacity to explore and exploit the infinite gradations of luminosity rather than by imitating the technique of the draughtsman."47

Taken together, the points made by Doty and Coburn suggest that though pictorialists were unified in their battle to make photography a legitimate fine art, there were important differences among them. One of the crucial but seldom recognized differences concerned the type of, and approach to, the subject matter used. In some sense, this difference was analogous to the conflict between literary realism and romanticism. One group of pictorialists did just what Doty noted: photographic artists such as Robert Demachy sought to emulate painters by utilizing methods such as soft focus lens effects and textured printing processes like gum bichromate (figure 43). Such methods allowed photographers to manipulate their images to look like chalk, pencil, and charcoal drawings as well as water color paintings. One pictorialist, Frank Eugene, even scratched his negatives in order to give his prints an etched appearance. Besides using such imitative printing methods, these photographers also often composed their scenes and subjects in ways that were reminiscent of the pictorial styles that were dominant and popular during the late nineteenth century, idealizing and romanticizing their subjects in the most didactic manner. The results were often highly imitative and sometimes melodramatic and pretentious in effect.

The other approach to pictorial photography also used the soft focus lens and even resorted to printing with processes that exuded handcraft qualities; but the subject matter presented in most of these images was allowed to retain the quality of realism. Art-photographers adopting this approach took their subject matter directly from the streets, or when they made portraits, they made it obvious that their subjects were contemporary persons. Studio artificiality and *tableau vivant* effects were, for the most part, eschewed. In this instance, the photographer's job was difficult because of the need to select good pictures from the usually chaotic streets, but when they succeeded, the results were refreshingly convincing and often astonishingly beautiful. And as they developed their approach, they turned more and more away from manipulated printing and, ultimately, even the soft focus lens. Their stylistic evolution was analogous to that of literary

Figure 43.   Robert Demachy, *Struggle*
             Camera Work, January 1904.
             (Courtesy of University Art Museum, University of
             New Mexico.)

realism in that they slowly rid their works of excess idealization and romanticism. The pioneer in this "realist" branch of pictorialism had, of course, been P. H. Emerson, the English photographer and theoretician whose brilliant studies of life in East Anglia—made during the 1890s—proved that the world itself could be a source for beautiful, penetratingly authentic images.[48] Following Emerson's lead was Alfred Stieglitz, who in Coburn's words, "made memorable photographs, especially of street scenes" (figure 44).[49] To do this, Stieglitz pioneered in the use of the hand camera for artistic purposes and in the process helped liberate art-photography. He turned his camera on life of all kinds, from the commonplace to the sordid.[50]

Though Coburn had studied initially with F. Holland Day, he acknowledged that Stieglitz was an important influence.[51] Coburn's photographic style utilized soft focus, but—like Stieglitz—he turned directly to contemporary life for his subject matter—be it landscape, cityscape, or portraiture (figures 45 and 46). Coburn's effects, though softly focused, were never pretentious, never artificial. He printed his negatives on platinotype paper, giving his images a soft, warm luster—an exquisiteness not unlike the daguerreotype's effect. Then, on the same prints, he brushed dark brown gum bichromate and reprinted the images. The second printing created the rich, dark tones that could not be brought out in straight platinotype prints. As a result of this double printing, Coburn's photographs contained the soft atmospheric gleam of platinum with its heightened whites *and* the contrasting darks made possible by gum bichromate. Together, these processes enabled Coburn to capture the highest contrast and fullest tonal range possible in a photograph without resulting in brashness. The overall image, though soft and ambiguous, was nonetheless photographic instead of painterly (figures 47 and 48).

Like Stieglitz, Coburn was also interested in carefully structured scenes that were selected from the world itself, pictures that caught and framed reality most dramatically and harmoniously (figures 49 and 50). And, like James, Coburn found and captured such scenes and then transformed them through his imagination and craft into art. As early as 1900, his eye saw the aesthetic possibilities in a Boston trash heap, and through his eye and imagination, his camera and printing skill, Coburn transformed that vulgar, banal scene into an atmospheric, shimmering image of asymmetrically balanced forms floating in space (see figure 39). A few years later, during his wanderings among the Liverpool shipyards, Coburn visualized the potential beauty implicit in the men working among the shapes and forms of the ships and machines, and he created ambiguously striking but concrete scenes of ongoing life (figures 51 and 52). As critic Sadakichi Hartmann wrote of

Figure 44.   Alfred Stieglitz, *The Street — Design for a Poster
Camera Work*, July, 1906.
(Courtesy of University Art Museum, University of
New Mexico.)

Figure 45.   A.L. Coburn, *The Bridge—Sunlight
Camera Work*, July 1906.
(Courtesy of University Art Museum, University of
New Mexico.)

Figure 46.   A.L. Coburn, *Notre Dame*
Camera Work, January 1908.
(Courtesy of University Art Museum, University of
New Mexico.)

Figure 47.   A.L. Coburn, *Wier's Close — Edinburgh*
Camera Work, January 1906.
(Courtesy of University Art Museum, University of
New Mexico.)

Figure 48.   A.L. Coburn, *The Bridge—Venice*
Camera Work, January 1908.
(Courtesy of University Art Museum, University of
New Mexico.)

Figure 49.   A.L. Coburn, *Gables*
Camera Work, April 1904.
(Courtesy of University Art Museum, University of
New Mexico.)

Figure 50. A.L. Coburn, *The Bridge—Ipswich*
Camera Work, April 1904.
(Courtesy of University Art Museum, University of
New Mexico.)

Coburn, he was able "to see objects, insignificant in themselves, in a big way."[52]

All of the Coburn images referred to in this chapter were made before the collaboration between Henry James and Coburn occurred. Indeed, most of them were included in the London exhibition of Coburn's work that James attended in 1906. Upon seeing these, James must have understood that, like his own, Coburn's art transformed moments from life into beauty and meaning. Coburn's portraits caught his sitters as they were expressing their own natural forces and presences, selecting the angle and framing that would allow their individual qualities to emerge most dramatically and effectively. They are stylized, certainly, yet they are utterly without any note of stiffness or falseness. Coburn's landscapes and cityscapes froze the formal beauty that inherently exists at different moments in nature and society: he sensed at what points of view and angles things fell into the most harmonious relation to each other. As Coburn wrote, "There are countless things in the world waiting to be recognized and captured, and the photographer has unique opportunities for recording . . . aspects of the world around him, in subtle gradations of lights and form not possible in any other medium."[53] Of course, Coburn understood that "photography demands great patience: waiting for the right hour, the right moment, and recognising it when you see it. . . . The artist-photographer must be constantly on the alert for the perfect moment, when a fragment of the jumble of nature is isolated by the conditions of light and atmosphere, until every detail is just right.[54]

Coburn's approach to photography was utterly compatible with James's perceptual/conceptual approach to the world. Writing about the experience of making with Coburn the images for *The Golden Bowl*, recall that James wrote of one, "it awaited us somewhere." Of the other, he explained, "we had . . . simply to recognize. . . . The thing was to induce the vision of Portland Place *to* generalize itself. . . . at a given moment the great featureless Philistine vista would itself perform a miracle, would become interesting, for a splendid atmospheric hour, as only London knows how; and that our business would be then to understand."[55] Coburn's photography unquestionably exhibited an artistic sensibility and craft that James could respect. It was based on direct observation, yet selective in the inclusion of details and in the organization of the scene and was not blunt in the presentation of that scene. His images contained strong form and balance, avoiding the merely picturesque. Never were they sentimental or melodramatic, nor were they ever didactic idealizations. Instead, they expressed the mysterious and dramatic through ambiguity and contrasting light and dark. Compositionally radical, they were nonetheless balanced. Design was

Figure 51.   A.L. Coburn, *The Rudder*
Camera Work, January 1908.
(Courtesy of University Art Museum, University of
New Mexico.)

Figure 52.   A.L. Coburn, *Spider Webs*
Camera Work, January 1908.
(Courtesy of University Art Museum, University of
New Mexico.)

always clear, conception was always simple. Finally, the print quality of all Coburn's images suggested a concern for the highest craft — they were, and remain, beautiful creations.

Almost uncannily, the critic Sadakichi Hartmann discussed Coburn's art in words that could have been used to characterize James's art. Hartmann wrote, "Coburn is an extreme. His delicate and poetical pictorial fancies are not for the public at large."[56] Discussing Coburn's portraits, Hartmann continued: Coburn "shows us forms and faces as we may see them in a dream immaterialized as it were, and yet in a strongly decorative manner."[57] In Hartmann's view, "To be transformed into a pictorial phantasm may grant an acute sensation to the fastidiously inclined, but I prefer line and clear modeling to vagueness."[58] Yet, Hartmann conceded,

> It is Coburn's merit to have developed this vagueness of effect into a style of his own. . . .
> As I looked at his Rodin in scull cap with flowing beard; at his Arthur Symons, very
> thoughtful-looking with one hand at his chin; and his Chesterton, all washy and blurred,
> it seemed to me that I did not merely see the faces of three distinct personalities, but
> something beyond; something of their life, their occupation, etc.; a vague impression,
> such as we may get of the personality of an author perusing one of his books.[59]

Wondering about this, Hartmann asked, "is it not rather curious that a photograph can set your imagination going in such a direction? It seems so to me. Steichen never accomplished it. . . . Coburn is subtler, more poetic and elegant. . . . His Shannon, Carpenter, James, Solomon Solomon, Shaw, Meredith, Sargent, etc., have what the critic calls soul quality. They give us more than we see at the first glance, yet we feel that all has not been said."[60] "Coburn," Hartmann added, "is not so much an impressionist as a symbolist. He knows that the character of a great man cannot be conveyed fully in one portrait; he therefore creates before our eyes an elegant and graceful vision, suggestive by its very formlessness of something subtly intellectual, and lets us add with the help of our imagination what the picture lacks in actual facts."[61] Hartmann found it extraordinary that he could write in this manner about a photographer, concluding that "Coburn is an artist, but the term portrait photography cannot be applied to such delicate fantasies as he has chosen to do."[62] It is not surprising that a photographer whose work possessed all the qualities Hartmann noted would appeal to James.

A photographic style that could depict concrete things without making them too direct or brash, that could present things clearly enough to be recognized yet softened enough to make them allusive, suggestive, turned out to be perfect for James's needs. In the right hands, the medium could select and capture, in James's words, "a concrete, independent, vivid instance,"[63] which was exactly what he wanted for his Edition's frontispieces. Coburn's photographic artistry was precisely the sort that could give the "rendering," in James's word, of places or things which would work as generalized symbols of aspects in his works, resulting in images that were "distilled and intensified."[64] Of course, "if the 'painter's eye' had persisted creatively in James," John L. Sweeney queries, "might he not have been tempted to illustrate his own text; to cultivate two gardens in one plot?"[65] Perhaps. But James did not have that kind of talent — one that would have given him full creative control over his Edition. However, he did have a photographer's eye and memory, and so he could do — and did — the next best thing. He collaborated with an artist whose medium was inclusive. "Even more than in painting," art critic Max Kozloff argues, "it is not so much *by* the photographer's eye but *in* that of the beholder that the experience is decisively shaped."[66] With his photographer's eye, James participated in the creation of the optical symbols that were used in his Edition. He directed his cameraman, like a film director directs his cinematographer, to make the images he saw in his mind or that he and Coburn found during their London outings. Once the images were made and printed, James then selected the ones that best fit the image he held in his mind. As Coburn put it, James "was . . . always displaying an unquenchable and contagious enthusiasm over every detail concerning these illustrations."[67] That would not have been an easy thing to do if the Edition had been illustrated by hand-rendered art.

James characterized himself early in his career in a letter to his brother William: "I have a constant impulse to try experiments of form."[68] By the time the New York Edition was being planned, James may well have decided that the photographic frontispieces would be a good experiment — a visual extension of the literary symbolism he had been using. Perhaps he was ripe for such a visual experiment for other reasons as well, because he wrote to his friend Grace Norton in early 1903, "I am so weary of pictures and questions of pictures, that it is the most I can do to drag myself for three minutes every three years to the National Gallery."[69]

The choice of Coburn — and photography — was indeed an experiment, a brave one. And as we look again at the images the two artists created, we must conclude that it was a worthwhile one, visually. As we shall see, it was also a successful experiment in terms of the way the pictures work with the texts they accompany.

8

Photographs as Symbols in the New York Edition

Recall that in the preface to *The Golden Bowl*, Henry James wrote, "The essence of any representational work is of course to bristle with immediate images; and I, for one, should have looked askance at the proposal, on the part of my associates in the whole business, to graft or 'grow,' at whatever point, *a picture by another hand on my own picture*—this being always, to my sense, a lawless incident" (emphasis added).[1] At the time he wrote these words—after the illustrations for the Edition had been made—James clearly understood that photography had been the right medium to use for illustrating his New York Edition. To avoid the "lawless incident" of grafting "a picture by another hand on my own picture," he had resisted the pressure to use handmade illustration. After Coburn arrived on the scene, James must have begun to recognize that photography would allow him to do this, that the right photographer could be directed by himself to capture whatever image his mind imagined—that is, his "own picture." The camera's art required what James's possessed—a good eye and visual memory. Understanding this, James conceived the solution of collaborating with a young camera-artist who had not only a good eye but whose aesthetics and artistic skill were admirable as well as compatible with his own. James discovered that by collaborating with the gifted photographer, Alvin Langdon Coburn, he could become—in a partial but important sense—his own illustrator, for no other "hand" would intervene and interfere with James's own literary picture. It was a stroke of genius.

"Nothing in fact could more have amused the author," James explained in his *Golden Bowl* preface,

than the opportunity of a hunt for a series of reproducible subjects—such as might best consort with photography—the reference of which to Novel or Tale should exactly be *not* competitive and obvious, should on the contrary plead its case with some shyness, that of images always confessing themselves mere optical symbols or echoes, expressions of no particular thing in the text, but only of the type or idea of this or that thing. They were to remain at the most small pictures of our "set" stage with the actors left out; and what was above all interesting was that they were first to be constituted.[2]

Each picture, in James's view, was to be "a concrete, independent, vivid instance,"[3] while at the same time each was to convey "the aspect of things or the combination of objects that might, by a latent virtue in it, speak enough for its odd or interesting self."[4] The images had to be concrete but not too specific, containing just enough ambiguity and generality to shroud their documentary quality so they would work well as symbols. Use of a documentary medium like photography for this purpose was both a perfect solution and a problematic one.

Fortunately at the turn of the century, as John Szarkowski has noted, "there were two possible ways of dealing with photography's preference for the particular: One could accept the fact and make use of it (as Atget did), or one could find ways partially to evade it, or at least soften its hard edges."[5] Coburn, of course, took the latter approach, becoming "one of the first — perhaps the first — to pursue consciously the possibilities of photography as a tool for exploring abstract form."[6] Through Coburn's work, James learned that even a camera-artist could create beautiful and strongly formal images of places and things and yet depict these with sufficient softness and vagueness to allow them to work as symbols. Coburn's style of making photographs fully suited James's needs.

There are two interrelated aspects in James's picture-text aesthetics that are expressed in *The Golden Bowl* preface. The first has to do with what James termed, "the general acceptability of illustration."[7] The second concerns what it was that James felt pictures ought to do in their relation with texts. As is evident from James's attitudes, explored earlier, illustration was — in James's words — "a competitive process."[8] He wanted no pictures by another person's hand grafted onto his own pictures, because visual images would very likely repeat, even possibly reinterpret, his own verbal images. James would not tolerate illustration that sought to "keep, or . . . pretend to keep, anything like dramatic step with their suggestive matter."[9] To be acceptable, illustration had to "stand off and on its own two feet and thus, as a separate and independent subject of publication, carrying its text in its spirit, just as that text correspondingly carries the plastic possibility, become a still more glorious tribute."[10]

James avoided using competitive illustration in two ways. Of course, as already argued, he used a medium and artist whose creative results he himself could direct and control, making certain that the images made were, to a great extent, his own creations. Coburn's camera faithfully recorded what James saw — at times, in his memory, other times, in person — and directed him to photograph. Coburn's artistry and printing skills took up where James's left off, creating the soft, atmospheric interpretations of the scenes and objects he was directed to record. In this way, James's imagined impressions were not altered in any basic way by another's hand. Competitive illustrations were also avoided through James's decision regarding the way they were function. Instead of calling into being visually descriptive, populated scenes — which, conventionally, would only repeat the dramatic content of the scenes in the text — James chose "images always confessing themselves mere optical symbols or echoes, expressions of no particular thing in the text, but only of the type or idea of this or that thing. They were to remain at the most small pictures of our 'set' stage with the actors left out."[11] And in doing this, James was merely extending his own well established literary practice of using symbols.

The literary symbol, according to William Flint Thrall and Addison Hubbard, "is in IMAGE which evokes an objective, concrete reality and has that reality suggest another level of meaning. However, the *symbol* does not 'stand for' the meaning; it evokes an object which suggests the meaning."[12] The symbol, in its allusiveness, contributed much to the development of James's indirect literary style, and his fiction abounds in the use of places and things which serve important symbolic purposes. It is through places and things, in Charles R. Anderson's view, the James's characters arrive at their various, and progressively more penetrating, understandings, of each other.[13] As Anderson simplifies it into a clear formula, "character *a* does not understand character *b* until he comes to understand object *x*, which he assumes is symbolic of character *b* — the inherent ambivalence of the symbol being a chief complicating factor."[14] "Object," of course, refers to all sorts of concrete things and places that are capable of being utilized as symbols. Anderson's examples are many, but for the purposes of this point, one will suffice. Isabel Archer, in *The Portrait of a Lady*, first perceives her future husband, Gilbert Osmond, through his Tuscan villa and his collection of Italian antiquities, and she comprehends him as an appreciator — a refined sensibility who loves the beautiful for the insights it can give into beauty and the creative life. Isabel, however, is mistaken in her initial understanding, for as she ultimately comes to recognize, Osmond is really a collector and exploiter — one who possesses things only in order to embellish his own sterile ego and power. It is through Osmond's possessions and his relation to them — Isabel becomes one, too — that Osmond is defined and given final meaning.

The photographic frontispieces are images of places and things, and they work in the same way James's verbal symbols do. But it is important to note that each picture is a "concrete, independent, vivid instance" which seldom repeats a symbol already appearing in the text. Often the visual symbols are drawn from objects or places — especially places — that appear in the text in less concrete ways and consequently serve less clear verbal symbolic functions. For instance (to continue to use *The Portrait of a Lady* example), although the country house called "Gardencourt" is a vitally important place in the evolution of Isabel Archer's fictional life—it is the place where she is launched into her life of "independence"—it works symbolically in a much more ambiguous and indirect way than does the gilt cup in *The Golden Bowl*. Not surprisingly, James chose not to use an image of a flawed golden bowl as a frontispiece for the latter book, but instead used an image of the "shop of the mind" (figure 23) where the cup was first encountered by the Prince and Charlotte and later purchased by Maggie. Though the illustration is related to the golden bowl, it is still free to function as a somewhat separate, broader symbol of Maggie and her father and their relationships with the Prince and Charlotte. On the other hand, for the frontispiece to the first volume of *The Portrait of a Lady*, James chose to use a photograph of the facade of a large country house, entitled simply "The English Home" (figure 3). In this instance, what was originally not a singularly vivid symbol in the text is turned into a distinct visual symbol, suddenly throwing into focus the place that represents important turning points in Isabel's life. By making visual symbols of these sorts for frontispieces, James expanded his use of symbolism in his collected Edition, often creating new symbols that work to evoke additional meanings or essences to be found in the works accompanied.[15]

James's use of places and things was brilliant in its insight into, and revelation of, how human consciousness and cultures work. Human beings actually do reflect something of themselves in their objects, and they do read meanings into material places and things. The photograph, as James perceived it is an object as well as being of objects, and it is thus capable of working symbolically. James also understood that visual images work differently than words. As E. H. Gombrich argues, "the visual image is supreme in its capacity for arousal," but as regards expression of ideas, "its use . . . is problematic, and . . . unaided it altogether lacks the possibility of matching the statement function of language."[16] No picture alone can tell us about something "past, present or future, observable or distant, actual or conditional."[17] Consequently, to understand the intended meaning of a visual image, we must have access to what Gombrich calls "the code, the caption, and the context."[18] If we do know and understand these, the picture will communicate its meaning instantly—just as a stoplight does in twentieth-century American automobile culture. Once the key to the picture's meaning is understood, the picture works faster than words in conveying that meaning.

The frontispieces put into practice Gombrich's point. If we look at one of them before we have read the story, we are aroused but uncertain as to its meaning. Each image is a striking and mystifying signal that has something to do with the story it accompanies. Yet, what that something is is not clear. Of course, since many of the pictures are of objects like bridges, doors, and houses that already have symbolic cultural meanings in the Western mind, we are not completely baffled. We have been given a cultural clue of what to look for as we read the text; and as we do read the story, we find that the visual image begins to take on meaning: we are acquiring a context for understanding it more explicitly. Finally, when we look at the image after completing the novel or tale, we find that it works as a gestalt, giving us an instant, direct summation of a meaning that is crucially present in the work. Instead of attempting to describe action, appearances, or dramatic scenes, each frontispiece represents an idea and communicates it symbolically. As symbols, all the frontispieces work quite effectively upon the reader who has understood the meanings and nuances of James's texts.

James evidently sensed that in seeking "optical symbols or echoes," he was using visual images for the function they could best serve, and a discussion of several examples of the picture-text combinations should illuminate how well James understood the differences between written language and visual language. Because of his insight, James was successful in his endeavor to reinvent a kind of illustration that had not been used for a long time—one that avoided competition with the words and instead proffered lovely visual symbols that complemented each of the individual verbal texts and added beauty to the entire New York Edition.

The only image of a person appearing among the New York Edition frontispieces is the portrait of Henry James (figure 1), accompanying the first volume of the collection, *Roderick Hudson*.[19] By its use, James created the largest, most complex symbol to be found in the entire Edition, since it works as a symbol for the whole Edition as much as it does for *Roderick Hudson*. The portrait is a profile of James in which the mature author's face looks toward the right, in the direction of the text of *Roderick Hudson* and toward the entire set of volumes that follow. It should not be surprising that a portrait of James, as a mature artist, begins the Edition: the New York Edition was James's masterwork, his monument, and inclusion of the portrait whose subject casts his gaze, as it were, on his entire life's achievement was an appropriate as well as brilliant conception. The Edition, with its revised texts and newly created prefaces and frontispieces, was called forth by the artist portrayed. Though it is a cliché to say so, James was obviously "the master of all he surveyed," yet when this ordinarily trite notion is suggested visually—as it is through the use of this portrait—it rises above cliché, becoming a fresh symbol that evokes exactly that truth. It is a tribute to the experimental quality of James's genius that in using photography and Coburn's unique talent, he discovered the most perfect, all pervasive symbol for use at the beginning of his Edition—his own explicit yet ambiguously powerful photographic profile.

The picture we specifically know to be James's own likeness achieves its symbolic meaning partly because of what we know about James as the artist who created the Edition. But that is only part of the context we need to interpret and appreciate the complexity of this symbol. We are given a deeper context by the text that James's portrait overlooks. *Roderick Hudson* is a novel about an artist and his patron. Roderick Hudson, the artist, is discovered in a small New England town by Rowland Mallet, a man who perceives Roderick to be potentially a great sculptor. Rowland, the center of consciousness in the book, becomes Roderick's patron, giving him money and advice that he hopes will enable the young man to study and create great works. Roderick accompanies Rowland to Rome, and the young artist creates some scuptures that are precociously good. Ultimately, however, Roderick fails as an artist, and the story traces his struggle and fall.

Without becoming an aesthetic tract, James's *Roderick Hudson* fictionally examines the aesthetic issues and problems facing the serious artist in James's day—indeed, facing James himself when he began to write and recognize that he had to make choices regarding his directions. Two aesthetic approaches are opposed in the story, and a third is unfolded as the way to knowledge for the nonartist, Rowland, as well as for his protege, Roderick. One view is the classical, personified by Rowland Mallet, a man who believes that it is his mission in life to pursue the noble ideal. His ideal, of course, is the realization of Roderick's talent as a great artist. Rowland, though he denies it at first, is attempting to mold Roderick into his conception of an artist who, through discipline and order, will develop his genius. When Roderick says, "you believe in me!" Roland answers, "I believe in you if you're prepared to work and to wait and to struggle and to exercise a great many virtues" (I, 35). But Roderick is not a disciplined person; rather, he is the opposite of Rowland—a personification of the extreme romantic view of the artist.

The book's action involves the unfolding struggle between these two individuals (and the mental cameras they possess) and the experiences they face in life. Both must face the real world, with its unfolding experience, and both are changed by it—though each in a different way. Roderick, the romantic figure, indulges himself in an impossible romance with Christina Light, and as a consequence of his indulgence, he ceases to work and grow as a sculptor. Though Roderick affirms that he must experience life in order to create—"an artist can't bring his visions to maturity unless he has a certain experience" (I, 224)—he spends more time living than working on his art. Finally, when life fails to deliver what he most wants—marriage to Christina—Roderick responds melodramatically, first by dejectedly refusing to work and ultimately by committing suicide.

Despite the fact that he pays homage to experience, Roderick—the consummate romantic—learns nothing from it except defeat. Rowland, however, acquires new consciousness as the result of his experience with Roderick. Though Rowland at first refuses to believe that he is trying to direct Roderick's life, he comes to recognize his own complicity and responsibility. "I took you from your mother and that young lady," Rowland tells Roderick, "and it seems to me my duty to restore you to their hands" (I, 319). And when Rowland later accompanies Roderick, Mrs. Hudson, and Mary to Florence, Italy, he reflects on his experience: "he said to himself that he would see it through but must never court again such perils" (I, 446). Rowland learns the price of trying to make over someone else's life according to his own ideal, but the important thing to note is that he does learn from his experience in spite of its painfulness.

Through experience, Roderick falls from genius because he refuses to reflect on its meaning; but Rowland grows into knowledge because he faces it directly. James, the mature artist whose image not only looks ahead at his completed life's work but also looks back in time at his first successful novel, is the antithesis of Roderick. James, as a young artist, once faced Roderick's choices, but unlike Roderick, he disciplined himself, made his art, and achieved his potential. Moreover, like Rowland, he learned from his experience and imparted his knowledge to his characters throughout his fiction. Hence, James could display his photographic image so that it looks back at an artist's beginnings, with all the possibility and precariousness inherent in such, and at the same time, looks ahead toward the successful fulfillment of his own potential, thereby creating a symbol of extraordinarily far-reaching complexity and subtlety. Where Roderick failed, the photograph tells us, James succeeded.

One of the great themes of James's fiction is characterized by Rowland Mallet's attempt to liberate the life of another person. James's characters often believe they are capable of freeing another only to learn ultimately that their action has ironically been a kind of manipulation. Of course, the "good" manipulators usually acquire knowledge as the result of their actions but often not until it is too late. This theme is a major one in *The Portrait of a Lady*,[20] and the frontispieces James conceived symbolize two opposing aspects of the theme. Isabel Archer is the manipulated heroine, but unlike Roderick Hudson, she reflects on her experience, accepts its lessons, and lives by her knowledge.

Symbolizing the beginning of Isabel's experience is the frontispiece to the first volume of the novel, "The English Home" (figure 3). This frontis-piece is, of course, a visual image of the imagined Gardencourt, but in spite of its specific connection, it does not work competitively by merely repeat-ing the place described by James in the text. It works in a more general way as a summary of Gardencourt's initial importance in Isabel's life, suggesting one aspect of Gardencourt's dual role in the book. Regarding Gardencourt's other aspect, the frontispiece provides a contrast, emphasizing the paradox-ical role the contry house plays in Isabel's life. It is almost as though there are two points of view regarding the meaning of the place—one of possibil-ity, symbolized by the frontispiece, and one of actuality, revealed ultimately through the text.

"The English Home" depicts a stately, somewhat forbidding, house sitting behind a beautiful, open garden. The picture is one of a vista that suggests the possibilities that open up for Isabel during her initial stay at Gardencourt. This is the Gardencourt that greets her, fresh from America, and offers her an unexpected wide, expansive freedom. Gardencourt, indeed, introduced Isabel to almost all of the possibilities her life would hold for her—good and bad. It is there that she meets Lord Warburton, whose proposal she rejects—thus casting aside one possibility. And it is there that she is given a large inherence through the generous mediation of Ralph Touchette—the gift that appears to give her real freedom to experi-ence life fully and acquire knowledge. But it is also there that she meets Madame Merle, the woman who introduces Isabel to Gilbert Osmond, another of life's possibilities and one that she ultimately chooses. Unfortu-nately, her marriage to Osmond would turn out to be one of the tragic possibilities in her life, though she becomes aware of this too late.

Finally, it is at Gardencourt—during her midnight vigil with the dying Ralph—that Isabel later reflects on her life and recognizes what she failed to understand earlier. She realizes that Ralph Tochette was correct in his initial judgment that Osmond is an exploiter. Moreover, she understands that it is Ralph who is the appreciator and who has been in love with her all along. Ralph would have given her room to grow; Osmond, on the other hand, will only attempt to crush her spirit. She has acquired knowledge, but she recognizes that she has crossed a bridge in her life and cannot go back, cannot leave Osmond—though her knowledge may give her the strength to stand on her own within the marriage.

Isabel's final understanding is symbolized by the frontispiece to volume two of the novel, "The Roman Bridge" (figure 4). She has crossed a bridge and discovered "the infinite vista of a multiplied life to be a dark, narrow alley with a dead wall at the end" (IV, 189). The road she chose led from the light, open vista at Gardencourt to the dark Roman palace she now shares with Osmond. "The English Home" suggests the seeming possibilities Isabel once had; and "The Roman Bridge" evokes the path of actuality Isabel chose and feels bound to accept. Once again, the idea implicit in the second frontispiece borders on cliché—"crossing bridges" and "water under the bridge"—yet when it is represented through a visual image, cliché is transcended and a beautiful symbol emerges. Just as he transformed melodrama and romance into serious art, James proved capable of doing the same with cliché.

Like those to *The Portrait of a Lady*, the *The Princess Casamassima*[21] frontispieces connect generally with the texts—more so than is implied by the second frontispiece's caption. And in contrast to the image in volume one of *Portrait*, neither of these symbols duplicates any of the specific places in the text in which action takes place. "The Dome of St. Paul's" (figure 5) adorns volume one of *Casamassima*, and as a symbol it attaches itself to Hyacinth Robinson's evolving political and moral consciousness, acquired mostly during his developing friendship with Paul Muniment. Muniment is involved with the revolutionary anarchist movement in London, and Hyacinth becomes involved in it through Paul. As Hyacinth sees himself, he is "Paul's pupil and devotee" (V, 262), but as Jay Martin notes, Paul is actually Hyacinth's "revolutionary father."[22]

When Hyacinth and Paul first meet, they walk to Paul's home. The flat is a dismal low rent place, but there is one pleasant thing about it: "from the back windows you could see the dome of St. Paul's" (V, 120). Building upon this foreshadowing aside, James created a visual symbol that works brilliantly though subtly by expanding a brief textual detail into a larger representation. What is alluded to by James use of "The Dome of St. Paul's" is the religious quality implicit in the revolutionary politics of the day. What Lewis Feuer has noted with reference to Marxism, applies equally to its heretical kin, anarchism, in spite of their being secular ideologies: "Marxism has often been described as a religion. . . . If Marx was its Messiah, Lenin was its St. Paul."[23] Feuer's observation is an acute one, and James perspicuously understood its import and appropriateness with regard to the nineteenth-century anarchist movement. In *The Princess Casamassima*, however, Hyacinth's St. Paul is Paul Muniment. Obviously, then, "The Dome of St. Paul's" is a perfect symbol. The image itself is one of the most stunning of the whole group of New York Edition frontispieces and one of the least direct and most complex. The dome is faintly seen in the hazy distance behind the far more prominent bridge. The dome suggests Hyacinth's secular "religious" quest with Paul as his leader. The bridge must be crossed if the dome—evoking the ambiguous utopia—is to be reached.

Symbolically, Hyacinth crosses that bridge when he commits himself to obey whatever "calling" is given to him by the movement. And he has no second thoughts about the rightness (or righteousness) of his commitment until, with his small inheritance, he goes to Paris—the home of his maternal ancestors. The experience of Paris complicates Hyacinth's life, and adds a new dimension to his consciousness and the knowledge that emerges from it. Symbolizing these is the frontispiece to the second volume, "'Splendid Paris, Charming Paris'" (figure 6). This image is a magnificent view of the Arc de Triomphe, and its caption quotes—though it does not merely repeat—Hyacinth's emotional response to Paris and the knowledge which that brings: "'Ah Paris!' he almost wailed at last" (VI, 115). As he is sitting in Tortoni's cafe terrace on the Boulevard, he begins to sense the meaning of his new experience:

> He knew about Tortoni's from his study of the French novel, and as he sat there he had a vague sense of fraternising with Balzac and Alfred de Musset: there were echoes and reminiscences of their works in the air, all confounded with the indefinable exhalations, the strange composite odour, half agreeable, half impure, of the boulevard. "Splendid Paris, charming Paris"—that refrain, the fragment of an invocation, a beginning without an end, hummed itself perpetually in Hyacinth's ears; the only articulate words that got themselves uttered in the hymn of praise his imagination had been addressing to the French capital from the first hour of his stay. He recognised, he greeted with a thousand palpatations, the seat of his maternal ancestors. . . . (VI, 120–21)

Hyacinth discovers the past and recognizes that it has a complex value in that it offers beauty and knowledge which must be allowed to survive. The Arc de Triomphe symbolizes this new recognition, visually acting as the gateway to what Hyacinth senses that the past has to offer: "What was supreme in his mind to-day was not the idea of how the society that surrounded him should be destroyed; it was much more the sense of the wonderful previous things it had produced, of the fabric of beauty and power it had raised" (VI, 124–25).

James chose two visual symbols that serve to represent the two poles that tug at Hyacinth—the revolutionary "religious" commitment he has made and his discovery of a civilization "that appeared to transport him to still wider fields of knowledge, still higher sensations" (VI, 121). Hyacinth is trapped in a paradox: he is committed to fight an economically unjust civilization; but he has conceived a deep appreciation for that civilization's achievements. It is Hyacinth's new consciousness with its seemingly unreconcilable opposites that forces him to destroy himself rather than carry out his anarchist mission to commit a political murder, a mission that he knows will contribute to the destruction of civilization. Ironically, both the "good" and the "evil" of civilization are implicit in the objects depicted in the frontispieces. "The Dome of St. Paul's" is one of the masterworks of the "corrupt" civilization whose utopian replacement it symbolizes. It is a product of the past that Hyacinth initially wants to destroy. And the Arc de Triomphe, the symbol of Hyacinth's new found respect for civilization's genius, was begun in 1806 in honor of Napoleon I, and thus it is also an Imperial symbol that affirms a grandeur and power made possible only through the political enslavement of people. Hyacinth's suicide implies that neither alternative offered by life is acceptable. Instead of being an escape, his suicide takes on the quality of protest — a refusal to live with the paradox he has discovered.

Clearly, the frontispieces work quite well as evocations of broad meanings of the long, complexly developed texts that make up James's novels. We may wonder, though, how well the visual symbols work when read alongside the shorter works. In one sense, the nouvelles and tales caused James some difficulty, regarding both their final organization and the choice of the frontispieces that were to accompany each volume. Because of the demands of space the stories dealing with similar subject matter were not always grouped together. Consequently, James could not conceive of a single frontispiece that would symbolically connect in some way with all of the tales and nouvelles appearing in the same volume. James, therefore had to settle for frontispieces that connected only with one of the texts in each book, though he usually invented a frontispiece idea that would symbolize the story beginning the particular volume.

The frontispiece, "By St. Peter's" (figure 18), links with the first tale in volume eighteen of the Edition — "Daisy Miller."[24] The young heroine of this tale, Daisy Miller, was conceived by James as being "pure poetry."[25] So it is entirely appropriate that "By St. Peter's" is one of the most purely poetic frontispieces in the entire series. "Daisy Miller," in F. W. Dupee's words, is a story that exhibits James's "methods of economy and suggestion . . . methods which appealed so little to a public accustomed to the Victorian abundance" that was his age's usual fare.[26] In that sense, the story is like Coburn's beautiful frontispiece. Daisy, only softly focused for us by James, is seen through the mediating eye and consciousness of Winterbourne, a Europeanized American. Daisy is the archetypal American, innocent and anarchical, who confronts a Europe that is filled with limits, conventions, traditions, manners — social taboos. Her innocence is radical and ultimately fatal, for she pays no heed to Europe's "wisdom." She is the natural American force in the midst of a world that does not believe in enduring innocence, freedom, or nature. Yet, while she appears to be free of constraints, she is only so because she is ignorant of consequences. Hence, she is vulnerable.

In short, she is Coburn's fountain scene, "By St. Peter's" — she is water spraying abundantly from a fountain into the air, ostensibly free but in actuality a prisoner to the wind that throws her about and the gravity that pulls her down to the hard stone pavements below. She is a fresh spray, suspended in the air, framed by a column on the left, St. Peter's in the background, and the beautifully patterned stone pavement below — the old world of traditions and restraints, a world which is more enduring finally than the fountain spray that is destined to fall to the ground and evaporate quickly in the sun. Yet perhaps, in spite of its fragility, it will continue to flow in some sense — in Winterbourne's mind and in unknown and unnamed persons' spirits. Coburn's fountain scene, indeed, captures the spirit of Daisy, her refusal to obey European social constraints, and the consequences of her experience; it symbolizes the idea, as James wished. The frontispiece is delightfully beautiful and powerfully evokes both the joy of Daisy's innocence and the sadness of her inability to learn life's limits, both the freshness of Daisy's being and the frailty and ephemeralness of her existence.

Another short tale, "Europe," is similarly though not so beautifully symbolized.[27] Unlike "Daisy Miller," this tale is not the story with which the volume begins. To attempt to connect the frontispiece with any other tale in this grouping is difficult, for though "The New England Street" (figure 16) is of an ambiguously located scene, it is explicitly tied to the text of "Europe" by its caption. Once again, James set up an opposing dichotomy of symbols, but in this instance the frontispiece symbol is opposed to the symbol that recurs often in the text — Europe.

The Rimmle sisters are three spinsters who care for their mother in Brookbridge, a New England town. They have never traveled, and so their lives have been limited to the narrow experience available in their town. Once, their mother and father took a grand tour of Europe, but their only knowledge of what Europe has to offer comes to them through stories about that trip. Hence, they dream of going to Europe themselves, but they are continually held back by their aged, infirm, and demanding mother. Finally, one of the sisters, Jane, goes; and once she experiences Europe, she refuses to return to "The New England Street." As a result of her decision, Jane is considered by her mother to be dead. At the end of the story, when one of the remaining sisters actually does die, the mother remarks that she has gone "To Europe" (XVI, 369).

Old Mrs. Rimmle is a personification of New England with all its narrow and rigid moralities. And "The New England Street" symbolizes that New England, a pleasant, quiet, well-ordered place with white picket fences that genteelly try to keep out life. Europe, on the other hand, offers experience and the pleasures and risks that accompany it. "Europe" is a charming though disquieting tale, and its accompanying frontispiece expands ironically the symbolism found in the text.

So far, I have mostly explicated the content of Coburn's images, content that James himself conceived of as being most appropriate for symbolizing his texts. The images' content does indeed make them work brilliantly as symbols, yet it is important to recognize that the formal aspects of the images — attributable to Coburn's framing eye and printing skill — contribute to their success as symbols. Form and content are consciously merged so that the former works to bring into being or emphasize the latter. Formally, the photographs' subjects are structured in a manner that is carefully designed and brilliantly executed. The placement of objects in relation to each other suggests a stillness — "set stage" — yet never is there a static quality to be found in Coburn's scenes. Rather, there is a completeness in the images that comes from Coburn's careful choice of objects and their successful unification into meaningful wholes.

Coburn was faced with a difficult artistic problem. He had to make images of things and places that inherently lent themselves to the expression of symbolism in relation to the texts they were to accompany. But these symbolic relationships had to be expressed with subtle and indirect force. Consequently, James and Coburn initially had to select the objects and places that might best lend themselves to the artists' purposes. Then decisions had to be made with regard to what to include in the scene and what point of view would best bring out the meanings they sought to express. In all but the English scenes, Coburn made the final choices without James's presence — though James did have several different images to choose from after Coburn returned. With his unique, pictorialist photographer's eye, Coburn made images in which all matter that might dilute, or distract from, the pictures' meanings was excluded from the picture planes. Also Coburn understood that each subject possessed formal characteristics which could only express certain meanings when seen from a specific distance and taken from a particular point of view.

A look at some examples will illuminate Coburn's success. Coburn realized that not only the massive gate but the wall and some glimpse of a house were necessary if the essence of *The American*[28] was to be symbolized by "Faubourg St. Germain" (figure 2). These objects had to be put into a careful relation with each other if they were to function as the apt equivalent of the metaphorical wall between Christopher Newman's world and that of the Bellegarde's. An oblique shot was necessary in order for Coburn to depict visually this relationship. And an oblique viewpoint was also necessary if Coburn was to capture the exact quality of the barrier's force against Newman. Though the Bellegarde's opposition to Newman's successful suit of Madame de Cintré is formidable, this is expressed in a somewhat indirect way in the text. The Bellegardes break up the match, although precisely how they do so is ambiguous; the gate of the *porte-cochére* is closed to Newman, he is kept out of the Bellegarde's—and Madame de Cintré's—world. An image that depicted the wall through a head-on view would have contradicted the text: it had to be oblique.

On the other hand, the frontispiece to the first volume of *The Wings of the Dove*,[29] "The Doctor's Door" (figure 19), is a head-on view. Unlike "Faubourg St. Germain," however, it is intended to symbolize something in the text that is quite direct—the knowledge by Milly Theale of her own inevitable death. That death—an entrance into an unfamiliar room and an exit from a cherished life—is something that must be faced directly, and Milly does so. Only a rather monolithic frontal view of Sir Luke Strett's door (he was the bearer of the news that demands facing) could depict the bluntness of this fact. Yet, in spite of the directness of that image, the objects also allude to meanings which are subtle when expressed in pictorial form. Closed doors not only allude to Milly's soon to be closed life, but also to the closed lives of Merton Densher and Kate Croy. In this sense, the door not only suggests an ending but also a beginning, for Merton Densher's life is changed in ways that will open him up to new possibilities.

"Juliana's Court" (figure 12) is the frontispiece to *The Aspern Papers*,[30] and its expression of meaning also emerges from its formal structure. In this picture, the relationship between the small potted tree in the foreground and the partially concealed doorway in the background is crucial, and again it was set up by photographing from an oblique point of view. The small tree dominates within the picture's frame, standing just to one side of the doorway and covering the top half of it. The small tree and the doorway work as a double-edged symbols: first, the tree may be read as Juliana, and the doorway as her dark past into which we cannot gain entrance; second, we may also read the tree as Juliana's niece, Tina, and the doorway as Juliana, her dark past, and the letters that might provide a key to that past. In both readings, the tree—be it Juliana or Tina—shields the doorway, and although we can see part of it, we cannot get past the tree and penetrate the secrets that the doorway leads to. Both readings, moreover, are linked: in order to get to the Aspen papers the narrator must get to, and then by, Juliana; and in order to get to Juliana the narrator must get past Tina. The readings seem to be suggested by the caption, "Juliana's Court," a title that works as a pun. On the one hand, it describes a place owned by someone named Juliana, and it is part of the set stage for the story; but it also alludes to a courtship or wooing, and in this sense, it may refer to the unnamed narrator's wooing of Juliana's niece in order to get hold of the Aspern papers. Of course, the court fails, for the narrator does not marry Tina nor does he get the papers—and Aspern's secrets remain beyond the dark doorway.

James and Coburn succeeded again and again in creating meanings through the right combination of the formal structure of their pictures and the content. And it is clear that Coburn's contribution—the intelligent structuring of these images—was as important as the subject matter that was reproduced.

It is fitting that a discussion of the frontispiece to *The Golden Bowl*[31] should end this chapter, for this work was the last complete novel James wrote, and it is the work with which James himself chose to end his Edition. The frontispiece to these two volumes are the only ones he discussed in his prefaces, and his comments give us insight into to what these images meant in James's mind. Thus, his words are worth repeating. About the frontispiece to the first volume, "The Curiosity Shop," James wrote:

> On the question . . . of the proper preliminary compliment to the first volume of "The Golden Bowl" we easily felt that nothing would so serve as a view of the small shop in which the Bowl is first encountered.
>
> The problem thus was thrilling, for though the small shop was but a shop of the mind, of the author's projected world, in which objects are primarily related to each other, and therefore not "taken from" a particular establishment anywhere, only an image distilled and intensified, as it were, from a drop of the essence of such establishments in general, our need . . . prescribed a concrete, independent, vivid instance, the instance that should oblige us by the marvel of an accidental rightness. It might so easily be wrong—by the act of being at all. It would have to be in the first place what London and chance and an extreme improbability should have made it, and then it would have to let us truthfully read into it the Prince's and Charlotte's and the Princess's visits.[32]

And regarding the second volume's frontispiece, "Portland Place," James continued:

> It was equally obvious that for the second volume of the same fiction nothing would so nobly serve as some generalised vision of Portland Place. Both our limit and the very extent of our occasion, however, lay in the fact that, unlike wanton designers, we had, not to "create" but simply to recognise—recognise, that is, with the last fineness. The thing was to induce the vision of Portland Place *to* generalise itself. This is precisely, however, the fashion after which the prodigious city, as I have called it, does on occasion meet halfway those forms of intelligence of it that *it* recognises. All of which meant that at a given moment the great featureless Philistine vista would itself perform a miracle, would become interesting, for a splendid atmospheric hour, as only London knows how; and that our business would be then to understand.[33]

The most ambitious symbol in *The Golden Bowl's* text is the object referred to in the novel's title. This object is a gilt crystal bowl which has a crack in it. It is first discovered by the Prince and Charlotte in the shop depicted in the first frontispiece, "The Curiosity Shop" (figure 23). Because it is flawed, they do not buy it. Much later, however, this object is purchased by Maggie, the Prince's husband, and its purchase leads Maggie eventually to discover that the Prince and Charlotte were, and are, lovers. It is this knowledge that enables Maggie and her father to decide to live apart and give their respective marriages a chance finally to develop into fuller human relationships.

Though the frontispiece depicts the shop where the symbolic golden bowl is found, it serves an even broader symbolic purpose. For long before Maggie purchases the bowl, it is apparent that her father and she had purchased one other European treasure that was like the bowl—the Prince. Shortly after Maggie and the Prince are married, Adam Verver says to the Prince, "As it is, for living with, you're a pure and perfect crystal" (XXIII, 138)—and a gilded one at that. The Prince responds with a foreboding note that he is glad he is perfect, for occasionally crystal is flawed even when it appears to be perfect. Though Prince Amerigo is indeed flawed despite his apparent surface perfection, he is at first regarded as a precious object to the Ververs. He had been obtained from Europe—which in itself is a kind of "shop of the mind" to the Ververs. Hence, the marriage between the Prince and Maggie is more proprietary and aesthetic in nature than it is human. Only when Maggie learns that both the Prince and their marriage have—like the golden bowl—cracks, can she move beyond her fascination with surfaces, approach the Prince as a human being, and try to save her marriage.

The other frontispiece, "Portland Place" (figure 24), is an equally subtle symbol, and it is just as shrewdly related to the text's symbolism as the first frontispiece is. Visually, it alludes to two things in the text. The obvious one is a set stage of the book—Portland Place is where the Prince and Maggie reside. The second allusion is more complex, however, and what is symbolized relates to a reverie that Maggie has. Shortly after the Prince and Charlotte have returned from a trip to the country, Maggie finds herself alone. The quality of the relationships among Adam Verver, Charlotte, the Prince, and Maggie have just been described. This family is compared to a four-wheeled coach: Charlotte's appearance on the scene was needed to provide the fourth wheel for the coach so that it would ride smoothly. And this has lightened Maggie's load, for now that her father has a wife (Charlotte), Maggie can rest. Suddenly, Maggie's thinking is jarred by an absurd, fantastic vision:

> She might have been watching the family coach pass and noting that somehow Amerigo and Charlotte were pulling it while she and her father were not so much as pushing. They were seated inside together, dandling the Principino and holding him up to the window to see and be seen, like an infant positively royal; so that the exertion was *all* with the

others. Maggie found in this image a repeated challenge; again and yet again she paused before the fire: after which, each time, in the manner of one for whom a strong light has suddenly broken, she gave herself to a livelier movement. She had seen herself at last, in the picture she was studying, suddenly jump from the coach; whereupon, frankly, with the wonder of the sight, her eyes opened wider and her heart stood still for a moment. She looked at the person so acting as if this person were somebody else, waiting with intensity to see what would follow. The person had taken a decision. . . . Only how was the decision to be applied? — what in particular would the figure in the picture do? (XXIV, 23-24)

Suddenly, as Maggie looks toward the middle of the room, Amerigo reappears, and the vision is broken. As the result of her vision, and Amerigo's sudden reassuring presence, Maggie vows to try and right her neglect of her husband and Charlotte, but her decision is complicated by her subsequent discovery of their adulterous relationship.

The problem is ultimately dealt with when Maggie's father decides to leave England, taking Charlotte with him. It is this act that is symbolized by the frontispiece. A two-wheeled coach is pictured from behind as it is leaving Portland Place. We immediately understand that the family cannot remain as a single four-wheeled coach; it must divide itself and ride in separate two-wheeled coaches, each going its separate way, each wheel carrying its share of the burden. So it is with the two marriages, though where each marriage will go, we are not told. We are only left with the recognition that new knowledge has been acquired and that, like the haze the coach is moving toward in the frontispiece, there are unknown possibilities ahead. The frontispiece is an extraordinary summary of these things, a perfect echoing of the quality and atmosphere implicit in the family's decision to separate.

It is also, on another level, an utterly appropriate image with which to end the Edition. A stunning black coach, hiding its passengers from our view, moving away not only from the reader's view but also from the streets that gave Henry James so much material for his fictions. Whether James conceived that the symbol might also work in this larger way is unclear; yet, it does work that way for us — the artist, James, with his masterwork completed, being carried out of his Edition, his collection of his life's work, into an ambiguous future.

It is entirely possible that my explications of the pictures and texts have occasionally been pushed too hard, culling implausible meanings from the visual-verbal relationships that James called into being. But it is also possible that the picture-text meanings have been underexplicated. There is inherently a problem in interpreting the symbolism represented in two separate but related media — the one visual, the other verbal. As Gombrich points out, they are so different in the way they function, and consequently when they are put together, an unrecognized problem may emerge regarding their working relationship. By appearing alongside verbal texts and being explicitly related to those texts through captions (their titles do work as captions), the frontispiece pictures are given contexts that help guide us in our interpretation of their meanings. In practice, though, the pictures often open up the meanings of the texts, too — as for example in the frontispiece to volume two of *The Princess Casamassima*, discussed above. This is because, as photographs of recognizable objects and places, the frontispieces' contexts are broadened by the reader's knowledge of the world. They have meanings that exist outside the ones provided by the text and the author. To complicate things even further, a larger, broader literary context exists, because the images are also part of a whole — a selected edition of Henry James's works. Taken together, these contexts ensure that readers will respond to the frontispieces in more open ended ways, bringing to their interpretations thoughts and insights that could not have been predicted by the images' makers. (This is, of course, true of verbal images too.) Yet, though these additional, unpredictable contexts of meanings inevitably attach themselves to the texts, visual and verbal, and allow meanings that my go beyond the author's intentions, it nonetheless must be understood that there are limits to interpretation — it must not go beyond what the visual and verbal texts themselves may reasonably suggest.

To what extent James recognized the problematic aspect of interpreting visual and verbal texts is unclear. Obviously, by using symbolic photogravure frontispieces, James introduced a new dimension of meaning into his works, occasionally altering the meanings of his verbal texts and violating his own cautionary rule about the use of illustration. Still, if he did not fully understand this, it does not particularly matter, since he was the dominant cocreator of the new symbols. His vision contributed importantly to their making, and if a new dimension of meaning was the result, it was entirely in keeping with the spirit of the texts and the subtle, multilayered meanings already present in his art. In the final analysis, Henry James's New York Edition — his most ambitious garden — was not disturbed by another's cultivating hands and mind. It maintained its integrity. It remains essentially *James's* garden in the end.

Epilogue

When Henry James began planning his New York Edition, his enthusiasm was high. "My idea," he wrote Scribner's on 30 July 1905, "has been to arrange for a handsome 'definitive edition' of the greater number of my novels and tales"; he wanted "to revise everything carefully"; he wished to include in each volume "a frank critical talk about its subject, its origin, its place in the whole artistic chain, and embodying, in short, whatever of interest there may be to be said about it."[1] Finally, he desired "a single very good plate in each volume, only one, but of thoroughly fine quality."[2] To one of his friends, he wrote with delight about the "matter of a 'handsome' collective (and *selective*) Edition Définitive of my writings."[3] And when the first volumes began to appear in 1907, he communicated his enormous "pleasure" to his publisher: "I am delighted with the appearance, beauty and dignity of the Book—am in short almost ridiculously proud of it. The whole is a perfect felicity, so let us go on rejoicing."[4] However, less than a year later, on 23 October 1908, James registered deep disappointment to his agent, James B. Pinker, regarding the sales of the Edition: "I am afraid my anti-climax *has* come from the fact that since the publication of the Series began no dimmest light or 'lead' as to its actualities or possibilities of profit has reached me."[5] And near the end of his life, he would lament that his "monument (like Ozymandias) . . . has never had the least intelligent critical justice done to it—or any sort of critical attention at all paid to it."[6]

James was correct about the critical response to the New York Edition. Only the first few volumes were reviewed in periodicals like *Dial*, *Nation*, *Outlook*, *Literary Digest*, and the *New York Times*—all in 1908.[7] And these reviews generally expressed mixed feelings about James's late manner, acknowledging James's accomplishments as a writer but somehow expressing disapproval. "Mr. James's world," wrote Edward E. Hale, Jr., "may seem to many a sequestered, perverted, exasperating world, and yet to him it evidently lives."[8] The problem, as Hale saw it, was that "James wrote better English thirty years ago than he writes to-day. But he does not think so himself, and so he has done his best to put the old dears into modern dress."[9] Another reviewer noted James's "exasperating style," yet still found the prefaces interesting.[10] Indeed, the reviewers spent much time discussing the prefaces, and one even suggested that these furnished "the key to the whole admirable work; and show it as a goodly structure, reared upon a coherent plan, tho years have been expended in the fashioning of it."[11] Reviewers also dwelled upon the textual revisions James had made, and spent much space summarizing the novels under review.

The frontispieces, however, were barely noticed by reviewers. The *Literary Digest* reviewer noted approvingly, "Nothing could be more satisfactory to the lover of a great writer's work than the fine, ample, and dignified volumes that make up this edition. The type . . . is beautifully simple and clear, the paper of agreeable texture. . . . The initial volume contains a fine portrait of Mr. James; the others it is promised, will present as frontispieces 'portraits' of some scene, situation, view, edifice, or monument actually existing and more or less completely representative of the *local* of the text. All these are specimens of the work of that sensitive artist-photographer, Alvin L. Coburn."[12] And Hale, in his *Dial* review, ended with a very complimentary discussion of Coburn's images—though without mentioning Coburn by name. "It was a very happy idea," he noted,

> to illustrate each volume with "portraits of some scene, situation, etc., representative of the locality of the text," and the execution has admirably carried out the plan: the pictures are an immense addition to the novels. Such as are accustomed to impressions of the spirit of place will look long and with intense pleasure at the picture of the Faubourg Saint Germains [*sic*] in "The American,"—it almost takes the place of the novel. People who feel they have lost something in the modernistic text may feel that they have gained something here, and so almost with some of the others. The spirit of place,—how much it may be in a novel![13]

The frontispieces, then, were viewed either as decoration—like the typeface—or as "visual aids" that might help some readers grasp the meaning of the particular book.

No, James could not have been pleased with such reviews. They were uncomprehending; somehow they missed the point of James's monumental achievement as he summed it up in 1915: "the artistic problem involved in my scheme was a deep and exquisite one, and moreover, was as I held, very effectively solved. Only it took such time—*and* such taste—in other words such aesthetic light. No more commercially thankless job of the literary order was (Prefaces and all—*they* of a thanklessness!) accordingly ever achieved."[14] He had agonized over those prefaces, meticulously revised his texts, and consciously brought into being the lovely frontispieces made by

Coburn. He had every right to be disappointed with the public response to his "Edition Définitive."

Eventually, the New York Edition grew into twenty-six volumes, the last two being added to the collection in 1917 after James's death. These volumes, *The Ivory Tower* and *The Sense of the Past*, were uncompleted works at the time James died and were never intended to become a part of the Edition. Nonetheless, they were edited by Percy Lubbock and added to the original twenty-four. These last two books also contain frontispieces – but not ones made by Coburn. Whether or not James would have been satisfied with the images themselves or with the way they work with their respective texts is an unanswerable question. One thing is clear, though. These additional images were not a part of the fruits of the collaboration between Henry James and Alvin Langdon Coburn. For that reason, they really have little place in my discussion of the collaboration.

It is clear that James *chose* Alvin Langdon Coburn to illustrate his Edition. And James was extremely satisfied with the results, commemorating Coburn's achievement in the preface to *To Golden Bowl* and acknowledging Coburn as "my fellow artist."[15] James *had* changed his views sufficiently to recognize that photography could be an art. But lest too much be implied by that change of heart, it is only fair to note that James still held reservations about the medium. Though he admired Coburn's work very much, he could still make the following observation: "Your clouds are very artful and beautiful," James wrote Coburn in 1912, but "Photography insists, for me, in remaining, at best but photography."[16] Photography had been admitted into "the Palace of Art" by Henry James – but not into its upper chambers.

Despite the reception of the Edition by the public and by reviewers, despite the posthumous interference with the Edition's final shape, and despite James's reservations about photography, the conception and execution of the New York Edition was masterful. The decision to use photographic frontispieces was courageous and displayed an uncanny aesthetic insight into the potential of the medium. The wedding of photographs and texts in a symbolic, as opposed to descriptive, way was ingenious. With its inception, a new art form was suggested – one that has only occasionally been pursued. *Let Us Now Praise Famous Men* (1941) by James Agee and Walker Evans is one example of this hybrid art; so too are the photograph-text experiments by Wright Morris, works such as *God's Country and My People* (1968). Perhaps the wedding of photographs and texts has not been much done because of the modern dominance of the cinema, another literary-visual form. Perhaps it is another "lost art." Whatever the case,

Henry James's use of photographic symbols as illustrations for his master-work is still an important landmark in the history of art.

Notes

Prologue

1. Review of *The Novels and Tales of Henry James*, New York Edition, *Literary Digest* 36 (1908), p. 418.

2. Edward E. Hale, Jr., "The Rejuvenation of Henry James." Review of *The Novels and Tales of Henry James*, New York Edition, *Dial* 44 (1908), p. 174.

3. Leon Edel, *The Life of Henry James: The Master (1901–1916)*, vol. 5 (Philadelphia and New York: Lippincott, 1972), pp. 131–32.

4. Letter from Henry James to Elizabeth Robins, 28 March 1906. In *Theater and Friendship, Some Henry James Letters*, ed. Elizabeth Robins (New York: Putnam's, 1932), p. 256.

5. See letter from Henry James to W. D. Howells, 17 August 1908. In *The Letters of Henry James*, vol. 2, ed. Percy Lubbock (New York: Scribner's, 1920), p. 99.

6. For a succinct description of the process, see Beaumont Newhall, *The History of Photography: From 1839 to the Present Day*, 4th ed. (New York: Museum of Modern Art, 1964), p. 98.

7. Henry James, "Preface to *The Golden Bowl*." In *The Art of the Novel* by Henry James, ed. R. P. Blackmur (1934: rpt. New York: Scribner's 1947), pp. 331–33.

8. See Neil Harris, "Iconography and Intellectual History: The Half-Tone Effect." In *New Directions in American Intellectual History*, eds. John Higham and Paul K. Conkin (Baltimore and London: Johns Hopkins University Press, 1979), pp. 196–211.

9. Robert Doty, *Photo-Secession: Photography as a Fine Art* (Rochester, N. Y.: George Eastman House, 1960), p. 9; see also, William Innes Homer, *Alfred Stieglitz and the Photo-Secession* (Boston: Little, Brown and Company, 1983), passim.

10. See Henry James, "Black and White." In *Picture and Text* by Henry James (New York: Harper and Brothers, 1893), pp. 1 ff. See also Betsy Lynn Jablow, "Illustrated Texts from Dickens to James," Ph.D. diss. Stanford Unviersity, 1978, pp. 1–7, 8 ff.

11. James, "Preface to *The Golden Bowl*," pp. 331–33.

12. This is James's term for illustration of this type (Henry James, *A Small Boy and Others* [New York: Charles Scribner's Sons, 1913], p. 261).

Chapter 1

1. Alvin Langdon Coburn, "Illustrating Henry James by Photography," London: B.B.C. Third Programme, 17 July 1953, p. 1. I am indebted to Beaumont Newhall for a copy of the B.B.C. broadcast transcript. See also *Alvin Langdon Coburn, Photographer: An Autobiography*, eds. Helmut and Alison Gernsheim (London: Faber and Faber, 1966), pp. 52–60. All biographical data on Coburn comes from this source unless otherwise noted. Finally, see unpublished letter from Henry James to Alvin Langdon Coburn, 27 January 1905, in the Henry James Collection, Clifton Waller Barrett Library, University of Virginia. For other discussions of the collaboration itself, see Joseph J. Firebaugh, "Coburn: Henry James's Photographer," *American Quarterly* 7 (1955), pp. 215–33; Edel, *The Master*, vol. 5, pp. 333–39; Jablow, "Illustrated Texts," pp. 172 ff; and Charles Higgins, "Photographic Aperture: Coburn's Frontispieces to James's New York Edition," *American Literature* 53 (1982), pp. 661–75.

2. Coburn, "Illustrating Henry James," p. 1.

3. Edel, *The Master*, vol. 5, p. 333. All biographical data on Henry James comes from this source unless otherwise noted.

4. James to Scribner's, 12 June 1906. In Leon Edel, ed., *Henry James Letters, 1895–1916*, vol 4 (Cambridge, Mass. and London: Harvard University Press, 1984), p. 408. See unpublished letters from W. C. B[rownell] to James, 1 June 1906; and from W. C. B. to James, 28 August 1906 — both in the Charles Scribner's Sons Archive, Princeton University Library.

5. Edel, *The Master*, vol. 5, p. 334. See James to Scribner's, 12 June 1906, and James to James B. Pinker, 14 June 1906, for expressions of James's reluctance (in Edel, ed., *Henry James Letters*, vol. 4, pp. 407–11). Regarding the photographic frontispieces, see W. C. B. to James, 28 August 1906, Scribner's Archive, Princeton, for an expression of Brownell's approval.

6. Coburn, "Illustrating Henry James," p. 1. Evidently, James agreed, for his fourth letter to Coburn (of fifty such pieces of correspondence) was warm and personal (see James to Coburn, 11 July 1906, in James Collection, Virginia).

7. After all, James felt intensely close to sculptor Hendrick Anderson but did not respect his work (see Edel, *The Master*, vol. 5, pp. 100–104).

8. Edel, *The Master*, vol. 5, p. 334.

9. Coburn, "Illustrating Henry James," p. 1.

10. Edel, *The Master*, vol. 5, p. 334.

11. Nancy Newhall, "Introduction." In *A Portfolio of Sixteen Photographs* by Alvin Langdon Coburn, ed. Nancy Newhall (Rochester, N.Y.: George Eastman House, 1962), p. 7.

12. See particularly, James to Scribner's, 9 May 1906; W. C. B. to James, 1 June 1906; Pinker to Scribner's, 13 July 1906; W. C. B. to James, 28 August 1906 — all in Scribner's Archive, Princeton; and, James to Scribner's, 12 June 1906 (in Edel, ed., *Henry James Letters*, vol. 4, pp. 407–9).

13. James to Coburn, 23 March 1906, James Collection, Virginia.

14. James to Scribner's, 9 May 1906. In Edel, ed., *Henry James Letters*, vol. 4, pp. 402–4.

15. James to Coburn, 8 June 1906, James Collection, Virginia; and James to Scribner's, 12 June 1906 (in Edel, ed., *Henry James Letters*, vol. 4, pp. 407–9).

16. Coburn's recollection puts the date at 12 June (see Coburn, "Illustrating Henry James," p. 1). The letter from James to Scribner's, 12 June 1906, records the date as 11 June (in Edel, ed., *Henry James Letters*, vol. 4, pp. 407–9).

17. See James to Coburn, 26 June 1906, James Collection, Virginia. James had earlier been hopeful that this second sitting would yield good results (James to Scribner's, 12 June 1906, in Edel, ed., *Henry James Letters*, vol. 4, pp. 407–9).

18. See James to Pinker, 14 June 1906 (in Edel, ed., *Henry James Letters*, vol. 4, pp. 409–10). The exact date Coburn was invited to engage in the collaboration remains unclear. Coburn simply says that after the making of the portrait of James at Rye, the author "subsequently suggested that I should make photographs to be used in other volumes of the edition" (Coburn, "Illustrating Henry James," p. 1). See also Pinker to Scribner's, 13 July 1906; and W. C. B. to James, 28 August 1906—Scribner's Archive, Princeton.

19. James to Coburn, 26 June 1906, James Collection, Virginia.

20. Pinker to Scribner's, 13 July 1906, Scribner's Archive, Princeton.

21. Coburn, "Illustrating Henry James," p. 3; James to Coburn, undated [11 July 1906], James Collection, Virginia.

22. James to Coburn, 3 September 1906, James Collection, Virginia.

23. Coburn, "Illustrating Henry James," p. 2.

24. James to Coburn, 2 September 1906 (but not mailed until 2 October 1906), James Collection, Virginia.

25. Coburn, "Illustrating Henry James," p. 2. See unpublished manuscript by Henry James, "For the Paris Subjects" [2 October 1906]. In Edel, ed., *Henry James Letters*, vol. 4, pp. 416–18.

26. James, "For the Paris Subjects." See also, Coburn, "Illustrating Henry James," p. 2.

27. James to Coburn, "For the Paris Subjects." In Edel, ed., *Henry James Letters*, vol. 4, p. 417.

28. Ibid.

29. Ibid, p. 412.

30. Ibid., pp. 417–18.

31. Ibid.

32. James, "Preface to *The Golden Bowl*," p. 333.

33. James to Coburn, 9 October 1906, James Collection, Virginia.

34. Coburn, "Illustrating Henry James," p. 2.

35. Permission was granted. See unpublished document from Hertford House to Henry James, "Wallace Collection. Permission to Photograph," 8 December 1906, James Collection, Virginia.

36. James to Coburn, 6 December 1906; and James to Coburn, 7 December 1906. In Edel, ed., *Henry James Letters*, vol. 4, pp. 426–30. An odd and unexplainable thing occurred in the latter letter. James listed the number of novels that were to appear in two volumes, the number that were to appear in only one volume, and the number of short novels and tales that were to appear in one volume. These add up to twenty-three volumes in all. He also asserted that a total of twenty-three frontispieces were required. But before going into all this, James wrote, "there *are* meanwhile, to be Twenty-Four Volumes." Perhaps it was merely a slip of the pen, for as late as 5 March 1907, he wrote to Grace Norton that there were going to be twenty-three volumes in the edition (in Lubbock, ed., *Letters of Henry James*, vol. 2, p. 70). Perhaps, though, it was not just a mistake; perhaps James was already feeling the pressure — subconsiously — to expand the edition into twenty-four volumes.

37. James to Coburn, 7 December 1906. In Edel, ed., *Henry James Letters*, vol. 4, pp. 429–30.

38. James to Coburn, 9 December 1906. In Edel, ed., *Henry James Letters*, vol. 4, pp. 4–31.

39. Edel, *The Master*, vol. 5, p. 321.

40. James to Coburn, 22 October 1906, James Collection, Virginia.

41. James to Coburn, 11 December 1906, James Collection, Virginia. Evidently, "St. John's Wood," "The Curiosity Shop," and "Portland Place" were photographed, too (see James to Coburn, 6 December 1906. In Edel, ed., *Henry James Letters*, vol. 4, p. 428).

42. Coburn, "Illustrating Henry James," p. 3.

43. Ibid.

44. He was also an inveterate bicycler. See Edel, *The Master, V*, pp. 21–24. See also Ralph F. Bogardus, "The Photographer's Eye: Henry James and *The American Scene*," *History of Photography* 8 (1984), pp. 179–96. The term *flâneur* is applied to Walker Evans by Robert Sobieszek, "Another Look at Walker Evans," *Art in America* 60 (March-April, 1972), pp. 120–22.

45. James to Coburn, 6 December 1906. In Edel, ed., *Henry James Letters*, vol. 4, p. 426.

46. Ibid., pp. 426–27.

47. The phrase is W. D. Howells's (see W. D. Howells, *London Films* [New York and London: Harper, 1905], p. 2).

48. James to Coburn, 6 December 1906. In Edel, ed., *Henry James Letters*, vol. 4, p. 427.

49. Ibid, p. 428.

50. James to Coburn, 27 December 1906, James Collection, Virginia.

51. James to Coburn, 2 January 1907, James Collection, Virginia.

52. Compare this with James's response to Joseph Pennell, regarding the illustrations made for "London" (1888), in which James indicates that he was fully aware that he could not share in the hand artist's work: James wrote, resignedly, "as for the illustrations I have really nothing to suggest save that you follow your own fancy . . . do your own London, and it will be sufficiently mine" (James to Pennell, 6 January 1888. In *Selected Letters of Henry James*, ed. Leon Edel [New York: Farrar, Straus and Cudahy, 1955], p. 92).

53. Coburn, "Illustrating Henry James," p. 3

54. James, "Preface to *The Golden Bowl*," pp. 331–33.

55. Ibid., p. 333.

56. Coburn, "Illustrating Henry James," pp. 3–4. The exact time is unclear from the record. What is clear is that by 6 December 1906, at least three London subjects were made (see James to Coburn, 6 December 1906. In Edel, ed., *Henry James Letters*, vol. 4, p. 428).

57. James, "Preface to *The Golden Bowl*," p. 333.

58. Ibid., p. 335.

59. Coburn, "Illustrating Henry James," p. 4.

60. James, "Preface to *The Golden Bowl*," p. 334.

61. Coburn, "Illustrating Henry James," p. 4.

62. Ibid.

63. Ibid, p. 5.

64. Ibid. It must be noted that there is some discrepancy regarding which English images Coburn was referring to. He identified them as "The English House" (for volume of *The Portrait of a Lady*) and "Some of the Spoils" (for *The Spoils of Poynton*). But recall that the letter from James to Coburn, 11 December 1906, James Collection, Virginia, makes it clear that the latter photograph was made in early December 1906.

65. James to Howells, 17 August 1908. In Lubbock, ed., *Letters of Henry James*, vol. 2, p. 100.

66. Edel, *The Master*, vol. 5, p. 323. Edel also discusses why James originally settled on twenty-three (pp. 321–23).

67. Ibid., pp. 323–24, for the reasons why James was disappointed.

68. James to Coburn, 19 December 1908, James Collection, Virginia.

69. Ibid.

70. Ibid.

71. James to Coburn, 22 January 1909, James Collection, Virginia.

72. James to Coburn, 29 April 1913, James Collection, Virginia.

73. Ibid.

74. James to Coburn, 2 May 1913, James Collection, Virginia.

75. Edel, *The Master*, vol. 5, pp. 433–34.

76. James to Gosse, 25 August 1915. In Lubbock, ed., *Letters of Henry James*, vol. 2, p. 497.

77. James to Gosse, 25 August 1915.

78. James to Coburn, 22 January 1909, James Collection, Virginia.

79. James, "Preface to *The Golden Bowl*," p. 333.

80. Ibid., p. 331.

81. Quoted in Edel, *The Master*, vol. 5, p. 324.

82. Ibid.

Chapter 2

1. Hale, "The Rejuvenation of Henry James," p. 176.

2. James, "Preface to *The Golden Bowl*," p. 331.

3. Ibid., pp. 332–33.

4. Ibid., p. 333.

5. Ibid.

6. Ibid.

7. Ibid., p. 334.

8. Regrettably, the frontispieces were excluded from the third printing of James collected works. See Henry James, *The Novels and Tales of Henry James: New York Edition*, 26 vols. (1907–09, 1917; rpt. New York: Charles Scribner's Sons, 1937). Occasionally, some of the images have been reproduced separately — for example, three of the frontispieces were included in Coburn, *Alvin Langdon Coburn, Photographer*; two appeared in Coburn, *A Portfolio of Sixteen Photographs*, ed. Nancy Newhall — but never has the entire set been published apart from the Edition.

Chapter 3

1. James, "Preface to *The Golden Bowl*," pp. 331–33.

2. William Wordsworth, "Illustrated Books and Newspapers." In *The Complete Poetical Works of William Wordsworth: Grasmere Edition*, vol. 9 (Boston and New York: Houghton Mifflin and Co., 1911), p. 246. The overwhelming presence of illustrated literature is attested to by the number of essays and books on the subject that were written during the 1880s and 1890s. See for example, Charles T. Congdon, "Over-Illustration," *North American Review* 139 (1884), pp. 480–91; Sidney Fairfield, "The Tyranny of the Pictorial," *Lippincott's Monthly Magazine* 55 (1895), pp. 861–64; Philip Gilbert Hamerton, "Book Illustration." In *Portfolio Papers* by Philip Gilbert Hamerton (London: Seeley and Co., 1889), pp. 283–386; Henry James, *Picture and Text*; Gleeson White, *English Illustration, "The Sixties": 1855–1870* (1897; rpt. Bath: Kingsmead Reprints, 1970); and Alfred Pollard, *Early Illustrated Books*, rev. ed. (1897; rpt. New York: Haskell House, 1968). As the first epigraph to part two of this study shows, W. D. Howells was also aware of the medium (see W. D. Howells, *A Hazard of New Fortunes* [1890; rpt. New York: New American Library, 1965], pp. 13, 122).

3. The Chinese also produced illustrated books from about the thirteenth or fourteenth centuries B.C. See David Bland, *A History of Book Illustration: The Illustrated Manuscript and the Printed Book* (Berkeley and Los Angeles: University of California Press, 1969), pp. 20 ff. See also E. H. Gombrich, *Art and Illusion: A Study in the Psychology of Pictorial Representation* (1960; rpt. Princeton: Princeton University Press, 1969), pp. 78 ff.

4. See Percy Muir, *Victorian Illustrated Books* (London: B. T. Batesford, Ltd., 1971), p. 1; Pollard, *Early Illustrated Books*, *passim*; Geoffrey Wakeman, *Victorian Book Illustration: The Technical Revolution* (Detroit: Gale Research Co., 1973), *passim*; Frank Weitenkampf, *The Illustrated Book* (Cambridge, Mass.: Harvard University Press, 1938), p. 16; and Congdon, "Over-Illustration," pp. 480–81. David Bland suggests, "Drawing and writing . . . developed simultaneously from a common origin" (*History of*

Book Illustration, p. 15). He is speaking, of course, of the ideogram. Bland goes on: "In a sense then all art is illustrative and in that sense illustration preceded literature. The earliest illustration was simply aimed to reach those who could not read, and this function continued right down to the fifteenth-century days of the printed block books" (*History of Book Illustration*, p. 15). Information regarding the history of illustration comes from these sources unless otherwise noted.

5. Blake's *The Marriage of Heaven and Hell* (1792) is a notable example. See W. J. Thomas Mitchell, *Blake's Composite Art: A Study of the Illuminated Poetry* (Princeton: Princeton University Press, 1978).

6. James R. Harvey, *Victorian Novelists and Their Illustrators* (New York: New York University Press, 1971), p. 8.

7. Ibid., pp. 12, 15.

8. See J. H. Plumb, "Henry Fielding: The Journey through Gin Lane," *Horizon* 6 (Winter 1964), pp. 78–79. Alain-René LeSage's *Histoire de Gil Blas de Santillane* (1835) and Miguel de Cervantes Saavedra's *L'Ingenieux hidalgo Don Quichotte de la Manche* (1836–37) were illustrated by Louis Viardot (see Beaumont Newhall, "The Vignetists," *American Magazine of Art* 28 [January 1935], pp. 31–35). An edition of Goethe's *Faust* was illustrated by Delacroix in 1828 (see Weitenkampf, *Illustrated Book*, p. 144). The original edition of James Fenimore Cooper's *The Pioneers* (1823) was also published with illustrations (see Henry Nash Smith, *Virgin Land: The American West as Symbol and Myth* [1950; rpt. Cambridge, Mass.: Harvard University Press, 1970], p. xv). Finally, an 1831 edition of Tobias Smollett's *The Expedition of Humphrey Clinker*, 2 vols. (London: Cochrane and Rickersgill), was illustrated by Cruikshank. This edition was owned by James, and is part of a collection of James's books housed at the Houghton Library, Harvard.

9. Muir, *Victorian Illustrated Books*, p. 89.

10. Harvey, *Victorian Novelists*, p. 44. An example of this is found in the work of Mrs. Trollope.

11. Harvey attests to this (p. 50).

12. Muir, *Victorian Illustrated Books*, p. 123. See also Muir, p. 100; and Mason Jackson, *The Pictorial Press: Its Origin and Progress* (London: Hurst and Blackett, 1885), pp. 284 ff.

13. Jablow, "Illustrated Texts," p. 2.

14. Christoph K. Lohmann, "The Pictorial Revolution: Text, Picture, and Photography in American Magazines, 1875–1900." Unpublished manuscript read at the meetings of the American Studies Association, Philadelphia, 4 November 1983, pp. 12–13.

15. Beginning with the 1860s, mechanization of the illustration industry took place also when the processes used were revolutionized. It became widespread practice to transfer drawings onto wood blocks (used for wood engravings) through the photographic process. The real revolution, however, occurred when the halftone process began to be used in the late 1880s and 1890s. For a thorough discussion of the changes in the reproduction processes during the nineteenth century, see Estelle Jussim, *Visual Communication and the Graphic Arts* (New York: Bowker, 1974), pp. 21–76. See also, Wakeman, *Victorian Book Illustration*, pp. 69 ff.; and Harris, "Halftone Effect," passim.

16. See Arnold Hauser, *The Social History of Art: Naturalism, Impressionism, the Film Age,* *vol. 4* (1951; rpt. New York: Vintage-Random, n.d.), for an analysis of this phenomenon. See also, Herbert J. Muller, *Freedom in the Modern World: The 19th and 20th Centuries* (New York: Harper-Colophon, 1966), pp. 38, 249. Dickens, for example, was often read to workers during the workday; they would collect a few coins and hire someone to read to them on the factory floor (Hauser, *Social History, vol. 4,* pp. 123-24.

17. Harvey, *Victorian Novelists,* p. 3.

18. Weitenkampf, *Illustrated Book,* p. 144. Certainly, there are exceptions; for example, William Blake, Delacroix, and Doré.

19. Other gifted caricaturists were Gillray and Rowlandson. For an analysis of caricature, see E. H. Gombrich, *Art and Illusion,* pp. 330-58. Daumier's achievement is discussed in Henry James, "Honoré Daumier." In *The Painter's Eye: Notes and Essays on the Pictorial Arts* by Henry James, ed. John L. Sweeney (London: Rupert Hart-Davis, 1956), pp. 229-43. Gavarni is discussed in Charles Baudelaire, "Some French Caricaturists." In *The Mirror of Art: Critical Studies* by Charles Baudelaire, ed. Jonathan Mayne (London: Phaidon, 1955), pp. 171-73.

20. James, *Small Boy,* p. 117; see also, pp. 118-20. It should be noted that memoirs, because written well after the events took place and hence based on memory, do contain distortions of emphasis as well as of fact. Still, they give us an approximate sense of the details of one's life as well as important insight into the developing mind of the subject.

21. Ibid., p. 63.

22. Henry James, *Notes of a Son and Brother* (New York: Charles Scribner's Sons, 1914), pp. 18, 23, 336; Henry James, "London," *Century* 37 (1888), p. 220.

23. James, *Small Boy,* p. 261.

24. Ibid., pp. 262-63.

25. Ibid., p. 96.

26. Ibid., p. 113.

27. Ibid, p. 204.

28. Ibid., pp. 64-65.

29. Ibid., pp. 309-10. James not only vividly and fondly recalled the work of "Phiz," Cruikshank, and Hogarth, but also remembered that of George DuMaurier, J. S. Millais, and Gavarni (see James, *Notes of a Son,* pp. 18, 23, 336). James also mentioned Bancroft as an illustrator (James, *Notes of a Son,* pp. 336-39). Gavarni is discussed in James, *Small Boy,* pp. 18-19. See also, Henry James, "George DuMaurier." In *Partial Portraits* by Henry James (1888; rpt. New York: Haskell House, 1968), p. 327, where James remembered himself as "a silent devotee of *Punch*," the magazine in which DuMaurier's work appeared so often.

30. James, *Small Boy,* p. 263. See also, Leon Edel, *The Life of Henry James: The Untried Years (1843-1870),* vol. 1 (Philadelphia and New York: Lippincott, 1953), pp. 161-63.

31. James as an art critic is intelligently discussed in Viola Hopkins Winner, *Henry James and the Visual Arts* (Charlottesville: University Press of Virginia, 1970), pp. 48-58. For a collection of James's art criticism, see Sweeney, ed., *Painter's Eye.*

32. Harvey, *Victorian Novelists*, pp. 162–63. For a penetrating discussion of the differences between caricature and drawing that strives to be literal in its representation, see Gombrich, *Art and Illusion*, pp. 345–55.

33. Holbrook Jackson, *The Eighteen Nineties: A Review of Art and Ideas at the Close of the Nineteenth Century* (London: G. Richards, 1913), p. 279.

34. Ibid., pp. 280–81; Harvey, *Victorian Novelists*, pp. 160–61. Walter Crane, whose book on illustration originally came out in 1896, blamed the new techniques of photographic reproduction for the change. Photographic reproduction methods "transformed the system of reproduction of illustrations and designs for books, magazines, and newspapers," Crane wrote; and though he praised the fidelity of the new technique as valuable, he added, photography's "influence, however, on artistic style and treatment has been, to my mind, of more doubtful advantage . . . . It has led in illustrative work to the method of painting in black and white, which has taken the place very much of the use of line . . . [and] concentrated artistic interest on the literal realization of certain aspects of superficial facts, and instantaneous impressions instead of ideas, and the abstract treatment of form and line" (Walter Crane, *Of the Decorative Illustration of Books Old and New*, 3rd ed. [1905; rpt. Detroit: Gale Research Co., 1968], p. 178).

35. Both Pennell and White are quoted in Harvey, *Victorian Novelists*, p. 161. These critics failed to note, as Harvey puts it, that "the naturalism of the later mode was qualified by a marked tendency to idealize" (p. 162). Illustration in the new style was achieving greater favor among editors and critics, because they sensed its growing popularity. The American editor Horace E. Scudder, for example, believed that there was likely "no class of books which feels the whiffs of fashion so quickly as illustrated books," yet he was pleased "to point out the steady advance toward what may be called happy marriages between art and literature" (Horace E. Scudder, "Some Holiday Books," *Atlantic Monthly* 71 [1893], 123). And Philip Gilbert Hamerton noted that "an illustrated edition is a confirmation of his [the writer's] fame" ("Book Illustration," p. 294).

36. Leon Edel, *The Life of Henry James: The Conquest of London (1870–1881), vol. 2* (Philadelphia and New York: Lippincott, 1962), p. 342. It is interesting to note that among the many well known periodicals published during the second half of the nineteenth century, only *Atlantic Monthly* refused to use illustration.

37. Leon Edel, *The Life of Henry James: The Middle Years (1882–1895)*, vol. 3 (Philadelphia and New York: Lippincott, 1962), p. 156. An appreciation of Robert Louis Stevenson, for example, was held up for nearly a year by the illustrator (Edel, *Middle Years*, vol. 3, pp. 242–43). James's attitudes are not discussed by Edel in other than these rather brief, general terms. Winner, *Henry James*, p. 62, also treats Henry James and illustration with brevity, agreeing that James objected to "the fact that illustration invaded the writer's domain."

38. Quoted in Edel, *Middle Years*, vol. 3, pp. 156–57.

39. James to Howells, dated 22 January 1894, in Lubbock, ed., *Letters of Henry James*, vol. 1, p. 231.

40. James to Shorter, dated 6 May 1896, in Edel, ed., *Selected Letters of Henry James*, p. 98.

41. James to Howells, dated 11 December 1902, in Lubbock, ed., *Letters of Henry James*, vol. 1, p. 408. Of course, as will be shown in chapter four, James was not the only important artist and critic to raise hard questions about the illustration of literature (see

for example, Scudder, "Some Holiday Books," p. 123; and Hamerton, "Book Illustration," p. 295).

42. Daumier was the exception. Interestingly, Winner has suggested by implication that some of these appreciative evaluations were the result of James's friendships with the artists (Winner, *Henry James*, p. 62); but James was not one to engage in puffing publically undeserved reputations, even those of his close friends. As will be shown, these appreciations are not without criticism.

43. Edel, *Middle Years*, vol. 3, p. 157.

44. James, "Black and White." In *Picture and Text*, pp. 1–2.

45. James, "Charles S. Reinhart." In *Picture and Text*, p. 63.

46. Ibid., p. 67.

47. James, "Black and White." In *Picture and Text*, p. 22.

48. Ibid., p. 37.

49. Ibid.

50. Ibid., p. 14.

51. Ibid., p. 20.

52. James, "Charles S. Reinhart." In *Picture and Text*, p. 77.

53. James, "Black and White." In *Picture and Text*, p. 33. Even here, James was careful to qualify his praise.

54. Ibid., pp. 33–34.

55. Henry James, "Washington Square," *Cornhill Magazine* 41 (1880), pp. 641–64; 42 (1880), pp. 107–28, 129–52, 364–84, 385–403, 616–40. This is discussed in chapter 4.

56. James, "Alfred Parsons." In *Picture and Text*, p. 90.

57. James, "Honoré Daumier." In *Picture and Text*, p. 133.

58. Ibid., p. 138.

59. James, "John Singer Sargent." In *Picture and Text*, p. 100.

60. James, "Honoré Daumier." In Sweeney, ed., *Painter's Eye*, p. 224. Daumier's drawings were believed to be of the highest art (p. 240), and DuMaurier's best work was held by James to be his caricatures (James, "George DuMauier." In *Partial Portraits*, p. 335).

61. James, "Black and White." In *Picture and Text*, p. 335.

62. James, "Charles S. Reinhart," p. 75.

63. James, "Black and White," p. 15.

64. Winner, *Henry James*, p. 62.

65. James, "After the Play." In *Picture and Text*, pp. 153–54.

66. Ibid., p. 156.

67. Ibid., pp. 157–58.

68. Ibid., p. 173.

69. Ibid., p. 175.

70. Henry James, "The Real Thing." In *The Real Thing and Other Tales* by Henry James (New York: Macmillan and Co., 1893), pp. 1–41.

71. Ibid., p. 4. It is also an irony—certainly one not likely lost on James himself—that this story was first published in the 16 April 1892 issue of *Black and White* (3 [1892], pp. 502–7), and was illustrated by Rudolf Blind. The story is not only an intelligent discourse on realism and on the illustration of literature but also a critique of photography and a deft satire on the nineteenth-century social types represented by the bourgeois couple, the Monarchs.

72. See Edel, *Untried Years*, vol. 1, pp. 161–63. If the status of illustration was low, photography was not even considered by many to be an art at all. James himself never seemed to have thought of photography as a fine art until his use of it in the New York Edition.

73. James, "Real Thing," p. 4.

74. Ibid., p. 7. Interestingly, the germ for this story is attributed by James to an experience related to him by George DuMaurier, who was once visited by such a couple (see James, "Preface to 'Daisy Miller,'" in *Art of the Novel*, pp. 283–84; and F. O. Matthiessen and Kenneth B. Murdoch, eds., *The Notebooks of Henry James* [1947; rpt. New York: Oxford-Galaxy, 1961], pp. 102–5).

Chapter 4

1. Leon Edel and Dan H. Laurence, *A Bibliography of Henry James* (London: Rupert Hart-Davis, 1961), pp. 50–52. The others were an American limited edition of "Daisy Miller," published by *Harper's* in 1982 (illustrated by Harry W. McVicker); and *Julia Bride*, published by *Harper's* in 1909 (illustrated by W. T. Smedley). Oddly, the American serialization of *Washington Square*, in *Harper's Monthly* 61 (1880), pp. 287–301, 413–26, 593–607, 753–66, 907–18; 62 (1880), pp. 129–44, did not include illustrations.

2. As Edel points out, James reserved his best fiction for the unillustrated *Atlantic* (Edel, *Conquest of London*, vol. 2, p. 342). Other examples of James's illustrated serialized works are: "The Seige of London," *Cornhill Magazine* 47 (1883), pp. 1–34, 225–26, illustrated by W. Small; "Louisa Pallant," *Harper's Monthly* 76 (1888), pp. 336–55, illustrated by C. S. Reinhart; "The Real Thing," *Black and White* 3 (1892), pp. 502–7, illustrated by Rudolf Blind; "Greville Fane," *Illustrated London News* 101 (1892), pp. 361–63, 393–95, illustrated by A. Forestier; "The Turn of the Screw," *Collier's Weekly* 20 (27 January–2 April, 1898) and 21 (9–16 April, 1898), n.p., illustrated by John LaFarge and Eric Pape. See Edel and Laurence, *Bibliography*, pp. 281–343, for a listing of those works which were and were not illustrated: Of 582 separate listings—essays and fiction, signed and unsigned work—only forty-nine were illustrated. Of these, many were essays on artists that contained illustrations of works discussed or portraits of the artists discussed.

3. See Edel and Laurence, *Bibliography*, p. 319.

4. For example, the illustration of DuMaurier, facing p. 34, and that of Alfred Parsons, facing p. 86, in James, *Picture and Text*.

5. Edel and Laurence, *Bibliography*, pp. 26–29. This was unusual for a Tauchnitz edition.

6. Ibid., pp. 60–63.

7. Ibid., pp. 63–67.

8. Henry James, "Preface." In *A Little Tour of France*, 2nd ed. (Boston and New York: Houghton, Mifflin and Co., 1900), p. v.

9. Henry James, "London," pp. 219-39.

10. James to Pennell, 6 January 1888, in Edel, ed., *Selected Letters of Henry James*, p. 92.

11. Ibid.

12. Henry James, *English Hours* (Boston and New York: Houghton, Mifflin and Co., 1905). See Edel and Laurence, *Bibliography*, pp. 95-96; pp. 126-27, 130-32.

13. Quoted in Edel, *The Master*, vol. 5, p. 23. A careful reading of *The American Scene* suggests that James was right to keep illustration out; it is an extraordinarily visual book (see Henry James, *The American Scene*, ed. Leon Edel [1907; rpt. Bloomington: Indiana University Press, 1968]; see also, Bogardus, "Photographer's Eye").

14. James to Coburn, 11 October 1909, James Collection, Virginia.

15. James, *Small Boy*, p. 69.

16. James, *Notes of a Son*, p. 246.

17. James, "Preface to *The Golden Bowl*," p. 331.

18. Ibid., p. 332.

19. Ibid., pp. 332-33.

20. Ibid., p. 333.

21. Ibid.

22. Ibid.

23. Henry James, "George DuMaurier," *Harper's Monthly* 95 (1897), 605. Yet, James also believed that in DuMaurier's *Peter Ibbetson*, the illustrations contributed to the text: "They are part of the delicacy of the book," James wrote, "and unique as an example of illustration at its happiest; not one's own idea, or somebody else's, of how somebody looked or moved or some image was constituted, but the lovely mysterious fact itself, precedent to interpretation and independent of it" (p. 606).

24. James, *Small Boy*, p. 120.

25. Harvey, *Victorian Novelists*, pp. 3-4. In Dickens, Harvey notes, illustration acted often as an additional paragraph might (p. 16). Moreover, according to Harvey, Dickens was aware of the competition. When Dickens and Cruikshank were working on *Oliver Twist*, Harvey tells us, there were difficulties between them: Dickens realized that, in Harvey's words, "There was a real risk . . . of being overshadowed" (p. 33). Indeed, Harvey continues, some critics "felt that the highest praise they could bestow on Dickens was to say that he was as good as his illustrator" (p. 33).

26. Congdon, "Over-Illustration," p. 489. After citing an editorial also entitled, "Over-Illustration," in *Harper's Weekly* 55 (1911), p. 6, Neil Harris remarks, "Articles about 'over-illustration' had been appearing since the 1880s" (Harris, "Halftone Effect," p. 210, n. 17).

27. Fairfield, "Tyranny of the Pictorial," pp. 863-64.

28. Recall from chapter 3 that Horace E. Scudder, in "Some Holiday Books," p. 123, expressed such a mixed view. And though Tudor Jenks respected what he thought to be proper illustration, he worried over the increasing decadence of the medium ("The Deca-

dence of Illustration," *Independent* 51 [1899], pp. 3487-89). Pennell is quoted in Jackson, *Eighteen Nineties*, p. 285.

29. Jackson, *Eighteen Nineties*, p. 103.

30. Ibid., p. 279.

31. Hamerton's influence is alluded to in Gordon C. Ray, *The Illustrator and the Book in England from 1790 to 1914* (New York and London: Oxford University Press, 1976), pp. 141-42. James himself wrote at least two reviews of books by Hamerton (see Henry James, unsigned review of *Round My House: Notes of a Rural Life in France in Peace and War*, Nation 22 (3 February 1876), pp. 85-86; and Henry James, "An English Critic." In Sweeney, ed., *Painter's Eye*, pp. 33-42). These essays indicated that James did not feel that Hamerton was a particularly brilliant critic, to be ranked, for example, with John Ruskin. Nonetheless, James believed that Hamerton exhibited "common sense . . . and in dealing with aesthetic matters he never ceases to be clear and precise" (James, "An English Critic," p. 37).

32. Hamerton, "Book Illustration," passim.

33. Henry James, "After the Play," p. 175.

34. See Henry James, "DuMaurier and London Society," *Century Magazine* 26 (1883), pp. 51-65. (Subsequently, in 1888, this was reprinted under the title, "George DuMaurier," in *Partial Portraits*—but without the illustrations.) Here, James recognized that DuMaurier's work was very different from Daumier's—for instance, it was gentler; still, DuMaurier's best caricatures deftly satirized their subjects. The following year (1884), James also wrote and published an exhibition catalogue essay on DuMaurier titled, *Notes on Drawings by George DuMaurier* (see listing in Edel and Laurence, *Bibliography*, p. 63).

35. James, "DuMaurier and London Society," p. 55. Note that this was published three years after *Washington Square*. Gordon C. Ray, *The Illustrator and the Book*, p. 125, finds it surprising that Henry James believed DuMaurier to be the best to be found in *Punch*.

36. James, "DuMaurier and London Society," p. 55.

37. The DuMaurier caricature shown in the text (figure 28) is taken from James, "DuMaurier and London Society," p. 57. James chose all of the illustrations by DuMaurier that were to exemplify DuMaurier's qualities. Even though the *Washington Square* illustration (figure 27) lacks the bite of the caricature found in *Punch* (figure 28), it is still—when compared with so many other artists' efforts during the age—a graceful and charming sketch. It possesses none of the stolidness or awkwardness that exists in so many of the naturalistic representations found in the illustrated literature of the day.

38. Henry James, *Washington Square* (New York: Harper & Brothers, 1881), p. 141. It must be noted that the way DuMaurier's illustrations were used by the publisher is not necessarily the fault of either the artist or the writer. Recall that, at this time, neither had firm control over the design and presentation of his work.

39. Henry James, "Louisa Pallant," *Harper's Monthly* 76 (1888), pp. 336-55.

40. Henry James, "The Real Thing," pp. 502-7.

41. Henry James, "Greville Fane," pp. 361-63, 393-95.

42. Henry James, "The Beldonald Holbein," *Harper's Monthly* 103 (1901), pp. 807-21.

43. See Henry James, "Julia Bride," pp. 489-502, 705-13. This story contains four illustrations by W. T. Smedley.

44. Henry James, "London," is an excellent example of this.

45. See Morton Dauwen Zabel, "Introduction." In *The Art of Travel: Scenes and Journeys in America, England, France, and Italy from the Travel Writings of Henry James,* ed. Morton Dauwen Zabel (Garden City: Doubleday, 1958), pp. 1-48, for an excellent discussion of James's travel literature.

46. Recall James's letter to Pennell, 6 January 1888, where James wrote, "do your own London, and it will be sufficiently mine."

47. James, "London," p. 220.

48. Ibid., p. 221.

49. Part of the problem undoubtedly lay in the reproduction medium itself. Also, when hand drawn illustration was used, a third person intervened: the engraver. This complicated the process, and often illustrators were as critical of the engravers' alterations of their work as some authors were critical of their illustrators (see Jablow, "Illustrated Texts," pp. 12 f., 25 f.). But though illustrators like Pennell complained that the quality of their drawings could not judged by the published illustrations, Bland argues that "it is impossible to judge a drawing apart from its reproduction since the reproduction *is* the illustration" (*History of Book Illustration*, p. 17). Joseph Pennell has been placed among the group of American Impressionists who were active around the turn of the century. Evidently, Pennell had an allegiance to the work of Whistler—its "soft line and broad interplay between highlights and shadows" were influences (*Impressionism in America* [Albuquerque University of New Mexico Press, 1965], p. 18). Though certainly an important illustrator and cultural figure, Pennell has never been considered a major American artist by art historians.

50. James, "Preface." In *Little Tour*, p. v.

51. Ibid., p. vi.

52. James, *English Hours*; Henry James, *Italian Hours* (Boston and New York: Houghton Mifflin and Co., 1909). Apparently, James regarded the latter book as a potboiler (see unpublished letter from James to Howells, 3 May 1909, in James Family Papers, Houghton Library, Harvard University).

53. James, "DuMaurier and London Society," pp. 48-65.

54. John L. Sweeney, "Introduction." In Sweeney, ed., *Painter's Eye*, p. 23.

Chapter 5

1. James, *Small Boy*, p. 86.

2. Ibid., pp. 87-88.

3. Ibid., p. 87. James also saw the daguerreotype as documenting "my father's cultivation of my company" on the occasions when they tramped "the queer empty dusty smelly New York of midsummer" (ibid., p. 69).

4. Reuben Gold Thwaites, ed., *Original Journals of the Lewis and Clark Expedition, 1804-06*, vol. 2 (New York: Dodd, Mead & Co., 1904), p. 150. The scene was the Shoshone Falls, located at the head waters of the Missouri River.

5. For extensive discussions of the prehistory of photography, see Peter Galassi, *Before Photography: Painting and the Invention of Photography* (New York: Museum of Modern Art, 1979), pp. 11-31; and Joel Snyder, "Picturing Vision," *Critical Inquiry* 6 (1980), pp. 499-526. Lewis's experience was not unique. William Henry Fox Talbot, an inventor of the calotype process, expressed a similar need for photography when visiting Lake Como in Italy in 1833 (see William Henry Fox Talbot, "A Brief Historical Sketch of the Invention of the Art." In Alan Trachtenberg, ed., *Classic Essays on Photography* [New Haven: Leete's Island Books, 1980], pp. 27-36).

6. See Newhall, *History of Photography*, chapters 1 and 3. Basic information about the history of photography comes from this source unless otherwise noted. See also, Snyder, "Picturing Vision," 510 ff., for a full discussion of the *camera obscura*.

7. See generally, Aaron Scharf, *Art and Photography* (Harmondsworth: Penguin, 1968), chapter 1. Frenchman Joseph Nicéphore Niépce was working on the problem in 1816, but it is not known for certain when he succeeded in first fixing an image (Newhall, *History of Photography*, pp. 13-14). L.J.M. Daguerre and William Henry Fox Talbot began working on the problem in the 1820s and 1830s, respectively (ibid., pp. 14 ff., 31 ff.). Daguerre entered into a joint effort with Niépce in 1829 that ended when Niépce died in 1833; Daguerre continued their work alone. Hippolyte Bayard, another French-man, succeeded in the late 1830s in creating another process, but his discovery was completely eclipsed by Daguerre's (ibid., p. 44). Sir John Herschel, the English astrono-mer and scientist, worked on the problem too, and he came up with the solution that became universally used to fix images — sodium thiosulphate or "hypo" (ibid., p. 32). Meanwhile, in Brazil, Hercules Florence apparently succeeded in fixing images (see Weston Naef, "Hercules Florence 'Inventor do Photographia,'" *Artforum* 14 (February 1976), pp. 57-79). See also, Helmut and Alison Gernsheim, *The History of Photography, 1687-1914* (New York: McGraw-Hill, 1969), pp. 88 ff.

8. Oliver Wendell Holmes, "The Stereoscope and the Stereograph," *Atlantic Monthly* 3 (1859), p 739.

9. See Arago's "Report." In Trachtenberg, ed., *Classic Essays on Photography*, pp. 15-25. Oddly enough, Daguerre was able to copyright his process in England, and consequently its use there never reached the magnitude that it did elsewhere. The calotype was used for the most part in the British Isles and British colonies.

10. Richard Rudisill, *Mirror Image: The Influence of the Daguerreotype on American Society* (Albuquerque: University of New Mexico Press, 1971), p. 48.

11. Newhall, *History of Photography*, p. 22.

12. Rudisill, *Mirror Image*, p. 4

13. Robert Taft, *Photography and the American Scene* (1938; rpt. New York: Dover, 1964), p. 63. Regarding the popularity of the medium, see Taft, *Photography*, chapters 4 and 5; Gernsheim, *History of Photography*, chapters 10 through 16; and Newhall, *History of Photography*, chapter 4.

14. See Alan Thomas, *Time in a Frame: Photography and the Nineteenth-Century Mind* (New York: Schocken, 1977), chapter 1, for a lucid summary of the evolving uses of photography throughout the nineteenth century. See also, Gail Buckland, *Reality Recorded: Early Documentary Photography* (Greenwich, Conn.: New York Graphic Society, 1974), passim. Regarding the popularity of stereographs, see William Culp Darrah, *Stereo Views: A History of Stereographs in American and Their Collection*

(Gettysburg: Times and News, 1964), pp. 8, 12. See also, Richard N. Masteller, "Western Views in Eastern Parlors: The Contribution of the Stereograph Photographer to the Conquest of the West," *Prospects* 6 (1981), pp. 56–59.

15. For discussion of the collodion process and what followed, see Newhall, *History of Photography*, pp. 47 ff. For discussion of the issue of photography and the rise of mass culture, see Reese V. Jenkins, "Technology and the Market: George Eastman and the Origins of Mass Amateur Photography," *Technology and Culture* 16 (January 1975), pp. 1–19; and Harris, "Half-Tone Effect."

16. See Walter Benjamin, "The Work of Art in the Age of Mechanical Reproduction." In *Illuminations* by Walter Benjamin, ed. Hannah Arendt and trans. Harry Zohn (1955; rpt. New York: Schocken, 1969), pp. 217–51, for a brilliant discussion of the point. Benjamin also urges that photography levelled the art object by making it more accessible through reproduction and thus reduced the aura surrounding it. Interestingly, Oliver Wendell Holmes made a similar point ("Sun-Painting and Sun-Sculpture," *Atlantic Monthly* 8 [1861], p. 13).

17. Paul Valéry, "The Centenary of Photography." In *The Collected Works of Paul Valéry: Occasions*, vol. 9, ed. Jackson Matthews and trans. Roger Shattuck and Frederick Brown (Princeton: Princeton University Press, 1970), pp. 160–61.

18. Robert Taft, *Photography*, p. 3.

19. See Rudisill, *Mirror Image*, p. 31, for a general discussion of this point. Susan Sontag, "Photography," *New York Review* (18 October 1973), notes, "there is something predatory in the act of taking a picture. To photograph people is to violate them, by seeing them as they never see themselves, by having knowledge of them that they can never have. To photograph is to turn people into objects that can be symbolically possessed . . . . Taking pictures is soft murder." It might be speculated that Henry James, unconsciously, sensed this and resented photography for "exposing" him.

20. Rudisill, *Mirror Image*, p. 32.

21. See Newhall, *History of Photography*, pp. 68–72, for a discussion of the photograph's realism. See also, Aaron Scharf, *Creative Photography* (New York: Van Nostrand Reinhold Co., and London: Studio Vista, 1965), pp. 31–32. See Newhall, *History of Photography*, pp. 60–61, for a discussion of the response to the realism even of a manipulated image—that of H.P. Robinson's "Fading Away" (1858). Sontag, "Photography," p. 59, notes that "a photograph seems to have a more innocent, and therefore, accurate, relation to visible reality than do other mimetic objects."

22. Valéry, "Centenary of Photography," p. 161.

23. Quoted in Beaumont Newhall and Robert Doty, *Image: The Bulletin of the George Eastman House of Photography* 21 (1962), p. 25.

24. Ibid. p. 26.

25. Quoted in Beaumont Newhall, "Foreword." In Doty, *Photo-Secession*, p. 3.

26. Quoted in Van Deren Coke, *The Painter and the Photograph, from Delacroix to Warhol* (Albuquerque: University of New Mexico Press, 1972), p. 7.

27. Ibid. p. 9.

28. Quoted in Scharf, *Art and Photography*, p. 102.

29. Edgar Allan Poe, *Edgar Allan Poe's Contributions to Alexander's Weekly Messenger*, ed. Clarence S. Brigham (Worcester, Mass.: American Antiquarian Society, 1943), pp. 20–21.

30. Henry David Thoreau, *The Journals of Henry D. Thoreau*, vol. 1, ed. Bradford Torrey and Francis H. Allen (1906; rpt. New York: Dover, 1962), p. 65.

31. Nathaniel Hawthorne, *The House of the Seven Gables* (1851; rpt. New York: Dell, 1960), p. 107. See Rudisill, *Mirror Image*, pp. 20–28, 127–28, for a discussion of Hawthorne's daguerreotypist.

32. Ralph Waldo Emerson, *Journals of Ralph Waldo Emerson, 1841–1844*, vol. 6, ed. Edward Waldo Emerson and Waldo Emerson Forbes (Boston and New York: Houghton Mifflin, 1912), p. 87.

33. Ibid., pp. 100–101.

34. Ibid., 110–11.

35. Oliver Wendell Holmes, "Stereoscope and Stereograph," pp. 738–48; "Sun-Painting," pp. 13–29; and "Doings of the Sunbeam," *Atlantic Monthly* 12 (1863), pp. 1–15.

36. Holmes, "Sun-Painting," p. 16.

37. Holmes, "Stereoscope and Stereograph," p. 741.

38. Holmes, "Doings of the Sunbeam," pp. 11–12.

39. Holmes, "Stereoscope and Stereograph," p. 747. This view is cogently explained by Susan Sontag, "Shooting America," *New York Review* (18 April 1974), pp. 17–24. Newhall, too, notes that "the depopulated aspect of the first daguerreotypes"—a surreal aspect — was "abhorred" by the public (*History of Photography*. p. 19). Other examples of individual responses to daguerreotypes as "a perfect transcript of the thing itself" and thus as a desireable substitute for the world may be found in Rudisill, *Mirror Image*, pp. 53–54. This idea foreshadows much later analyses regarding the influence of photography on the audiences' perception of, and response to, the world (see Daniel Boorstin, *The Image: A Guide to Pseudo-Events in America* [New York and Evanston: Harper Colophon, 1961]; and Walker Percy, "The Loss of the Creature." In *The Message in the Bottle* by Walker Percy [New York: Farrar, Straus and Giroux, 1977], pp. 46–63).

40. Charles Baudelaire, *The Mirror of Art: Critical Studies*, ed. and trans. Jonathan Mayne (London: Phaidon, 1955), p. 230.

41. Quoted in Beaumont Newhall, "Delacroix and Photography," *Magazine of Art* 45 (1952), p. 300.

42. Quoted in Coke, *Painter*, p. 12.

43. Quoted in Rudisill, *Mirror Image*, p. 55. Ruskin warned of this, too (see Scharf, *Art and Photography*, pp. 95–100).

44. This has been treated extensively in Scharf, *Art and Photography*, passim; and in Coke, *Painter*, pp. 3–15. See also, Newhall, "Delacroix and Photography."

45. See Coke, *Painter*, passim; and Scharf, *Art and Photography*, chapters seven and eight. See also, Hauser, *Social History*, vol. 4 pp. 222–25; and Wylie Sypher, *From Rococo to Cubism in Art and Literature* (New York: Random-Vintage, 1960), p. 257–88. For a dissenting view, see Kirk Varnadoe, "The Artiface of Candor: Impressionism and Photography Reconsidered," *Art in America* 68 (January 1980), pp. 66–78; and Varnadoe,

"The Ideology of Time: Degas and Photography," *Art in America* 68 (Summer 1980), pp. 96–110. See Walter Benjamin, "Paris, Capital of the 19th Century," *Dissent* 17 (1970), p. 442, for the view that photography freed painting from the bonds of realism, pushing painters toward abstraction. Regarding the relation between photography and Impressionism, as Donald Drew Egbert has argued, the Impressionists believed "that a picture should be a record of a moment," and they went about painting "moments" taken from life on their canvases—hence, their perceptual approach could certainly be said to have been like that of a photographer and their paintings an embodiment of instantaneous vision (Donald Drew Egbert, *Social Radicalism and the Arts* [New York: Knopf, 1970], p. 235). Varnadoe agrees that there was, indeed, a distinct stylistic approach to making art in the nineteenth century, and that this had much in common with instantaneous photographs; but he rejects the term "photographic style," because it implies (he believes) major influence, something which he has argued against. Yet since photography, more than any other medium of the period, embodied inherently the new spatial and temporal style of representing the world, and since this style became central to Impressionism and post-Impressionism, I feel that the term "photographic style" is entirely appropriate to use in reference to discussions of evolving modernist painting and literature (see Bogardus, "Photographer's Eye," passim).

46. Quoted in Linda Nochlin, *Realism: Style and Civilization* (New York and Baltimore: Penguin, 1971), p. 45.

47. See Ralph F. Bogardus, "A Literary Realist and the Camera: W.D. Howells and the Uses of Photography," *American Literary Realism, 1870–1910* 10 (1977), pp. 231–41; Dan Schiller, "Realism, Photography, and Journalistic Objectivity in 19th Century America," *Studies in the Anthropology of Visual Communication* 4 (Winter 1977), pp. 86–98; Ann Wilsher, "Photography and Literature: the First Seventy Years," *History of Photography* 2 (1978), pp. 223–34; and Johatan Kamholtz, "Literature and Photography: The Captioned Vision Vs. the Firm, Mechanical Impression," *Centennial Review* 24 (1980), pp. 385–402. See also, Alan Spiegel, *Fiction and the Camera Eye* (Charlottesville: University Press of Virginia, 1976), pp. 28 ff.; Leon Edel, "Novel and Camera." In *The Theory of the Novel: New Essays*, ed. John Halpern (New York, London, and Toronto: Oxford University Press, 1974), pp. 177–88; and Bogardus, "Photographer's Eye.") This relation is treated more extensively in chapter 6.

48. Quoted in Newhall, *History of Photography*, p. 59. See the discussion of "pictorial effect" in photography on pp. 59–65.

49. Ibid. p. 31.

50. Coke, *Painter*, p. 233.

51. Rudisill, *Mirror Image*, pp. 39–40, discusses the consequences of the visual conditioning of the existing painting conventions, causing many to react against the explicit detail, immediacy, and lack of idealization of the subject.

52. Henry James later became good friends with the Leslie Stephens, but nowhere did James mention the magnificent portrait of Mrs. Stephen taken by Cameron. See Newhall, *History of Photography*, pp. 62–63, for reproductions of the Cameron portraits of Mrs. Stephen and Sir John Herschel. Reproduced examples of Hill and Adamson portraits are found on pp. 37–39; of Southworth and Hawes portraits, p. 27; of Nadar's, pp. 54–56. Portraiture and the family album became quite important and widespread phenomena (see Thomas, *Time in a Frame*, chapter 3).

53. Newhall, *History of Photography*, p. 59.

54. Ibid.

55. Ibid., pp. 23, 25, 29; and Gernsheim, *History of Photography*, p. 127.

56. Holmes, "Doings of the Sunbeam," p. 8.

57. Thomas, *Time in a Frame*, p. 19.

58. The term is Scharf's; *Art and Photography*, p. 127.

59. Marcus Aurelius Root, *The Camera and the Pencil; or The Heliographic Art* (1864; rpt. Pawlet, Vt.: Helios, 1971), p. xv.

60. Rudisill, *Mirror Image*, p. 182.

61. See Scharf, *Creative Photography*, pp. 7 ff.

62. Newhall, *History of Photography*, p. 60.

63. Quoted in ibid., p. 61.

64. Cameron executed a series of dress theatricals for use as illustrations to Tennyson's *Idylls of the King*.

65. Doty, *Photo-Secession*, p. 11.

66. "Characteristics of the International Fair. Closing Days, Part 6," *Atlantic Monthly* 39 (1877), p. 94.

67. Ibid.

68. Ibid., 95.

69. Philip Gilbert Hamerton, "Style." In *Portfolio Papers*, p. 252.

70. Joseph Pennell, "Is Photography among the Fine Arts?" *Contemporary Review* 72 (1897), pp. 824–36.

71. Ibid., p. 824.

72. Ibid, p. 828.

73. Ibid., pp. 828–29. For a comparison, see "The Perils of Photography," *Nation* 85 (1907), pp. 28–29, where an anonymous essayist wrote, "In its infancy amateur photography was regarded as rather a mild pastime, not exactly effeminate but dilettante."

74. Pennell, "Is Photography among the Fine Arts?" p. 829.

75. Ibid., pp. 830–31.

76. Ibid., p. 832.

77. Ibid., p. 836. See a similar view by an anonymous reviewer of "Some Books on Art," *Nation* 73 (1901), p. 476, who, in assessing Charles H. Caffin's *Photography as a Fine Art*, said that the photographer's "landscapes, however modified in effect, must be always topographical; his figures must be starkly naturalistic in form, and with no other composition than accident or the painful tableau vivant may furnish. If he should attempt the serious alteration of form, his art, whatever else it might be, would cease to be photography, though it might utilize photography, as painters sometimes — too often — do."

78. Pennell, "Is Photography among the Fine Arts?," pp. 832–33.

79. Newhall, *History of Photography*, p. 176. See also Harris, "Half-Tone Effect," pp. 197–98, for a brief discussion of the process and its subsequent development and impact.

80. Fairfield, "Tyranny of the Pictorial," pp. 861–62

81. For extensive definitions of the different photomechanical processes, see Bernard C. Jones, ed., *The Encyclopedia of Photography* (1879; rpt. New York: Arno Press, 1974); and Gernsheim, *History of Photography*, pp. 539–53. See also, Jussim, *Visual Communication*, chapters two and three, for a full and brilliant analysis of the impact on perception of the use of these technologies.

82. See Harris, "Half-Tone Effect," pp. 205–9.

83. Newhall, *History of Photography*, p. 175. Wood engravings made after daguerreotypes were also used to illustrate Henry Mayhew, John Binney, et al., *London Labour and the London Poor*, published between 1851 and 1864 (p. 139).

84. "*Edinburgh Review*, January 1843." In Vicki Goldberg, ed., *Photography in Print: Writings from 1816 to the Present* (New York: Simon and Schuster-Touchstone, 1981), pp. 49–69; see particularly, p. 66. Some of these scenes were altered by hand; since the exposure time of the daguerreotype process was not yet fast enough to record people, they were drawn into some of the images.

85. See Beaumont Newhall, "Introduction." In *The Pencil of Nature* by William Henry Fox Talbot (1844–46; rpt. New York: DeCapo, 196), n.p. See Jussim, *Visual Communication*, chapters 3 and 4, for a full discussion of photography and illustration.

86. Scharf, *Art and Photography*, p. 98. Ruskin decided not to use them, because he felt that details were too often obliterated by the shadows in daguerreotypes. Though an early advocate of the use of photographs, he later repudiated this view (pp. 95–100).

87. See Jablow, "Illustrated Books," pp. 103 ff., for a discussion of the "extra-illustrated" Tauchnitz editions. See also, Simon Nowell-Smith, "Firma Tauchnitz 1837–1900," *Book Collector* 15 (1966), pp. 423–36.

88. Jussim, *Visual Communication*, pp. 96 ff. This book is better known as *The Marble Faun*. Later, when *The Marble Faun* was republished in an American edition in 1890, it was accompanied by photogravure illustrations.

89. Jablow, "Illustrated Books," pp. 103 ff.

90. Ibid., p. 60.

91. "Characteristics of the International Fair," p. 94.

92. Jablow, "Illustrated Books," p. 5.

93. Jacob A. Riis, *How the Other Half Lives* (New York: Charles Scribner's Sons, 1890). See Ferenc M. Szasz and Ralph F. Bogardus, "The Camera and the American Social Conscience: The Documentary Photography of Jacob A. Riis," *New York History* 55 (1974), pp. 409–36.

94. Mark Twain, *Pudd'nhead Wilson and Those Extraordinary Twins* (1894; rpt. New York and London: Harper & Brothers, 1899).

95. W. D. Howells, *Their Silver Wedding Journey*, 2 vols. (New York and London: Harper & Brothers, 1899). Though a travel book, Howells's *London Films* exhibits the same conflict.

96. Howells disliked having his books illustrated and no doubt had little to do with the manner in which pictures were used in his books (see letter from Howells to Frederick A. Duneka, 13 May 1914. In *W. D. Howells: Selected Letters*, vol. 6, ed. William M. Gibson and Christoph K. Lohmann [Boston: Twayne, 1983], p. 55). Recall, too, that beginning in the late nineteenth century, publishers dealt with the matter of illustration, generally keeping it out of the hands of authors.

97. See "Handsomely Illustrated," *Atlantic Monthly* 93 (1904), pp. 136–37; "A Growl for the Unpicturesque," *Atlantic Monthly* 98 (1906); rev. of "Holiday Books," *Atlantic Monthly* 67 (1891), pp. 121–26. See also, Larzer Ziff, *The American 1890s: Life and Times of a Lost Generation* (1966; rpt. Lincoln and London: University of Nebraska Press, 1979), pp. 121–22; and Christopher P. Wilson, "The Rhetoric of Consumption: Mass-Market Magazines and the Demise of the Gentle Reader, 1880–1920." In *The Culture of Consumption: Critical Essays in American History, 1880–1980*, eds. Richard Wightman Fox and T.J. Jackson Lears (New York: Pantheon, 1983), p. 47.

98. Quoted in Weitenkampf, *Illustrated Book*, p. 181

99. Hamerton, "Book Illustration," p. 333.

100. "Holiday Books," p. 126.

101. James John Hissey, *Untravelled England* (London and New York: Macmillan and Company, 1906), pp. vii–viii. Hissey's apology is odd, though, because many of the reproduced photographs in the volume are clearly retouched to make them look like wood engravings. They fail, of course, as successful imitations; and as a consequence of their retouching, their straightforwardness as photographs is diminished. For contemporary critical discussions of photographic illustration, see Congdon, "Over-Illustration"; Fairfield, "Tyranny of the Pictorial"; Jenks, "Decadence of Illustration"; "Some Books on Art," pp. 475–76; and "Handsomely Illustrated," pp. 136–37. For an opposite view, see Ella M. Boult, "The Illustration of Books by Artistic Photographs," *Independent* 61 (1906), pp. 1414–20.

102. Jablow, "Illustrated Books," pp. 13–14, indicates that photomechanical processes for printing illustration were used generally by the 1880s. See "A Symposium of Wood-Engravers," *Harper's New Monthly* 60 (1880), pp. 442–53.

103. "Symposium of Wood-Engravers," p. 447.

104. Ibid., p. 449.

105. Ibid., p. 453. Only one engraver, in a group of seven participants, disagreed. A. V. S. Anthony petulantly declared, "Which is better to engrave from, a photograph on the block or a drawing on the block? I most decidedly prefer the drawing, and I don't know an engraver who does not" (p. 444).

106. Jablow, "Illustrated Books," pp. 1, 12 ff., and 25 ff., discusses this point.

107. Crane, *Of the Decorative Illustration of Books*, p. 178.

108. Quoted in Coke, *Painter*, p. 205.

109. Harris, "Half-Tone Effect," p. 199.

110. Benjamin, "Work of Art."

111. Recall Fairfield, "Tyranny of the Pictorial."

112. See Alan Trachtenberg, *The Incorporation of America: Culture and Society in the Gilded Age* (New York: Hill and Wang, 1982), chapters 5, 6, and 7; Henry F. May, *The End of American Innocence: a Study of the First Years of Our Own Time, 1912-1917* (New York: Knopf, 1959); and Wilson, "Rhetoric of Consumption," passim.

113. "Newspaper Pictures," *Nation* 56 (1893), p. 307.

114. The twentieth-century arguments against mass culture that began with the members of the Frankfurt School, such as Theodor Adorno and Leo Lowenthal, and others such as Ortega y Gasset, really had their origins in earlier times—including, of course, the nineteenth century. See Patrick Brantlinger, *Bread and Circuses: Theories of Mass Culture as Social Decay* (Ithaca and London: Cornell University Press, 1984).

Chapter 6

1. "Handsomely Illustrated," p. 137.

2. See Marcia Jacobson, *Henry James and the Mass Market* (University, Ala.: University of Alabama Press, 1983), chapter 1.

3. Edel dates the inception of the style with the publication of *The Spoils of Poynton* (1896) (Leon Edel, *The Life of Henry James: The Treacherous Years, 1895-1902*, vol. 4 [Philadelphia and New York: Lippincott, 1969], p. 112). H. Peter Stowell, *Literary Impressionism, James and Chekhov* (Athens, Ga.: University of Georgia Press, 1980), pp. 161 ff., dates it even earlier, arguing that the late phase began to emerge in 1881 in *The Portrait of a Lady*. For a discussion of James's use of popular forms, see Jacobson, *James and Mass Market*, passim; Peter Brooks, *The Melodramatic Imagination: Balzac, Henry James, Melodrama, and the Mode of Excess* (New Haven, Conn.: Yale University Press, 1976); and, Leo Ben Levy, *Versions of Melodrama: A Study of the Fiction and Drama of Henry James, 1865-1897* (Berkeley and Los Angeles: University of California Press, 1957).

4. William James to Henry James, 22 October 1905. In *The Thought and Character of William James* vol. 1, ed. Ralph Barton Perry (Boston and Toronto: Little, Brown and Company, 1935), pp. 424-25.

5. William James to Henry James, 4 May 1907. In *The Letters of William James*, vol. 2, ed. Henry James (Boston: Atlantic Monthly Press, 1920), pp. 227-80. Henry's response to this last letter was quite forceful and apparently effective enough to make William soften his criticism in a subsequent letter (see William James to Henry James, 6 October 1907, in *Letters of William James* vol. 2, p. 229).

6. Stowell, *Literary Impressionism*, pp. 4, 17, 33, 59-68.

7. Recall that this was Coburn's one-person show in London, held during early 1906. James later remarked in an unpublished letter to Alvin Langdon Coburn, 22 October 1908, in the James Collection, Virginia, that he went to see another of Coburn's shows in 1908. This show also included the work of another pictorialist, Baron DeMeyer, whose work James also commented upon favorably in this same letter.

8. James, *Small Boy*, p. 88.

9. Ibid., pp. 122-23.

10. Henry James to William James, 1 December 1897. In Lubbock, ed., *Letters of Henry James* vol. 1, p. 265.

11. Quoted in Edel, *Treacherous Years*, vol. 4, pp. 48–49.

12. James to Mrs. Frank Mathews, 18 November 1902. In Lubbock, ed., *Letters of Henry James*, vol. 1, p. 406.

13. James, *Notes of a Son*, pp. 495–96. It is not reproduced; included instead is an illustration of a sketch of Minny Temple made by William James.

14. James to Robert Louis Stevenson, 5 August 1893. In Lubbock, ed., *Letters of Henry James*, vol. 1, p. 204.

15. James to Edith Wharton, 17 October 1914. In Lubbock, ed., *Letters of Henry James*, vol. 2, p. 415.

16. James, *Notes of a Son*, p. 431. It is unclear whether the photograph James was referring to was a portrait of Lincoln taken when he was alive or a death portrait of Lincoln. James continued the passage, confirming the fact that whatever the photograph contained, it was powerful: "No countenance, no salience of aspect nor composed symbol, could superficially have referred itself less than Lincoln's mould-smashing mask." (p. 431). See also a letter from James to Edith Wharton, 1 September 1914, in Lubbock, ed., *Letters of Henry James*, vol. 2, pp. 399–400; and a letter from James to Edward Marsh, 13 June 1915, in Lubbock, ed., *Letters of Henry James*, vol. 2, p. 474.

17. [Henry James] rev. of *Essays on Fiction*, by Nassau W. Senior, *North American Review* 99 (1864), p. 582.

18. [Henry James] rev. of *Miss Mackenzie*, by Anthony Trollope, *Nation* 1 (1865), pp. 51–52.

19. Sweeney, *Painter's Eye*, pp. 141–42.

20. Ibid., p. 240. In a letter from James to Charles Eliot Norton, 28 November 1899, in Lubbock, ed., *Letters of Henry James*, vol. 1, p. 342, James referred to an upcoming visit of the art collector, Mrs. Jack Gardner. James wrote, ironically, "I must rush off, help her to disembark, see all her Van Eycks and Rubenses through the Customs and bring her hither, where three water-colours and four photographs of the 'Rye school' will let her down easily."

21. The difficulties of making good portraits is discussed in Newhall, *History of Photography*, pp. 20–22, 47; and Rudisill, *Mirror Image*, p. 205.

22. Henry James, *The Novels and Tales of Henry James: The American*, vol. 2 (New York: Charles Scribner's Sons, 1907), p. 264. Since James revised his work for the New York Edition, sometimes extensively, it is interesting to note that only a slight revision was made in the passage quoted. In Henry James, *The American* (Boston: James R. Osgood and Co., 1877), p. 232, the passage reads, "You've a high spirit, a high standard; but with you it's all natural and unaffected; you don't seem to have stuck your head in a vise, as if you were sitting for the photograph of propriety." The use of a colon instead of a semicolon does not change the passage's meaning substantially.

23. Henry James, *The Novels and Tales of Henry James: The Aspern Papers, The Turn of the Screw, The Liar, The Two Faces*, vol. 12 (New York: Charles Scribner's Sons, 1908), p. 8. James altered his New York Edition text in this instance to clarify the import of the first clause in that statement. The first published text reads: "But it was a revelation to us that it was possible to keep so quiet in the latter half of the nineteenth century—the age of newspapers and telegrams and photographs and interviewers" (Henry James, *The*

Aspern Papers, In *The Complete Tales of Henry James*, vol. 6, ed. Leon Edel [Philadelphia and New York: J.B. Lippincott Co., 1963], p. 279).

24. See Jacobson, *James and the Mass Market*, pp. 10–11, for discussion of James's link with the nineteenth-century cultural elite.

25. Henry James, *The Novels and Tales of Henry James: What Maisie Knew, In the Cage, The Pupil*, vol. 11 (New York: Charles Scribner's Sons, 1908), p. 48. No textual changes were made in this instance.

26. James, *Maisie*, vol. 11, p. 49.

27. Ibid., p. 77.

28. Henry James, "Real Thing," p. 9.

29. Ibid., p. 21.

30. It is worth noting that James also was suggesting here a rather radical idea regarding the potential influence of photograph on human behavior. Oscar Wilde somewhere said, "Life imitates art," but in "The Real Thing," James suggested that in the photographic age, some people would project themselves as though imitating photographs.

31. See [George Eliot?] "The Progress of Fiction as an Art," *Westminster Review* 60 (1853), pp. 187–88.

32. See Hauser, *Social History*, vol. 4, pp. 3–60, 106–60.

33. Ibid., pp. 3–60; Nochlin, *Realism*, chapter 3; and Egbert, *Social Radicalism*, pp. 188–200, 228–37.

34. T.S. Perry, "American Novelists," *North American Review* 115 (1872), p. 367.

35. Ibid., p. 369.

36. Ibid., p. 378.

37. "Concerning *realism*," *Atlantic Monthly* 41 (1878), p. 130.

38. Ibid., p. 132.

39. "The Novels of Mr. Howells," *Nation* 31 (1880), p. 50.

40. Charles Dudley Warner, "Modern Fiction," *Atlantic Monthly* 51 (1883), p. 464. Brander Matthews, another important critic, agreed with Warner, in a review of *Huckleberry Finn*, by Mark Twain: "That Mr. Clemens draws from life, and yet lifts his work from the domain of the photographic to the region of art, is evident to anyone who will give his writing the honest attention it deserves" (Matthews, "Disolving Views." In *Americanisms and Briticisms, with Other Essays on Other Isms* by Brander Matthews [New York: Harper and Brothers, 1892], p. 161).

41. Emile Zola, *The Experimental Novel*. In *Documents of Modern Literary Realism*, ed. George J. Becker (Princeton: Princeton University Press, 1963), p. 168.

42. Frank Norris, "Zola as a Romantic Writer." In *American Thought and Writing: The 1890's*, ed. Donald Pizer (Boston: Houghton Mifflin Co., 1972), p. 98.

43. Interview with Samuel L. Clemens. In *Pittsburg Chronicle Telegraph*, 29 December 1884, p. 1.

44. Quoted in Hamlin Garland, "Mr. Howells's Latest Novels." In Pizer, ed., *American Thought*, p. 47. A year after this essay was written, Garland seems to have changed his mind, for in a lecture on Howells given on 17 August 1891, Garland was quoted as saying, "It is absurd to call him photographic. The photograph is false in perspective, in light and shade, in focus. When a photograph can depict atmosphere and sound, the comparison will have some meaning, and then it will not be used as a reproach" (quoted in Stephen Crane, "Howells Discussed at Avon-by-the-Sea," in Pizer, p. 52).

45. W.D. Howells, "A Case in Point," in Pizer, p. 61. See also W. D. Howells, "Criticism and Fiction," in *Criticism and Fiction*, ed. Clara Marburg Kirk and Rudolf Kirk (1892; rpt. New York: New York University Press, 1959), pp. 12–13, where Howells's famous grasshopper passage appears.

46. Especially his novels written and published during the 1880s. See Harold H. Kolb, Jr., *The Illusion of Life: American Realism as a Literary Form* (Charlottesville: University of Virginia Press, 1969), where the fictional works that James, Howells, and Twain wrote in the 1880s are discussed as examples of literary realism.

47. Review of *The Lady of the Aroostook*, by W. D. Howells, *Nation* 28 (1879), p. 205.

48. Review of *The Tragic Muse*, by Henry James, *Atlantic Monthly* 66 (1890), p. 419.

49. Ibid., p. 420.

50. Gombrich, *Art and Illusion*, p. 87.

51. Catherine Belsey, *Critical Practice* (London and New York: Methuen, 1980), p. 47. See Gombrich, *Art and Illusion*, pp. 63–90, 146–70, for discussion of these issues as they relate to the visual arts.

52. Belsey, *Critical Practice*, p. 51.

53. Ibid.

54. Warner, "Modern Fiction," p. 464.

55. See Robert Falk, *The Victorian Mode in American Fiction: 1865–1885* (East Lansing: Michigan State University Press, 1964), p. 160: "Anti-romanticism was still another form of realism, and Henry James became the master of transposed melodrama." An example of this is found in the ending of Henry James's tale, "The Pupil," in James, *Maisie*, vol. 11, pp. 509–77. See also, Kolb, *Illusion of Life*, p. xv.

56. Edel, *The Master*, vol. 5, p. 114.

57. Edgar Allan Poe, *Edgar Allan Poe's Complete Works: Marginalia*, ed. James A. Harrison, XVI (New York: Thomas Y. Crowell & Co., 1902), p. 164.

58. Ralph Waldo Emerson, "Art." In *Essays*, vol. 2, by Ralph Waldo Emerson, (1865; rpt. Cambridge, Mass.: Riverside, 1883), p. 351.

59. Kolb, *Illusion of Life*, p. 39.

60. Ibid., p. 40.

61. Naturalism tended to discount the role of the haphazard in the novel's causation. Psychology, too, was really only secondary. The primary causes of the characters' actions were heredity and environment, and their lives were impersonally swept along by forces about which they had little or no understanding and over which they had little control. Literary naturalism grew out of the scientific determinisms that were in vogue during the nineteenth century—Darwinism and Marxism, in particular. See Richard

Ellmann and Charles Feidelson, Jr., eds., *The Modern Tradition: Backgrounds of Modern Literature* (New York: Oxford University Press, 1965), pp. 229–378, for a discussion of these matters.

62. James, *Small Boy.* p. 243.

63. James, *Notes of a Son*, pp. 428–29.

64. James to The Deerfield Summer School [Summer 1889]. In Edel, ed., *Selected Letters of Henry James*, pp. 93–94.

65. R.P. Blackmur, "Introduction." In *Art of the Novel*, p. xv.

66. Henry James, "The Art of Fiction." In *Partial Portraits*, p. 384.

67. Ibid., p. 395.

68. Ibid., 408.

69. James, "Preface to *What Maisie Knew.*" In *Art of the Novel*, p. 143.

70. The term is Harold Kolb's in *Illusion of Life*. James recognized this clearly (see James, "Art of Fiction," p. 390).

71. James, "Art of Fiction," p. 388.

72. James to H. G. Wells, 10 July 1915. In Lubbock, ed., *Letters of Henry James*, vol. 2, p. 490.

73. Though not a painter, James responded to painting very much in the same way he did to fiction. He believed, for example, that Tintoretto's greatness emanated from that painter's pictorial ability to feel "the great, beautiful, terrible spectacle of human life very much as Shakespeare felt it poetically" (quoted in Edel, *Untried Years*, vol. 1, pp. 301–2). And Delacroix was "a man of imagination — of the richest" (Henry James, "The Letters of Eugene Delacroix." In *Painter's Eye*, p. 187). On the other hand, a Dutch painter, Van der Helst, lacked "invention blossoming into style," and he failed to "cross the line which separates a fine likeness from a fine portrait" (Henry James, "The Metropolitan Museum's '1871 Purchase.'" In *Painter's Eye*, p. 56). Winner sums up James's approach to painting: "In short, James valued most highly the painting he thought reflected the beauty to be found by the painter with imagination in an observable reality, but he could appreciate good painting as painting regardless of the offensiveness or inanity of the subject" (Winner, *Henry James*, p. 30). An example of this is James's response to the painting of the American, Winslow Homer (see James, "On Some Pictures Lately Exhibited." In *Painter's Eye*, pp. 96–97).

74. See Winner, *Henry James*, pp. 91–91, 94–126. See also Edel, *Untried Years*, vol. 1 p. 325.

75. Kirk, "Contemporary Essays," *Atlantic Monthly* 73 (1894), p. 267. Kirk added, however, that despite this, James still brought "real living creatures into a book" (p. 267).

76. James, *Notes of a Son*, p. 112.

77. James to Mrs. Henry James, Sr., 26 March 1870. In Edel, ed., *Selected Letters of Henry James*, p. 34. Thirty-two years later, James immortalized Minny Temple, drawing on her memory for one of his most beautiful realized heroines, Milly Theale, in *The Wings of the Dove* (1902). As James later put it in his memoirs, the image of Minny Temple's desire to live "was long to remain with me, [and it] appeared so of the essence of tragedy

that I was in the far off aftertime to seek to lay the ghost by wrapping it, a particular occasion aiding, in beauty and dignity of art" (James, *Notes of a Son*, p. 515).

78. W. D. Howells, "Henry James, Jr.," *Century* 25 (1882), p. 27.

79. Horace E. Scudder, Review of *The Tragic Muse*, by Henry James, *Atlantic Monthly* 66 (1890), p. 420.

80. Falk, *Victorian Mode*, p. 91. See also, Brooks, *Melodramatic Imagination*, passim.

81. F. O. Matthiesen and Kenneth B. Murdock, eds., *The Notebooks of Henry James* (New York: Oxford University Press, 1941), p. 102.

82. Sweeney, *Painter's Eye*, pp. 141–42. John Szarkowski, in *Looking at Photographs: 100 Pictures from the Collection of the Museum of Modern Art* (New York: Museum of Modern Art, 1973), p. 194, argues, "No mechanism has ever been devised that has recorded visual fact so clearly as photography. The consistent flaw in the system has been that it has recorded the wrong facts: not what we knew was there but what has appeared to be there. This Achilles' heel of the medium has long been recognized by theorists, and has been defined as 'superficial photographic accuracy,' or 'surface naturalism.'"

83. James, "Real Thing," p. 4.

84. Edel, *Treacherous Years*, vol. 4, p. 343.

85. La Farge is quoted by John L. Sweeney, "Introduction." In *Painter's Eye*, p. 9. Others have commented on James's acute visual sense. See Winner, *Henry James*, pp. 45, 60; and Edel, *Untried Years*, vol. 1, pp. 92–93.

86. For extensive discussions of these matters, see E. H. Gombrich, "The Visual Image," *Scientific American* 227 (September 1972), pp. 82–96; William M. Ivins, Jr., *Prints and Visual Communication* (1953; rpt. Cambridge, Mass., and London: M.I.T. Press, 1969), chapters 5, 6, and 7; and Jussim, *Visual Communication*, chapters 1, 2, and 3.

87. James, *Small Boy*, p. 53.

88. Ibid., p. 24; see also, pp. 178–79, for other examples.

89. James, *Notes of a Son*, p. 379.

90. Henry James, *The Middle Years*, ed. Percy Lubbock (New York: Charles Scribner's Sons, 1917), p. 6.

91. James, *Middle Years*, pp. 10–11.

92. James to Howells, 28 May 1896. In Lubbock, ed., *Letters of Henry James*, vol. 1, p. 48.

93. James, "Art of Fiction," p. 389.

94. *Compact Edition of the Oxford English Dictionary*, vol. 1 (Glasgow and New York: Oxford University Press, 1971), p. 310. See, for example the use of the word "impression" in Holmes, "Sun-Painting," p. 14. See also a letter from James to Mrs. Frank Mathews, 18 November 1902, in Lubbock, ed., *Letters of Henry James* vol. 1 p. 406, where James used the words "impression" and "image" to refer explicitly to photographs, a practice that seems to have recurred more often in James's writings after the turn of the century. Finally, note this usage by Stephen Crane in "The Blue Hotel" (1898): "During this pause, the Easterner's mind, like a film, took lasting impressions of three men." (*Stephen Crane: Stories and Tales*, ed. Robert Wooster Stallman [New York: Vintage-Random, 1952], p. 305).

95. James, *Middle Years*, p. 11.

96. James, *Small Boy*, p. 308.

97. Ibid., pp. 24-25.

98. Ibid., pp. 25-26. The Paris walks are described on p. 337.

99. Henry James, "Preface to *The Princess Casamassima*." In *Art of the Novel*, pp. 59-60; see also, p. 77.

100. Coburn, *Alvin Langdon Coburn, Photographer*, p. 58. It is important to note that we cannot clearly separate the influence of photography on nineteenth-century consciousness and perception from that of other technological innovations and experiences related to journalism and travel (the telegraph, quick sketch art made for wood engraved illustration, and so on). The influence of travel—particularly methods of travel—on the evolving consciousness is intriguing: a window of a coach or a train frames the world rather like a camera's viewfinder, and if the vehicle is moving, the scene changes almost as in a film. Can we say that nineteenth-century travel contributed to "photographic" and "filmic" perceptual consciousness? Reflect on the following: "Mr. James gave himself up to the little dreary pictures of Chicago life, which framed themselves on either hand in the square of cab door glass" (journalist's report of James's visit to Chicago, quoted in Edel, *The Master*, vol. 5, p. 276). See Emerson's journal entry of 29 August 1833, where he records an early (his first?) train ride (*The Journals and Miscellaneous Notebooks of Ralph Waldo Emerson*, vol. 4, ed. Alfred R. Ferguson [Cambridge, Mass.: Harvard-Belknap Press, 1964], p. 226).

101. Robert A. Sobieszek, "Photography and the Theory of Realism in the Second Empire: A Reexamination of a Relationship." In *One Hundred Years of Photographic History: Essays in Honor of Beaumont Newhall*, ed. Van Deren Coke (Albuquerque: University of New Mexico Press, 1975), p. 155.

102. The problem of definition always arises when we confront the various attempts to discuss realism in the disparate arts. See Susan Sontag, "Against Interpretation." In *Against Interpretation* by Susan Sontag (New York: Delta-Dell, 1966), pp. 3-14; and Erich Auerbach, *Mimesis: The Representation of Reality in Western Literature*, trans. Willard R. Trask (1946; rpt. Princeton: Princeton University Press, 1968). Though nineteenth-century painters such as Ingres, Delacroix, and Courbet were mimetic in their representations, only Courbet was considered a "Realist." Ingres was labeled a "Classicist," Delacroix a "Romantic." Courbet was a Realist partly because of the subject matter he used—everyday, ordinary social phenomena. Though each used mimetic representation, neither Sir Walter Scott nor James Fenimore Cooper were "realists" as nineteenth-century critics defined the term. On the other hand, "realism" was the label often applied to writers such as Howells, Tolstoy, James, Zola, Dreiser, and others. The latter group of writers are distinguishable from the former in that their attitudes toward the world were empirical and critical and they tended to embody their explorations and criticism in their works. They refused to idealize or romanticize the fictional lives they constructed—at least when compared with nineteenth-century practitioners of idealism and romance.

103. Recall E. H. Gombrich's remark, quoted earlier in the text: "All art originates in the human mind, in our reactions to the world rather than in the visible world itself, and it is precisely because all art is 'conceptual' that all representations are recognized by their style" (*Art and Illusion*, p. 87).

104. Egbert, *Social Radicalism*, p. 235. Recall, too, that Varnadoe, in "Artiface of Candor," pp. 71–76, does not dispute this proclivity; he just objects to photography being treated as a prime cause of this phenomenon.

105. Ralph Waldo Emerson, *Nature*. In *Selected Writings of Ralph Waldo Emerson*, ed. William H. Gillman (New York: New American Library, 1965), p. 193.

106. Walt Whitman, "Song of Myself." In *Complete Poems and Selected Prose* by Walt Whitman, ed. James E. Miller, Jr. (Boston: Riverside-Houghton-Mifflin, 1959), p. 32; see also, Whitman, "Cavalry Crossing a Ford." In *Complete Poems*, p. 215.

107. Numerous examples of this influence may be found in nineteenth-century literature. For instance, Stephen Crane's hero in *The Red Badge of Courage* (1895), as John Szarkowski has noted, "sees the War as though he were a camera: 'His mind took a mechanical but firm impression, so that afterward everything was pictured and explained to him, save why he himself was there'" (*Looking at Photographs* [New York: Museum of Modern Art, 1973], p. 26). Crane's book is filled with too many other examples of a photographic/cinematic sense of image and narrative structure to allow us to believe that such things are mere quirks. For extensive discussion of these matters, see Spiegel, *Fiction and the Camera Eye*, passim.

108. Sypher, *Rococo to Cubism*, p. 287.

109. See Sypher, pp. 257–94, for a discussion of cubism and the camera. Notable in this context are the scientific motion studies of Eadweard Muybridge (*Animal Locomotion* [1887]), Thomas Eakins, and Etienne Jules Marey. See also the early photo-interview of the French scientist, Michel-Eugène Chevreul, by Paul Nadar, appearing in the 5 September 1886 issue of *Le Journal illustré* (see Newhall, *History of Photography*, pp. 181–82). As mentioned in chapter five, the "picture-story" became common in mass magazines by 1900 (see F. B. Johnston, "The New Idea in Teaching Children," *Ladies' Home Journal* 17 [April 1900], pp. 20–21; and F. B. Johnston, "President Roosevelt's Children," *Ladies' Home Journal* 19 [August 1902], pp. 18–19).

110. See Scharf, *Art and Photography*, chapters 7 and 8. Compare Monet's Rouen cathedral series with Timothy O'Sullivan's series of photographs of the Grand Canyon (ca. 1872) that record a single scene at different times of the day (see Barbara Novak, "Landscape Permuted: From Painting to Photography," *Artforum* 14 [October 1975], p. 44). Manet's work also provides good examples of this pervasive phenomenon (see Nochlin, *Realism*, pp. 31–33).

111. See Sergei Eisenstein, "Dickens, Griffith, and the Film Today." In *Film Form Essays in Film Theory*, ed. and trans. Jay Leyda (New York: Harcourt, Brace and Co., 1949), pp. 195–272; and John L. Fell, *Film and the Narrative Tradition* (Norman: University of Oklahoma Press, 1974), pp. 3–86.

112. Joseph Frank, "Spatial Form in Modern Literature." In *The Widening Gyre: Crisis and Mastery in Modern Literature* by Joseph Frank (1963; rpt. Bloomington: Indiana University Press, 1968), pp. 8–9.

113. Sypher, *Rococo to Cubism*, p. 266. Arnold Hauser agrees: chapter eight in *Social History*, vol. 4, is entitled "The Film Age."

114. Sypher's words, *Rococo to Cubism*, p. 267.

115. Again, Sypher's words, p. 266.

116. Edel, *Treacherous Years*, p. 112.

117. Edel, *The Master*, vol. 5, pp. 77, 78.

118. Edel, "Novel and Camera," p. 181.

119. Compare Gertrude Stein's observations regarding the relation between cinema and prose when she began writing: "In the beginning . . . I was doing what the cinema was doing, I was making a continuous succession of the statement of what that person [in *Tender Buttons*] was until I had not many things but one thing.

    "I of course did not think of it in terms of the cinema, in fact I doubt whether at that time I had ever seen a cinema but, and I cannot repeat this too often any one is of one's period and this our period was undoubtedly the period of the cinema and series production. And each of us in our own way are bound to express what the world in which we are living is doing.

    "You see then what I was doing in my beginning portrait writing and you also understand what I mean when I say there was no repetition. In a cinema picture no two pictures are exactly alike each one is just that much different from the one before, and so in those early portraits there was as I am sure you will realize as I read them to you also . . . no repetition" (Gertrude Stein, *Lectures in America* [1935; rpt. New York: Vintage-Random, 1975], pp. 176–77).

120. James, "Preface to *Roderick Hudson*." In *Art of the Novel*, p 5.

121. James, "Preface to *The Portrait of a Lady*." In *Art of the Novel*, p. 46.

122. James, "Preface to *The Awkward Age*." In *Art of the Novel*, p. 101.

123. James, "Preface to *The Wings of the Dove*." In *Art of the Novel*, p. 289.

124. Winner, *Henry James*, p. 65. See James, "Preface to *The Wings of the Dove*," pp. 288–306, for an extensive discussion of this phenomenon.

125. Stowell, *Literary Impressionism*, p. 17. See Stowell, pp. 13–55, for an extensive discussion of literary impressionism in general, and pp. 169–239, for discussion of James as a literary impressionist. For a discussion of James as a literary cinematographer, see Spiegel, *Fiction and Camera Eye*, pp. 53–68; Edel, "Novel and Camera," passim; and Bogardus, "Photographer's Eye." The last offers an analysis of James's *The American Scene* as a photographic/cinematic book. James's subordination of chronology is noted in J. A. Ward, *The Search for Form: Studies in the Structure of James's Fiction* (Chapel Hill: University of North Carolina Press, 1967), p. 31 n. 7.

126. Sypher, *Rococo to Cubism*, p. 266.

127. William James to Henry James, 4 May 1907.

128. "Handsomely Illustrated," p. 137. The anonymous reader's remark appears on the first blank recto page in the front matter of a copy of the American first edition of Henry James's *The American Scene* that is in the collection of the Amelia Gayle Gorgas Library, The University of Alabama.

Chapter 7

1. This is suggested by James's apparent distaste for allegory in visual and, one might add, literary art. See Henry James, "The Picture Season in London (1877)," in *Painter's Eye*, p. 142, where he wrote that he believed "allegory, an uncomfortable thing in painting," even though a few succeeded at it — for example, G. F. Watts. Max Kozloff, "Critical and Historical Problems of Photography," in *Renderings: Critical Essays on a Century of Modern Art* by Max Kozloff (New York: Simon and Schuster-Clarion, 1969), p. 291,

suggests that, though photographs imply a narrative, still photography "cannot ultimately tell a story. The explanation for the ambiguity of the photographic presence, rather, is that it constantly jeopardizes our notion of reality by opposing the impersonal, unbiased evidence of a light-sensitized film to the unconsciously selected data processed by the human retina, and that to arrest the flux of the natural world is in large measure to change its character. One expects discrepancies between the seen and the recreated in painting; but in photography there is usually no such ritual allowance, and thus the divergent results of the camera often have a sinister fascination. Exactly because the level of recognizability in photographs is so high, their random and accidental lapses from that level form a very keen-edged exploration into the unknown."

2. Hugh Kenner suggested this dichotomy to me in a conversation some time ago. He attributed it to poet Basil Bunting. Kenner speculated that these impulses show up in language as well as in other ways. For example, Tennyson used what Kenner terms "soft-focus" language, choosing words like "moved" instead of "walked." Here, sound is more important than specificity of meaning. James's language could be said to be "soft focus" too.

3. See Blackmur, "Introduction." In *Art of the Novel*, pp. xiii ff.

4. Kozloff, "Critical and Historical Problems," p. 288.

5. James, "On Some Pictures Lately Exhibited," p. 97.

6. Ibid., p. 96.

7. Winner, *Henry James*, p. 52.

8. James mentioned seeing the pre-Raphaelites for the first time in 1855 and responding favorably to their work, especially that of Millais (James, *Small Boy*, p. 316). By 1897, however, James found pre-Raphaelite painting only agreeable and not particularly great, possessing only pleasantness and a sense of craft (see Henry James, "The New Gallery [1897]," in *Painter's Eye*, pp. 244–46; and Henry James, "Lord Leighton and Ford Madox Brown [1897]," in *Painter's Eye*, pp. 247–50). For discussion of James's changing preferences in painting, see Winner, *Henry James*, pp. 9–13. All information regarding James's responses to painting and painters comes from this source unless otherwise noted.

9. The best example of James's ability to grow in his aesthetic views is his response to Impressionism. He began by disliking it. Impressionists were "partisans of unadorned reality and absolute foes to arrangement, embellishment, selection . . . the beautiful" (Henry James, "The Impressionists [1876]. In *Painter's Eye*, p. 114). For a discussion of James's change of heart regarding Impressionism, see Winner, *Henry James*, pp. 45–48, 108. There is evidence that James saw an early exhibit of post-Impressionist painting in London, arranged by Roger Fry in 1912. According to Virginia Woolf, James responded to Picasso and Matisse with "disturbed hesitations" (quoted in Winner, p. 53). Fry tried to explain the new art to James, but we do not know with what success. Interestingly, there is an unconscious relation between some of Coburn's complexly structured pre-1907 photographs and post-Impressionist art (see figures 49, 51, and 52). James evidently approved of these protocubist images, for they were among those appearing in Coburn's 1906 London exhibition — the one James saw before deciding to use Coburn as a collaborator.

10. Quoted in Doty, *Photo-Secession*, p. 24.

11. Ibid., p. 25.

12. For a more extensive discussion of this important exhibition and of F. Holland Day, see Homer, *Alfred Stieglitz*, pp. 39–42.

13. Pennell, "Is Photography among the Fine Arts?" See also, "Is Photography among the Fine Arts: A Symposium," *Magazine of Art* 23 (1899), pp. 102–5, 156–58, 206–9, 253–56, and 369–73. Pennell's attack, it should be noted, also expressed a nasty strain of nativism.

14. Katheryn Staley, "Photography as a Fine Art," *Munsey's Magazine* 14 (1896), p. 582.

15. Ibid., p. 588. There are ten examples included in the article (see pp. 582–90).

16. Quoted in Homer, *Alfred Stieglitz*, p. 28.

17. This discussion of the beginnings of amateur art-photography comes largely from Homer, *Alfred Stieglitz*, pp. 31–33.

18. For a brief discussion of this period in Stieglitz's life, see Homer, *Alfred Stieglitz*, pp. 8–15.

19. Discussion of this aspect is found in Homer, *Alfred Stieglitz*, pp. 16–42.

20. Theodore Dreiser, "A Master of Photography," *Success* 2 (1899), p. 471. In another article published during the same year, Dreiser featured the Camera Club of New York: Theodore Dreiser, "The Camera Club of New York," *Ainslee's* (4 October 1899), pp. 324–35. Stieglitz's leadership was unchallenged by 1902. That he was a major force is evidenced not only by Dreiser's and Marsden's bestowal on him of the seal of *Success*, but also by the fact that he was mentioned frequently in articles about pictorialism and was himself published in non-art journals and magazines. See, for example, Theodore Dreiser, "A Remarkable Art," *The Great Round World* (3 May 1902), pp. 430–34; Alfred Stieglitz, "The New Photography: vol. 2. Modern Pictorial Photography," *Century* 64 (1902), pp. 822–26; and John Corbin, "The Twentieth Century City," *Scribner's Magazine* 30 (1903), pp. 259–72, an essay that was illustrated extensively from photographs by Alfred Stieglitz.

21. Homer, *Alfred Stieglitz*, pp. 36–37.

22. Ibid., p. 37.

23. Ibid., p. 39.

24. Ibid., pp. 39–42.

25. Ibid., pp. 39–40.

26. Ibid., p. 40.

27. This is discussed more extensively in Homer, *Alfred Stieglitz*, pp. 40–42.

28. Ibid., p. 42.

29. For a full discussion of the particulars of this, see Homer, *Alfred Stieglitz*, pp. 43–48.

30. Ibid., pp. 53–57.

31. Ibid., pp. 111–17.

32. Quoted in Homer, *Alfred Stieglitz*, p. 112.

33. Ibid., pp. 118–26.

34. Ibid., pp. 143–47.

35. Ibid., pp. 109–10.

36. Ibid., p. 142.

37. Coburn, *Alvin Langdon Coburn, Photographer*, pp. 14–20.

38. Biographical data on Coburn comes from Homer, *Alfred Stieglitz*, pp. 101–10, and Coburn, *Alvin Langdon Coburn, Photographer*, passim, unless otherwise noted.

39. Barbara Rose, *American Art since 1900*, rev. ed. (New York: Praeger, 1975), p. 33.

40. Ibid.

41. Thomas Harrison Cummings, "Some Photographs by Alvin Langdon Coburn," *Photo Era* 10 (March 1903), pp. 87–88; see also, pp. 90 ff.

42. Charles H. Caffin, "Some Prints by Alvin Langdon Coburn," *Camera Work* (April 1904), no. 6, p. 18.

43. Ibid., p. 19.

44. George Bernard Shaw, "Preface." In *Alvin Langdon Coburn Exhibition Catalogue, April 30 to May 19, 1906* (London: Royal Photographic Society, 1906), n.p.

45. Sadakichi Hartmann, "Alvin Langdon Coburn, Secession Portraiture." In *The Valiant Knights of Daguerre* by Sadakichi Hartmann, ed. Harry W. Lawton and George Knox (Berkeley and Los Angeles: University of California Press, 1978), p. 258.

46. Doty, *Photo-Secession*, pp. 29, 31.

47. Coburn, *Alvin Langdon Coburn, Photographer*, p. 20.

48. See Newhall, *History of Photography*, pp. 96–99.

49. Coburn, *Alvin Langdon Coburn, Photographer*, p. 18.

50. See Corbin, "Twentieth Century City," pp. 259–72, for a wide variety of street images by Alfred Stieglitz.

51. See Doty, *Photo-Secession*, pp. 43, 45.

52. Quoted in Nancy Newhall, "Introduction." In Coburn, *A Portfolio of Sixteen Photographs*, p. 5.

53. Coburn, *Alvin Langdon Coburn, Photographer*, p. 48.

54. Ibid., p. 44.

55. James, "Preface to *The Golden Bowl*," p. 335.

56. Hartmann, "Alvin Langdon Coburn, Secession Portraiture," p. 256.

57. Ibid.

58. Ibid.

59. Ibid., pp. 256, 259.

60. Ibid., pp. 259–60.

61. Ibid., p. 260.

62. Ibid.

63. James, "Preface to *The Golden Bowl*," p. 334.

64. Ibid.

65. Sweeney, "Introduction." In *Painter's Eye*, p. 22.

66. Kozloff, "Critical and Historical Problems," pp. 288–89.

67. Coburn, "Illustrating Henry James," p. 3.

68. Henry James to William James, 14 November 1878. In Lubbock, ed., *Letters of Henry James*, vol. 1, p. 66.

69. Quoted in Edel, *The Master*, vol. 5, p. 378.

Chapter 8

1. James, "Preface to *The Golden Bowl*," pp. 331–32.

2. Ibid., p. 333.

3. Ibid., p. 334.

4. Ibid., p. 333.

5. Szarkowski, *Looking at Photographs*, p. 62.

6. Ibid.

7. James, "Preface to *The Golden Bowl*," p. 331.

8. Ibid.

9. Ibid., p. 333.

10. Ibid., pp. 332–33.

11. Ibid., p. 333.

12. William Flint Thrall and Addison Hibbard, *A Handbook to Literature*, rev. C. Hugh Holman (New York: Odyssey Press, 1960), p. 478.

13. Charles R. Anderson, "Person, Place, and Thing in James's *The Portrait of a Lady*." In *Essays on American Literature in Honor of Jay B. Hubbell*, ed. Clarence Gohdes (Durham, N.C.: Duke University Press, 1967), p. 166. Viola Winner, agrees, stating that, "It is the relation of character to 'things' as well as to people that is for James the touchstone of moral sensibility" (p. viii).

14. Anderson, "Person, Place, and Thing," p. 166.

15. This is true even though verbal symbols like the golden bowl already work in this same way. There are a few verbal symbols that work in this holistic way—the spoils being one good example.

16. Gombrich, "Visual Image," p. 82.

17. Ibid.

18. Ibid., p. 86.

19. Henry James, *The Novels and Tales of Henry James: Roderick Hudson*, vol. 1 (New York: Charles Scribner's Sons, 1907). All references to works included in the New York Edition will, after their initial citation, be cited parenthetically in the text and identified by volume number.

20. Henry James, *The Novels and Tales of Henry James: The Portrait of a Lady*, vols. 3–4 (New York: Charles Scribner's Sons, 1908).

21. Henry James, *The Novels and Tales of Henry James: The Princess Casamassima*, vols. 5–6 (New York: Charles Scribner's Sons, 1908).

22. Jay Martin, *Harvests of Change: American Literature, 1865–1914* (Englewood Cliffs: Prentice-Hall, 1967), p. 336.

23. Lewis S. Feuer, "Introduction." In *Marx and Engels: Basic Writings on Politics and Philosophy*, ed. Lewis S. Feuer (Garden City: Doubleday-Anchor, 1959), p. x.

24. Henry James, *The Novels and Tales of Henry James: Daisy Miller, Pandora, The Patagonia, and Other Tales*, vol. 18 (New York: Charles Scribner's Sons, 1909).

25. Henry James, "Preface to *Daisy Miller*." In *Art of the Novel*, p. 270.

26. F. W. Dupee, *Henry James* (New York: William Sloane Assoc., Inc., 1951), p. 108.

27. Henry James, "Europe," In *The Novels and Tales of Henry James: The Author of Belraffio, The Middle Years, Greville Fane, and Other Tales*, vol. 16 (New York: Charles Scribner's Sons, 1909).

28. James, *The American*, vol. 2.

29. Henry James, *The Novels and Tales of Henry James: The Wings of the Dove*, vol. 19 (New York: Charles Scribner's Sons, 1909).

30. James, *Aspern Papers*, vol. 11.

31. Henry James, *The Novels and Tales of Henry James: The Golden Bowl*, vols. 23–24 (New York: Charles Scribner's Sons, 1909).

32. James, "Preface to *The Golden Bowl*," p. 334.

33. Ibid., p. 335.

Epilogue

1. Memorandum to Charles Scribner's Sons, 30 July 1905. In Edel, ed., *Henry James Letters*, vol. 4, pp. 366–67.

2. Ibid., p. 368.

3. James to Elizabeth Robins, 28 March 1906. In Robins, ed., *Theater and Friendship*, pp. 256–57.

4. James to Charles Scribner's Sons, 31 December 1907. In Edel, ed., *Henry James Letters*, vol. 4, p. 484.

5. James to Pinker, 23 October 1908. In Edel, ed., *Henry James Letters*, vol. 4, p. 498. See also James to Howells, 17 August 1908, James Family Collection, Henry James, Jr., Papers, Houghton Library, Harvard University, for the expression of disappointment at the public reception of the Edition.

6. Quoted in Edel, *The Master*, vol. 5, p. 339.

7. No reviews appeared in 1909 or 1910 (see *Book Review Digest* 5 [Minneapolis: H. W. Wilson Co., 1909], pp. 228–29; and *Book Review Digest* 6 [Minneapolis: H. W. Wilson Co., 1910], pp. 202–8).

8. Hale, "Rejuvenation of Henry James," p. 176.

9. Ibid., p. 175.

10. Review of *The Novels and Tales of Henry James, The New York Edition*, vols. 3–4," *Nation* 86 (1908), p. 215. See also review of *The Novels and Tales of Henry James, The New York Edition*, vols. 1–2, *Nation* 86 (1908), p. 11.

11. Review of *The Novels and Tales of Henry James, New York Edition*, vols. 1–6, *Literary Digest* 36 (1908), p. 418.

12. Review of *Novels and Tales, Literary Digest*, p. 418.

13. Hale, "Rejuvenation of Henry James," p. 176.

14. Quoted in Edel, *The Master*, vol. 5, p. 339. As if to add insult to injury, reviewers praised the reissued *Italian Hours* in 1909 and commented favorably on Pennell's illustrations (review of *Italian Hours, Independent*, 67 [1909], p. 1352; and review of *Italian Hours, Literary Digest* 39 [1909], p. 1073).

15. James, "Preface to *The Golden Bowl*," p. 333.

16. James to Coburn, dated 18 August 1912, James Collection, Virginia.

Bibliography

Abercrombie, Stanley. "Beaux-Arts at the Modern." *Artforum* 14 (February 1976), 52–56.

Anderson, Charles R. "Person, Place, and Thing in James's *The Portrait of a Lady*." In *Essays on American Literature in Honor of Jay B. Hubbell*, edited by Clarence Gohdes. Durham, N.C.: Duke University Press, 1967.

Arms, George W. "Howells' English Travel Books: Problems in Technique." *PMLA* 82 (1967), 104–16.

Baudelaire, Charles. *The Mirror of Art: Critical Studies*. Edited and translated by Jonathan Mayne. London: Phaidon, 1955.

Becker, George J., ed. *Documents of Modern Literary Realism*. Princeton: Princeton University Press, 1967.

Benjamin, Walter. "Paris, Capital of the 19th Century." *Dissent* 17 (1970), 438–47.

_____ , "A Short History of Photography." Translated by Phil Patton. *Artforum* 15 (February 1977), 46–51.

_____ . "The Work of Art in the Age of Mechanical Reproduction." In *Illuminations* by Walter Benjamin. Edited by Hannah Arendt, and translated by Harry Zohn. 1955. Reprint. New York: Schocken, 1969.

Black, Alexander. "The Camera and the Comedy." *Scribner's* 20 (1896), 604–10.

Bland, David. *A History of Book Illustration: The Illuminated Manuscript and the Printed Book*. Berkeley and Los Angeles: University of California Press, 1969.

Bogardus, Ralph F. "A Literary Realist and the Camera: W. D. Howells and the Uses of Photography." *American Literary Realism, 1870–1910* 10 (1977), 231–41.

_____ . "The Photographer's Eye: Henry James and *The American Scene*." *History of Photography* 8 (1984), 179–96.

Boorstin, Daniel. *The Image: A Guide to Pseudo-Events in America*. New York and Evanston: Harper-Colophon, 1961.

Boult, Ella M. "The Illustration of Books by Artistic Photographs." *Independent* 61 (1906), 1414–20.

Brooks, Peter. *The Melodramatic Imagination: Balzac, Henry James, Melodrama, and the Mode of Excess*. New Haven, Conn.: Yale University Press, 1976.

Buckland, Gail. *Fox Talbot and the Invention of Photography*. Boston: David R. Godine, 1980.

_____ . *Reality Recorded: Early Documentary Photography*. Greenwich, Conn.: New York Graphic Society, 1974.

Buckley, Jerome Hamilton. *The Victorian Temper: A Study in Literary Culture*. 1951. Reprint. New York: Vintage-Random, n.d.

Caffin, Charles H. *Photography as a Fine Art: The Achievements and Possibilities of Photographic Art in America*. New York: Doubleday, Page & Co., 1901.

_____ . "Some Prints by Alvin Langdon Coburn." *Camera Work*, No. 6 (April 1904), 17–19.

"Characteristics of the International Fair: Closing Days, VI." *Atlantic Monthly* 39 (1877), 94–100.

Chase, Richard. *The American Novel and Its Tradition*. Garden City: Doubleday-Anchor, 1957.

Coburn, Alvin Langdon. *Alvin Langdon Coburn, Photographer: An Autobiography*. Edited by Helmut and Alison Gernsheim. London: Faber & Faber, 1966.

———. "Illustrating Henry James." London: B.B.C. Third Programme, 18 July 1953, 9:50–10:15 p.m.

———. *Men of Mark*. New York: Mitchell Kennerley, 1913.

———. "New Portraits of a Group of British Authors." *Century* 70 (1905), 11–18.

———. *A Portfolio of Sixteen Photographs*. Edited by Nancy Newhall. Rochester, N.Y.: George Eastman House, 1962.

Coke, Van Deren. *The Painter and the Photograph, from Delacroix to Warhol*. Albuquerque: University of New Mexico Press, 1972.

Congdon, Charles T. "Over-Illustration." *North American Review* 139 (1884), 480–91.

"Contributor's Club. Concerning *realism*." *Atlantic Monthly* 41 (1878), 130–34.

Corbin, John. "The Twentieth Century City." *Scribner's* 30 (1903), 259–72.

Crane, Walter. *Of the Decorative Illustration of Books Old and New*. 3rd edition. 1905. Reprint. Detroit: Gale Research Co., 1968.

Cummings, Thomas Harrison. "Some Photographs by Alvin Langdon Coburn." *Photo Era* 10 (1903), 87–92.

Darrah, William Culp. *Stereo Views: A History of Stereographs in America and Their Collection*. Gettysburg: Times & News, 1964.

Doty, Robert. *Photo-Secession: Photography as a Fine Art*. Rochester, N.Y.: George Eastman House, 1960.

Dreiser, Theodore. "A Master of Photography." *Success* 2 (1899), 471.

———. "A Remarkable Art." *The Great Round World* (3 May 1902), 430–34.

———. "The Camera Club of New York." *Ainslee's* (4 October 1899), 324–35.

Duncan, Carol. "Neutralizing the Age of Revolution." *Artforum* 14 (December 1975), 46–54.

Dupee, F. W. *Henry James*. New York: William Sloane Assoc., Inc., 1951.

———. "Introduction." *Henry James: Autobiography*. Edited F. W. Dupee. New York: Criterion Books, 1956.

Edel, Leon, ed. *Henry James Letters*. 4 vols. Cambridge, Mass.: Harvard University Press, 1974–84.

———. *The Life of Henry James*. 5 vols. Philadelphia and New York: Lippincott, 1952–72.

———. "Novel and Camera." In *The Theory of the Novel: New Essays*. Edited by John Halpern. New York, London, and Toronto: Oxford University Press, 1974.

———, ed. *The Selected Letters of Henry James*. New York: Farrar, Straus and Cudahy, 1955.

———, and Dan H. Laurence, eds. *A Bibliography of Henry James*. London: Rupert Hart-Davis, 1961.

Edgerton, Giles [Mary Fanton Roberts]. "Photography as One of the Fine Arts: The Camera Pictures of Alvin Langdon Coburn a Vindication of This Statement." *The Craftsman* 12 (1907), 394–402.

Egbert, Donald Drew. *Social Radicalism and the Arts*. New York: Knopf, 1970.

Ellmann, Richard, and Charles Feidelson, Jr., eds. *The Modern Tradition: Backgrounds of Modern Literature*. New York: Oxford University Press, 1965.

Emerson, Ralph Waldo. "Art." *Essays* by Ralph Waldo Emerson. Vol. II. 1865. Reprint. Cambridge, Mass.: Riverside, 1883.

_____. *Journals of Ralph Waldo Emerson, 1841–1844*. Vol. VI. Edited by Edward Waldo Emerson and Waldo Emerson Forbes. Boston and New York: Houghton Mifflin, 1912.

Fairfield, Sidney. "The Tyranny of the Pictorial." *Lippincott's Monthly Magazine* 55 (1895), 861–64.

Falk, Robert. *The Victorian Mode in American Fiction: 1865–1885*. East Lansing: Michigan State University Press, 1964.

Fell, John L. *Film and the Narrative Tradition*. Norman, Okla.: University of Oklahoma Press, 1974.

Firebaugh, Joseph J. "Coburn: Henry James's Photographer." *American Quarterly* 7 (1955), 215–33.

Frank, Joseph. "Spatial Form in Modern Literature." In *The Widening Gyre: Crisis and Mastery in Modern Literature* by Joseph Frank. 1963. Reprint. Bloomington: Indiana University Press, 1968.

Gass, William H. "The High Brutality of Good Intentions." In *Fiction and the Figures of Life* by William H. Gass. 1971. Reprint. New York: Vintage-Random, 1972.

Gernsheim, Helmut and Alison Gernsheim. *The History of Photography, 1685–1914*. New York: McGraw-Hill, 1969.

Goldberg, Vicki, ed. *Photography in Print: Writings from 1816 to the Present*. New York: Simon and Schuster-Touchstone, 1981.

Gombrich, E. H. *Art and Illusion: A Study in the Psychology of Pictorial Representation*. 1960. Reprint. Princeton: Princeton University Press, 1969.

_____. "The Visual Image." *Scientific American* 227 (September 1972), 82–96.

Green, Jonathan, ed. *Camera Work: A Critical Anthology*. Millerton: Aperture, 1973.

"A Growl for the Unpicturesque." *Atlantic Monthly* 98 (1906), 140–43.

Hale, Edward E., Jr. "The Rejuvenation of Henry James." *Dial* 44 (1908), 174–76.

Hamerton, Philip Gilbert. "Book Illustraiton." In *Portfolio Papers* by Philip Gilbert Hamerton. London: Seeley & Co., 1889.

"Handsomely Illustrated." *Atlantic Monthly* 93 (1904), 136–37.

Harris, Neil. "Inconography and Intellectual History: The Half-tone Effect." In *New Directions in American Intellectual History*. Edited by John Higham and Paul K. Conkin. Baltimore and London: The Johns Hopkins University Press, 1979.

Hartmann, Sadakichi. "Alvin Langdon Coburn, Secession Portraiture." In *The Valiant Knights of Daguerre* by Sadakichi Hartmann. Edited by Harry W. Lawton and George Knox. Berkeley and Los Angeles: University of California press, 1978.

Harvey, J. R. *Victorian Novelists and Their Illustrators*. New York: New York University Press, 1971.

Hauser, Arnold. *The Social History of Art*. 4 vols. 1951. Reprint. New York: Vintage-Random, n.d.

Higgins, Charles. "Photographic Aperture: Coburn's Frontispieces to James's New York Edition." *American Literature* 53 (1982), 661–75.

Holmes, Oliver Wendell. "Doings of the Sunbeam." *Atlantic Monthly* 12 (1863), 1–15.

_____. "The Stereoscope and the Stereograph." *Atlantic Monthly* 3 (1859), 738–48.

_____. "Sun-Painting and Sun-Sculpture." *Atlantic Monthly* 8 (1861), 13–29.

Homer, William Innes. *Alfred Stieglitz and the Photo-Secession*. Boston: Little, Brown and Company, 1983.

Howells, W. D. "Editor's Study." *Harper's Monthly* 72 (1886), 972–76.

_____. "Henry James, Jr." *Century* 25 (1882), 25–29.

_____. *London Films*. New York and London: Harper & Brothers, 1905.

Ivins, William M. *Prints and Visual Communication*. 1953. Reprint. Cambridge, Mass.: M. I. T. Press, 1969.

Jablow, Betsy Lynn. "Illustrated Texts from Dickens to James." Ph.D. diss., Stanford University, 1978.

Jackson, Holbrook. *The Eighteen Nineties: A Review of Art and Ideas at the Close of the Nineteenth Century.* London: G. Richards, 1913.

Jackson, Mason. *The Pictorial Press: Its Origins and Progress.* London: Hurst and Backett, 1885.

Jacobson, Marcia. *Henry James and the Mass Market.* University, Ala.: University of Alabama Press, 1983.

James, Henry. *The American Scene.* London: Chapman and Hall, 1907.

––––––. *The American Scene.* Edited by Leon Edel. 1907. Reprint. Bloomington: Indiana University Press, 1968.

––––––. "The Art of Fiction." In *Partial Portraits* by Henry James. 1888. Reprint. New York: Haskell House Publishers, Ltd., 1968.

––––––. *The Art of the Novel: Critical Prefaces.* Edited by R. P. Blackmur. 1934. Reprint. New York: Scribner's, 1947.

––––––. "The Beldonald Holbein." *Harper's Monthly* 103 (1901), 807–21.

––––––. "DuMaurier and London Society." *Century* 26 (1883), 51–65.

––––––. *English Hours.* Boston and New York: Houghton, Mifflin and Co., 1905.

––––––. "George DuMaurier." *Harper's Monthly* 95 (1897), 594–609.

––––––. "Greville Fane." *Illustrated London News* (17 and 24 September 1892), 361–63, 393–95.

––––––. "Julia Bride." *Harper's Monthly* 116 (1908), 489–502, 705–13.

––––––. "London." *Century* 37 (1888), 219–39.

––––––. "Louisa Pallant." *Harper's Monthly* 76 (1888), 336–55.

––––––. *The Middle years.* Edited by Percy Lubbock. New York: Charles Scribner's Sons, 1917.

––––––. *Notes of a Son and Brother.* New York: Charles Scribner's Sons, 1914.

––––––. *The Novels and Tales of Henry James: New York Edition.* 26 vols. New York: Charles Scribner's Sons, 1907–09, 1917.

––––––. *Picture and Text.* New York: Harper & Brothers, 1893.

––––––. "The Real Thing." *Black and White* 3 (1892), 502–7.

––––––. "The Real Thing." In *The Real Thing and Other Tales* by Henry James. New York and London: Macmillan and Co., 1893.

[––––––]. Review of *Essays on Fiction* by Nassau W. Senior. *North American Review* 99 (1864), 580–87.

[––––––]. Review of *Miss Mackenzie* by Anthony Trollope. In *Notes and Reviews* by Henry James. Cambridge, Mass.: Dunster Hosue, 1921.

[––––––]. Review of *Round My House: Notes of a Rural Life in France in Peace and War* by Philip Gilbert Hamerton. *Nation* 27 (1876), 85–86.

––––––. *A Small Boy and Others.* New York: Charles Scribner's Sons, 1913.

James, Henry, ed. *The Letters of William James.* 2 vols. Boston: Atlantic Monthly Press, 1920.

Jenkins, Reese V. "Technology and the Market: George Eastman and the Origins of Mass Amateur Photography." *Technology and Culture* 16 (1975), 1–19.

Jenks, Tudor. "The Decadence of Illustration." *Independent* 51 (1899), 3487–89.

Jones, Bernard C., ed. *The Encyclopedia of Photography.* 1879. Reprint. New York: Arno Press, 1974.

Jussim, Estelle. *Visual Communication and the Graphic Arts: Photographic Technologies in the Nineteenth Century.* New York and London: R. R. Bowker Co., 1974.

Kamholtz, Jonathan. "Literature and Photography: The Captioned Vision Vs. the Firm, Mechanical Impression." *Centennial Review* 24 (1980), 385–402.

Keyes, Donald D. "The Daguerreotype's Popularity in America." *Art Journal* 26 (1976–77), 116–22.

Kirk, S. "Contemporary Essays." *Atlantic Monthly* 73 (1894), 262–69.

Kirstein, Lincoln. "Walt Whitman and Thomas Eakins: A Poet's and a Painter's Camera-Eye." *Aperture* No. 3 (1972), n.p.

Kolb, Harold H., Jr. *The Illusion of Life: American Realism as a Literary Form*. Charlottesville: University Press of Virginia, 1969.

Kozloff, Max. "Critical and Historical Problems of Photography." In *Renderings: Critical Essays on a Century of Modern Art* by Max Kozloff. New York: Simon and Schuster-Clarion, 1969.

Levy, Leo Ben. *Versions of Melodrama: A Study of the Fiction and Drama of Henry James, 1865–1897*. Berkeley and Los Angeles: University of California Press, 1957.

Lubbock, Percy, ed. *The Letters of Henry James*. 2 vols. New York: Scribner's, 1920.

Maddox, Jerald C. "Photography in the First Decade." *Art in America* 61 (July–August 1972), 72–79.

Margolis, Marianne Fulton, ed. *Camera Work: A Pictorial Guide*. New York: Dover, 1978.

Martin, Jay. *Harvests of Change: American Literature, 1865–1914*. Englewood Cliffs: Prentice-Hall, 1967.

Matthews, Brander. *Americanisms and Briticisms, with Other Essays on Other Isms*. New York: Harper & Brothers, 1892.

Matthiessen, F. O., and Kenneth B. Murdock, eds. *The Notebooks of Henry James*. New York: Oxford University Press, 1947.

May, Henry F. *The End of American Innocence: A Study of the First Years of Our Own Time*. New York: Knopf, 1959.

Miller, J. Hillis, and David Borowitz. *Charles Dickens and George Cruikshank*. Los Angeles: William Andrews Clark Memorial Library, University of California, 1971.

Mitchell, W. J. Thomas. *Blake's Composite Art: A Study of the Illuminated Poetry*. Princeton: Princeton University Press, 1978.

Muir, Percy. *Victorian Illustrated Books*. London: B. T. Batsford, Ltd., 1971.

Muller, Herbert J. *Freedom in the Modern World: The 19th and 20th Centuries*. New York: Harper-Colophon, 1966.

Mumford, Lewis. *The Brown Decades: A Study of the Arts in America, 1865–1895*. 1931: Reprint. New York: Dover, 1971.

Newhall, Beaumont. *The History of Photography: From 1839 to the Present Day*. 4th ed., rev. New York: Museum of Modern Art, 1964.

———. "The Vignettists." *American Magazine of Art* 28 (January 1935), 31–35.

Newhall, Nancy. "Introduction." In *A Portfolio of Sixteen Photographs* by Alvin Landgon Coburn. Edited by Nancy Newhall. Rochester, N.Y.: George Eastman Hose, 1962.

"Newspaper Pictures." *Nation* 56 (1893), 306–7.

Nochlin, Linda. *Realism: Style and Civilization*. New York and Baltimore: Penguin, 1971.

"The Novels of Mr. Howells." *Nation* 31 (1880), 49–51.

Nowell-Smith, Simon. "Firma Tauchnitz 1837–1900." *Book Collector* 15 (1966), 432–36.

Nye, Russel B. "Photography and American Culture." In *Towards a New American Literary History*. Edited by Louis J. Budd, Edwin H. Cady, and Carl L. Anderson. Durham, N.C.: Duke University Press, 1980.

O'Doherty, Brian. "The Silent Decade: 1900–1910." *Art in America* 61 (July–August 1973), 32.

Pennell, Joseph. "Is Photography among the Fine Arts?" *Contemporary Review* 72 (1897), 824–36.

"The Perils of Photography." *Nation* 85 (1907), 28–29.

Perry, Ralph Barton, ed. *The Thought and Character of William James*. 2 vols. Boston and Toronto: Little, Brown and Co., 1935.

Perry, T. S. "American Novelists." *North American Review* 115 (1872), 366–78.

"Photography: Its History and Applications." *Living Age* 92 (1867), 195–218.

Pizer, Donald, ed. *American Thought and Writing: The 1890s*. Boston: Houghton Mifflin, 1972.

Pollard, Alfred W. *Early Illustrated Books: A History of the Decoration and Illustration of Books in the 15th and 16th Centuries*. 1917. Reprint. New York: Haskell House Publishers, Ltd., 1968.

Ray, Gordon N. *The Illustrator and the Book in England from 1790 to 1914*. New York and London: Oxford University Press, 1976.

Review of "Holiday Books." *Atlantic Monthly* 67 (1891), 121–26.

Review of *The Novels and Tales of Henry James, The New York Edition, vol. I–VI. Literary Digest* 36 (1908), 418.

Review of *The Novels and Tales of Henry James, The New York Edition, vol. I–II. Nation* 86 (1908), 11.

Review of *The Novels and Tales of Henry James, The New York Edition, vol. III–VI. Nation* 86 (1908), 215.

Review of *The Novels and Tales of Henry James, The New York Edition, vol. VII–VIII. Literary Digest* 36 (1908), 376.

Review of *The Novels and Tales of Henry James, The New York Edition, vol. IX–X. Nation* 86 (1908), 511.

Review of *The Novels and Tales of Henry James, The New York Edition, vol. XI–XII. Nation* 87 (1908), 115.

Review of *The Novels and Tales of Henry James, The New York Edition, vol. I–II. New York Times* (11 January 1908), 13, 15.

Review of *The Novels and Tales of Henry James, The New York Edition, vol. III–IV. New York Times* (29 February 1908), 111.

Review of *The Novels and Tales of Henry James, The New York Edition, vol. V–VI. New York Times* (7 March 1908), 128.

Review of *The Novels and Tales of Henry James, The New York Edition, vol. VII–VIII. New York Times* (11 April 1908), 198.

Review of "Some Books on Art." *Nation* 73 (1901), 475–76.

Review of *The Lady of Aroostook* by W. D. Howells. *Nation* 28 (1897), 205.

Robins, Elizabeth, ed. *Theater and Friendship: Some Henry James Letters* New York: G.P. Putnam's Sons, 1932.

Robinson, H.P. *Pictorial Effect in Photography*. 1869. Reprint. Pawlet: Helios, 1971.

Root, Marcus Aurelius. *The Camera and the Pencil, or the Heliographic Art*. 1864. Reprint. Pawlet: Helios, 1971.

Rose, Barbara. *American Art since 1900*. Rev. ed. New York: Praeger, 1975.

Rosen, Charles, and Henri Zerner. "The Revival of Official Art." *New York Review* (18 March 1976), 32–39.

Rudisill, Richard. *Mirror Image: The Influence of the Daguerreotype on American Society*. Albuquerque: University of New Mexico Press, 1971.

Scharf, Aaron. *Art and Photography*. Harmondsworth: Penguin, 1968.

———. *Creative Photography*. New York: Van Nostrand Reinhold Co., and London: Studio Vista, 1965.

Schiller, Dan. "Realism, Photography, and Journalistic Objectivity in 19th Century America." *Studies in the Anthropology of Visual Communication* 4 (1977), 86–98.

[Scudder, Horace.] "A Few Story-Tellers, Old and New." *Atlantic Monthly* 72 (1893), 693–99.

[Scudder, Horace.] Review of *The Tragic Muse* by Henry James. *Atlantic Monthly* 66 (1890), 419–22.

[Scudder, Horace.] "Some Holiday Books." *Atlantic Monthly* 71 (1893), 123–25.

Shaw, George Bernard. "Preface." *Catalogue of the Alvin Langdon Coburn Exhibition, 5 February–31 March 1906.* London: Royal Photographic Society, 1906. n.p.

Snyder, Joel. "Picturing Vision." *Critical Inquiry* 6 (1980), 499–526.

Sobieszek, Robert A. "Photography and the Theory of Realism in the Second Empire: A Reexamination of a Relationship." In *One Hundred Years of Photographic History: Essays in Honor of Beaumont Newhall.* Edited by Van Deren Coke. Albuquerque: University of New Mexico Press, 1975.

Sontag, Susan. "Against Interpretation." In *Against Interpretation* by Susan Sontag. New York: Delta-Dell, 1965.

———. "Freak Show." *New York Review* (15 November 1973), 13–19.

———. "Photography." *New York Review* (18 October 1973), 59–63.

———. "Shooting America." *New York Review* (18 April 1974), 17–24.

Spiegel, Alan. *Fiction and the Camera Eye.* Charlottesville: University Press of Virginia, 1976.

Staley, Kathryn. "Photography as a Fine Art." *Munsey's Magazine* 14 (1896), 582–91.

Stieglitz, Alfred. "The New Photography: II. Modern Pictorial Photography." *Century* 64 (1902), 822–26.

Stowell, H. Peter. *Literary Impressionism, James and Chekkov.* Athens, Ga.: University of Georgia Press, 1980.

Sweeney, John L., ed. *The Painter's Eye: Notes and Essays on the Pictorial Arts* by Henry James. London: Rupert Hart-Davis, 1956.

"Symposium of Wood-Engravers." *Harper's New Monthly* 60 (1880), 442–53.

Sypher, Wylie. *From Rococo to Cubism in Art and Literature.* New York: Vintage-Random, 1960.

Szarkowski, John. *Looking at Photographs: 100 Pictures from the Collection of the Museum of Modern Art.* New York: Museum of Modern Art, 1973.

Szasz, Ferenc M., and Ralph F. Bogardus. "The Camera and the America Social Conscience: The Documentary Photography of Jacob A. Riis." *New York History* 55 (1974), 409–36.

Taft, Robert. *Photography and the American Scene: A Social History, 1839–1889.* 1938. Reprint. New York: Dover, 1964.

Talbot, William Henry Fox. *The Pencil of Nature.* 1844–46. Reprint. New York: DaCapo Press, 1969.

Thomas, Alan. *Time in a Frame: Photography and the Nineteenth-Century Mind.* New York: Schocken, 1977.

Trachtenberg, Alan. *The Incorporation of America: Culture and Society in the Gilded Age.* New York: Hill and Wang, 1982.

———, ed. *Classic Essays on Photography.* New Haven, Conn.: Leete's Island Books, 1980.

Twain, Mark. *Pudd'nhead Wilson and Those Extraordinary Twins.* 1894. Reprint. New York and London: Harper & Brothers, 1899.

Valéry, Paul. "The Centenary of Photography." In *The Collected Works of Paul Valéry: Occasions. XI.* Edited by Jackson Matthews, and translated by Roger Shattuck and Frederick Brown. Princeton: Princeton University Press, 1970.

Varnadoe, Kirk. "The Artifice of Candor: Impressionism and Photography Reconsidered." *Art in America* 68 (January 1980), 66–78.

———. "The Ideology of Time." *Art in America* 68 (Summer 1980), 96–110.

Wakeman, Geoffrey. *Victorian Book Illustration: The Technical Revolution.* Detroit: Gale Research Co., 1973.

Ward, J.A. *The Search for Form: Studies in the Structure of James's Fiction.* Chapel Hill: University of North Carolina Press, 1967.

Warner, Charles Dudley. "Modern Fiction." *Atlantic Monthly* 51 (1883), 464–74.

Weitenkampf, Frank. *The Illustrated Book.* Cambridge, Mass.: Harvard University Press, 1938.

White, Gleason. *English Illustration, "The Sixties": 1855–1870.* 1897. Reprint. Bath: Kingsmead Reprints, 1970.

Wilsher, Ann. "Photography and Literature: The First Seventy Years." *History of Photography* 2 (1978), 223–34.

Wilson, Christopher P. "The Rhetoric of Consumption: Mass Market Magazines and the Demise of the Gentle Reader, 1880–1920." In *The Culture of Consumption: Critical Essays in American History, 1880–1980.* Edited by Richard Wightman Fox and T. J. Jackson Lears. New York: Pantheon, 1983.

Winner, Viola Hopkins. *Henry James and the Visual Arts.* Charlottesville: University Press of Virginia, 1970.

Wordsworth, William. "Illustrated Books and Newspapers." In *The Complete Poetical Works of William Wordsworth, IX,* Grasmere edition. Boston and New York: Houghton Mifflin, 1911.

Zabel, Morton Dauwen. "Introduction." In *The Art of Travel: Scenes and Journeys in America, England, France and Italy from the Travel Writings of Henry James.* Edited by Morton Dauwen Zabel. Garden City: Doubleday, 1958.

Ziff, Larzer. *The American 1980s: Life and Times of a Lost Generation.* 1966. Reprint. Lincoln and London: University of Nebraska Press, 1979.

Index